STEEPED IN A CULTURE
OF VIOLENCE

STEEPED IN A CULTURE OF VIOLENCE

Murder, Racial Injustice, and Other
Violent Crimes in Texas, 1965–2020

Edited by Brandon T. Jett and
Kenneth W. Howell

TEXAS A&M UNIVERSITY PRESS
COLLEGE STATION

∞ This paper meets the requirements of ANSI/NISO Z39.48-1992
(Permanence of Paper).
Binding materials have been chosen for durability.
Manufactured in the United States of America

Library of Congress Cataloging-in-Publication Data

Names: Jett, Brandon T., editor. | Howell, Kenneth Wayne, 1967– editor.
Title: Steeped in a culture of violence : murder, racial injustice, and
    other violent crimes in Texas, 1965–2020 / edited by Brandon T. Jett and
    Kenneth W Howell.
Other titles: Elma Dill Russell Spencer series in the West and Southwest.
Description: First edition. | College Station : Texas A&M University Press,
    [2023] | Series: Elma Dill Russell Spencer series in the West and
    Southwest | Includes bibliographical references and index.
Identifiers: LCCN 2022043321 | ISBN 9781648431333 (cloth) | ISBN
    9781648431340 (ebook)
Subjects: LCSH: Violent crimes—Texas—History—20th century. | Violent
    crimes—Texas—History—21st century. | Murder—Texas—History. |
    Intimate partner violence—Texas—History. | Hate
    crimes—Texas—History. | Minorities—Violence against—Texas—History.
    | Gangs—Texas—History. | Prison violence—Texas—History. | Mass
    shootings—Texas—History.
Classification: LCC HV6533.T4 S74 2023 | DDC
    364.152/309764—dc23/eng/20221123
LC record available at https://lccn.loc.gov/2022043321

This book is dedicated to Jeff Adler and Dwight Watson for their inspiration, guidance, and support of my interest in the study of violence and criminal justice in American history.

—BRANDON T. JETT

I dedicate this book to all the victims of violent crimes in Texas and beyond. While the words written here will not ease the pain and suffering of the victims and their families, I hope this study will represent the next step in gaining a greater understanding of the issues associated with violent crimes and mark the beginning of nonpartisan discussions that can produce commonsense solutions to the violence that still plagues our society.

—KENNETH W. HOWELL

CONTENTS

ACKNOWLEDGMENTS

Although the editors of this volume got our names on the cover, anyone who edits a book such as this one acquires obligations and support from many people and organizations. Foremost, the authors of the individual chapters deserve all the credit for the success of this volume. This book was completed throughout the COVID-19 pandemic. Despite all of the hardships faced during these trying few years, the authors demonstrated an amazing willingness and commitment to complete their chapters and respond to feedback. We cannot thank them enough for their contributions to the volume.

The staff at Texas A&M University Press were incredibly supportive. From our initial conversations at the TAMU Press booth at the Southern Historical Association's annual conference, to the proposal, and through the publication of the book, Jay Dew has been a steadfast ally. Thom Lemmons helped steer the manuscript through board approval and final publication. There were also numerous members of the staff who we never met or corresponded with that aided throughout the publication process. Finally, TAMU Press found two wonderful reviewers who provided important feedback on the manuscript that fundamentally improved the work.

Through informal conversations over dinner at the AP US History grading sessions, Zoom chats, email exchanges, and casual conversations, friends and colleagues from across the country proved critical as we worked to complete the project. We would especially like to thank the members of the Community College Writing Support Group, whose reading of the manuscript improved the final version in myriad ways.

As any author knows, finding the time to sit down, think through arguments, and write is hard to come by. Florida SouthWestern State

College generously provided course releases to Brandon Jett that proved crucial to the completion of this project. We were supported by the East Texas Historical Association through the Lock Research Grant that allowed us the time and resources to complete the introduction. We are sincerely appreciative of the help, guidance, feedback, and support that everyone gave to this project.

Of course, we would like to thank our families for their constant support of our work. None of this would have been possible without them.

Finally, you, the reader. We cannot express how thankful we are that you are taking the time to read this collection. Thank you for your support and interest.

EDITOR'S NOTE

The editors came up with the date ranges for this book, 1965 to 2020, as part of a larger effort to understand the various trends in violence that occurred in Texas. As the authors completed their chapters and the manuscript underwent reviews and was edited by the press, rates of violence across the United States spiked after a long period of decline. The chapters that follow do not grapple with the recent spike that occurred between 2020 and 2022 because it was outside the purview of the collection when it was originally conceived in 2018. We did our best to bring the collection as close to the "present" as we possibly could.

Even more troubling, after this book went to press, the Lone Star State suffered another tragic and senseless act of violence. On May 24, 2022, a lone gunman entered the halls of Robb Elementary School in Uvalde, Texas, and opened fire, murdering nineteen children and two teachers and wounding seventeen others. This shooting is the deadliest school shooting in the state's history.

Though we were unable to incorporate the spike in violence and the Uvalde massacre into our book because of the ongoing uncertainties associated with these issues at the time of publication, we believe it is necessary to recognize that these violent realities continue to hurt the lives of so many people in the state and around the country.

Our hearts go out to all those affected by the violence in Texas, the community of Uvalde, and all those who lost loved ones during this horrific attack. We sincerely hope that in some small way this collection will contribute to a greater understanding of the violence that seems to plague the United States and spur substantive changes to address the underlying causes.

STEEPED IN A CULTURE
OF VIOLENCE

INTRODUCTION

Violence in Texas History

Brandon T. Jett and Kenneth W. Howell

Around 7:30 a.m. on May 18, 2018, a seventeen-year-old student armed with a shotgun and a pistol opened fire in an art class at Santa Fe High School, about thirty miles southeast of Houston. For around twenty-five minutes, the sound of gunfire echoed throughout the halls of the school until the suspect surrendered to law enforcement. When it was all said and done, ten people lost their lives and another ten suffered serious injuries.[1] This tragedy was the twenty-second school shooting to occur in the United States in 2018.[2]

The shooting at Santa Fe High School, as with other major school shootings in the United States in the last twenty years, prompted public debate over the causes and potential solutions to this type of violent act. On May 21, 2018, Oliver North, then president of the National Rifle Association, declared that a culture of violence is largely responsible for these killings. Summarizing the sentiments of those who oppose any restrictions on firearms in the United States, North stated, "The problem that we've got is we're trying like the dickens to treat the symptom without treating the disease. . . . The disease is youngsters who are steeped in a culture of violence." North continued, "Nearly all of these perpetrators are male, and they're young teenagers in most cases, and they've come through a culture where violence is commonplace. All we need to do is turn on a TV, go to a movie."[3] North is not alone in his assessment of American culture. The rise in the number of mass shootings over the last several decades has led to an apparent general consensus that Americans are ensconced in a culture of violence. Social commentators, journalists, and scholars point to violent video games and movies, the frequent glamorization of perpetrators of violent acts by the media, the widespread availability of firearms in the United States, the military-industrial complex, and an association between violence and masculinity in American society as evidence of this wider culture of violence.[4]

The focus on mass shootings and publicized violence in America has obscured the fact that from the early 1990s until 2018, rates of violence in the United States declined to some of the lowest points in history (see fig. 1).[5] The consensus regarding the culture of violence in America neglects a critical examination as to why homicides declined to historic lows despite the seeming encouragement of violence in our culture. While scholars amply demonstrated that industrialization and economic changes coupled with the expansion of state institutions in the late nineteenth and twentieth centuries worked to reduce the frequency and acceptance of violence across the country, the reactions to school shootings indicate that not everyone agrees. This dichotomy suggests instead that a culture of violence has emerged, or perhaps continued to

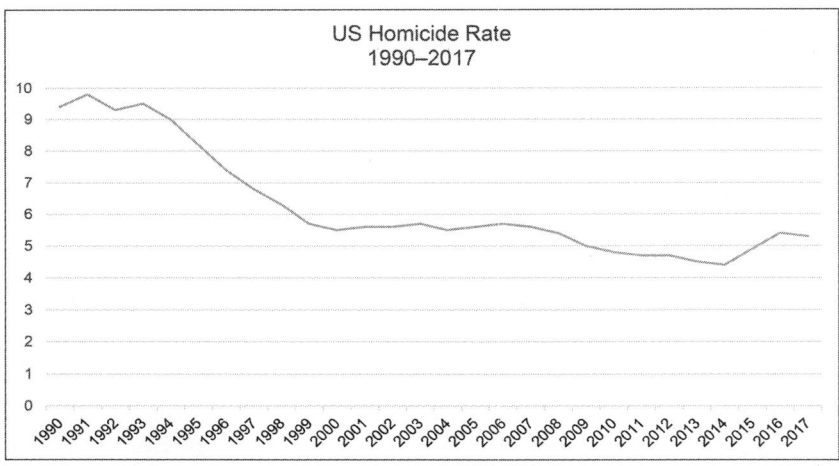

Figure 1. US homicide rate, 1990–2017. Data culled from the FBI's Uniform Crime Reports.

exist, despite the institutional, economic, and social changes that drove down rates of violence over the past 150 years.[6]

This collection of essays explores the question of whether a culture of violence exists through an examination of multiple trends in violence and the social and political responses to violent behavior in one state, Texas, from 1965 to 2020. For purposes of this study, a *culture of violence* refers to the set of attitudes, values, beliefs, and behaviors shared by a group of people that can be used to justify or legitimize acts of violence.[7] Texas provides an interesting context for the study of a culture of violence in the United States more broadly for several reasons. First, Texas underwent political, social, and demographic changes that mirrored those of the United States as a whole since the 1960s, including post–civil rights movement, economic changes related to deindustrialization, the urban crisis of the 1970s and 1980s, rise of conservatism, economic growth in the late twentieth century, and, perhaps most important for this study, numerous acts of violence that are similar to acts committed in other parts of the nation. The population of Texas also reflects the diversity found in urban and rural areas in other regions of the United States. Second, the emergence of Texas as one of the more politically, demographically, and economically important states in the country provides scholars a useful case study that can be used to contextualize the current issues related to violence in the United States. Finally, several scholars argue that a culture of violence existed historically in the state, but none of those works explore the issue past the 1960s.[8] All of these factors allow for an engaging study of multiple forms of violence in different geographical settings that provides insight into larger trends occurring in the United States because, as historian Robert Perkinson claims, "to a large extent, Texas stands for the country as a whole."[9]

For myriad reasons, the seven essays in this collection begin their examination of violent trends in Texas in 1965. While the specific year 1965 might seem arbitrary, scholars of violence have documented a drastic increase in violence across the country and in Texas beginning in the last half of the 1960s.[10] As such, using the midpoint of the decade is fertile ground for exploring the state and local reactions to this increase that, in many ways, set the stage for changes to the criminal justice apparatus that came in the late twentieth and early twenty-first centuries. Beginning the analysis in 1965 also allows each scholar to explore the fifty years of violence and state and local responses to it in their chapter. The story of changes in cultural, political, and economic reactions to violence in Texas traced in this collection, then, starts at the beginning of the spike in violence that occurred in the state in the late 1960s.

Yet, Texas history is steeped in brutality and bloodshed. Native Americans in Texas engaged in raids and warfare against other Native American groups as they vied for supremacy over each other or sought revenge for previous wrongs. While Native American warfare was usually limited in scope and targeted other warriors, the significance of warfare in their customs and society is found in the artifacts they left behind. Mississippian peoples, such as the Caddo, who lived in northeast Texas around the Red River, built fortified cities that offered defenses against perceived enemies, indicating a fear of violent attacks from other Native Americans. Equally important, however, is how Native Americans in Texas viewed warfare and violent confrontations. Several Native American groups in Texas glorified successes in battle in various forms of artwork.[11] Successful Caddo warriors also comprised an honored caste, called *amayxoya*. Violence played an important role in Native American life in the region that would become Texas, as warfare helped tribes establish dominion over certain territories and neighboring peoples, and many warriors and chieftains gained influence and authority based on their success in war.[12]

When Spanish explorers in 1528 first traversed the region that would become Texas, they introduced European notions of martial masculinity into the cultural milieu of Texas. Spanish conquistadors and the soldiers under their command engaged in warfare against Native Americans throughout North and South America and in the Caribbean beginning in the late fifteenth century. Violence and brutality, as well as disease, proved essential to the conquest of small Native groups and vast empires such as the Aztecs. For their efforts and military successes, the Spanish awarded conquistadors, such as Hernán Cortés, massive *encomiendas,* glory, titles, and riches.[13] The military victories of Cortés inspired other conquistadors to seek conquests of other peoples north and south of the Aztec capital at Tenochtitlan. Alonso Álvarez de Pineda first explored the Texas coast in 1519 as part of an exploratory expedition, and Álvar Núñez Cabeza de Vaca first crossed into what is now Texas in 1528 as part of the failed Spanish expedition to colonize Florida.[14] Francisco Vásquez de Coronado set out from Mexico City to find cities of gold in the present-day American Southwest. Between 1540 and 1541, the expedition entered into New Mexico and Texas and encountered several Native American peoples. In each of these encounters, Vásquez de Coronado read the Catholic *requerimiento* that demanded all Natives convert to Catholicism and pledge loyalty to the Spanish crown or face immediate death. According to one historian, "Coronado's men left a wake of death and destruction" across the Southwest, including modern-day Texas.[15] These first explorations of Texas did not lead to extensive colonization efforts by the Spanish, however, and were branded failures. Nonetheless, violence and disease devastated many Native Americans in the region. Death and destruction to Native Americans equated to domination and status for the Spanish. Through violence and warfare, the Spanish claimed one of the larger empires in world history in the sixteenth, seventeenth, and eighteenth centuries.[16]

Native Americans, of course, challenged Spanish claims to the region north of the Rio Grande for centuries. Perhaps the most successful challenges to Spanish dominion over the region came from the Comanche. Throughout the eighteenth century, the Comanche grew from a "small tribe of hunter-gatherers living in the rugged Canyonlands on the far northern frontier of the Spanish kingdom" into what Pekka Hamalainen called "the Comanche Empire."[17] This empire controlled most of present-day central and west Texas and was made up of "ferocious horse-riding warriors who forestalled Euro-American intrusions into the American Southwest well into the late nineteenth century."[18] The Comanche Empire grew as a result of their success in warfare and raiding against the Spanish, other European powers, and other Native groups. Violence and warfare permeated Comanche culture as they embraced kinship responsibilities that emphasized the obligation to avenge slain relatives.[19] Comanche raids against and outright warfare with the Spanish not only upended notions of European superiority in the Americas but also demonstrated the ways in which violence permeated Native culture in Texas. Warriors' status and identity within

Comanche tribes were often linked to their demonstration of acts of bravery and success in raids and warfare.[20]

Anglo settlement of Texas began in 1821 and ushered in a new era of violence and cultural embrace for it in the state. As historian Matthew Jennings argued, Anglo-Americans embraced a culture of violence with roots in the colonial period, and that culture "would spread with English colonization to points west."[21] Violent actions used in defense of perceived wrongs became ingrained in Texas lore during the Texas Revolution (1835–1836), the Mexican-American War (1846–1848), and the American Civil War (1861–1865). During these three wars, Anglo Texans became well versed in the use of violence during warfare but also celebrated the use of violence when confronted with perceived threats to notions of freedom and democracy by what they viewed as oppressive forces. During the Texas Revolution and the US war with Mexico, perceived threats to Anglo Texans presented themselves in the form of the Mexican government. When Mexican President Antonio López de Santa Anna assumed power, he attempted to centralize the Mexican government and reign in the localized control enjoyed by Mexicans and Anglos in Texas for quite some time. In the face of such threats, Anglo Texans and Tejanos alike revolted and eventually secured independence from Mexico. Similarly, the immediate cause of the Mexican-American War grew out of boundary disputes between Texas and the Mexican government. Texans and their American supporters claimed the Rio Grande as the southern border, while the Mexican government argued the boundary of Texas ended at the Nueces River. In late April 1846, a detachment of Mexican troops crossed the Rio Grande to enforce their border claims and engaged in open combat with a detachment of US cavalry. Americans and Texans decried what, in their eyes, was an act of aggression by the Mexican government. Congress declared war with Mexico, and as many as seven thousand Texans volunteered. The Treaty of Guadalupe-Hidalgo formally ended the war in 1848 and established the Rio Grande as the official boundary between Mexico and Texas. Finally, many Texans based their support for secession in 1861 around the notion that the election of Abraham Lincoln represented another challenge to the rights and honor of white men in the state. As such, Texans voted to secede from the Union in 1861, knowing full well that they would soon be called on to defend that decision in a bloody civil war. Following in the footsteps of the forebearers, twenty-five thousand Texans joined the Confederate military in response to Jefferson Davis's call for volunteers in the wake of Fort Sumter.[22]

The significance of the three wars in the mid-nineteenth century lay not only in the exposure to warfare and the justifications for it by Texans but also in the celebration of those wars and soldiers in the state. Much of Texans' collective memory was shaped by nineteenth-century interpretations that glamorized Anglo sacrifices at the Alamo, painted Mexico as a tyrannical government, and valorized Confederate heroism against the Union forces.[23] The Alamo in particular rose to almost mythical proportions in Texans' collective memory as a place where valiant white defenders of freedom from tyranny and oppression sacrificed their lives.[24] Even on a smaller scale, counties across the state erected monuments celebrating Confederate soldiers in the late nineteenth and early twentieth centuries. These monuments were part of a larger effort to ennoble the Confederate cause and promote the "lost cause" ideology of the Civil War.[25] This powerful legacy and memory of the efficacy of violence and valor associated with it resonated in the cultural ethos of Texas for the next century and a half.

Anglo settlement in Texas brought more than eventual revolution and armed struggle. These migrants also embraced the culture of honor and slavery that predominated in the antebellum US South. The southern culture of honor refers to "a system of values within which you have exactly as much worth as others confer upon you."[26] In the antebellum South, Texas included, honor was reserved for adult white males. When these adult white males felt their honor challenged, honor culture demanded they courageously, and at times violently, defend their reputation. The cultural embrace of honor led to countless brawls between backwoodsmen and poor white southerners, while planters and politicians turned to the duel.[27]

Honor blended with slavery to sow the seeds of a culture of violence in antebellum Texas. Slavery was perhaps the most important factor in determining the economic and ideological development in Texas prior to the Civil War. By 1861, the proportion of enslavers and enslaved people in the state mirrored that of Virginia. At a very basic level, violence sustained slavery. Enslaved people lived with the constant threat that they could be whipped, beat, raped, and abused at any time by their enslavers or overseers.[28] These abuses and punishments not only shaped enslaved peoples' lived experiences but also became part of white men's identity and understanding of themselves.[29] Exercising control and domination over others only increased one's honor in the antebellum South. As such, dominance over enslaved people, and the willingness to use violence to maintain that dominance, garnered enslavers' public reputations.

Honor and slavery contributed to violence beyond the punishments meted out against enslaved people. The southern criminal justice system remained weaker and more decentralized than that of northern states throughout the antebellum era. Despite the fact that the Texas legislature built the first state prison in Huntsville in 1848, most southerners opposed the idea of expanded criminal justice apparatus because of their distrust of state institutions and their conviction to deal with problems on their own that formed the basis of honor culture.[30] Weak state institutions ceded almost complete authority over punishment and control to enslavers, thereby contributing to a society that distrusted centralized state institutions and championed individual reliance on violence to maintain authority over subordinates.[31]

The familiarity with, reliance on, and celebration of violence in conjunction with a weak criminal justice system in mid-nineteenth-century Texas contributed to perhaps the most ferocious era in state history: 1865–1900. During the last four decades of the nineteenth century, Texans killed each other with frightening frequency. Even more problematic, state authorities and residents often accepted, respected, and participated the actions.[32] For these reasons, historian William Carrigan described this era as exhibiting "a robust culture of violence."[33] Following the Civil War, Anglo Texans engaged in a "relentless campaign of violence against the freedpeople and their white allies" during the Reconstruction era.[34] Historian Kenneth W. Howell described the widespread nature of the violence as nothing short of "a continuation of the Civil War" whereby Anglo Texans utilized guerilla tactics to reclaim control of the state.[35] While violence during the Reconstruction era was widespread, the significance also lay in the fact that it was effective at thwarting black Texans' push for equality and Republican efforts to limit the political power of former Confederates. Much like the celebratory histories of the Texas Revolution, Mexican-American War, and Civil War, the violence of Reconstruction became imbedded in the minds of future white Texans as heroic and worthy of celebration.[36]

The violence did not cease with the end of Reconstruction in 1877. On the contrary, for the next several decades, Texans engaged in an array of violent encounters. As with the rest of the American West, armed confrontation between Anglo Americans and Native Americans proliferated in the late nineteenth century. The main arena of conflict erupted between the Comanche, whose empire stretched across most of west Texas, and Texas settlers and cattle ranchers encroaching on Comanche territory. Beginning in 1870, Texas authorities worked in collaboration with the US Army to eliminate the Comanche's claims to lands in Texas. Texas officials initially established local militias to protect Anglo settlers from Comanche raids. These militias proved terribly ineffective in the eyes of Anglo Texans against the Comanche. The failures of militias led to the reinstatement of the Frontier Battalion of the Texas Rangers in 1874. For the next year, the Rangers engaged in a relentless campaign of violence deployed under the guise of legality against the Comanche that resulted in the collapse of the Comanche empire and the end of major confrontations between Anglo Texans and Native Americans. As with other violent episodes in this era of Texas history, the wars against the Comanche affected Texas culture in significant ways. Not only was Anglo violence once again framed as a defense against the violent incursions of outside forces, but the threat of Comanche raids and weakness of state institutions to protect settlers fostered a "tendency to violence." Settlers constantly carried guns and were prepared to use them in violent defense of their lives or livelihood.[37]

The violent tactics embraced by Texas militias and the Texas Rangers in the war against Native Americans were championed and celebrated by Anglo Texans, but it was Texans' embrace of extralegal violence that demonstrated how imbedded the culture of violence became in the late nineteenth and early twentieth centuries. During this era, Texans participated in as many as sixty vigilante movements that encompassed at least thirty-eight counties. Vigilantism involved organized groups "taking law into their own hands to reinforce existing power relationships" within communities.[38] Vigilante movements typically emerged in response to criminal events that members of the community felt formal institutions of criminal justice were incapable of punishing. Some of the Texas vigilante movements lasted a few weeks. Others went on for years. One of the most infamous examples came out of the tri-county area of Bastrop, Lee, and Williamson counties in 1883. In response to a number of outlaws and cattle thieves known as the Yegua Notch Cutters, local cattle ranchers and townspeople formed a vigilante group and hanged three members of the Yegua Notch Cutters on Christmas Eve and engaged in a shootout with two other members of the gang the following day. Local leaders, city officials, and law enforcement officials typically supported these movements and viewed them as necessary and legitimate forms of community self-protection.[39]

Feuds represented another form of extralegal violence that swept through the state in the late nineteenth century. From 1860 to 1900, at least eight major feuds erupted in Texas, which resulted in at least seventy-five deaths. These feuds were more than small family matters or disputes: they represented what historians identified as *community feuds*. Community feuds typically involved family loyalties and kinship ties but often extended beyond familial affairs to encompass entire communities. The origins of these feuds typically grew out of land disputes, local political issues, or racial conflicts. Some feuds last several years with dozens of fatalities, such as the Sutton-Taylor feud of DeWitt County (1867–1877), which claimed the lives of thirty-five people, and the Townsend-Stafford/Townsend-Reese feud of Colorado County (1890–1906) that left eleven people dead in its wake of destruction. Others lasted only a few years but could be just as deadly, including the Truitt-Mitchell feud of Hood County (1877) that ended with five fatalities, the Horrell-Higgins feud in Lampasas County (1888–1889) with two deaths, the Marlow-cattlemen feud in Young County (1888–1890) that resulted in seven killings, the Jaybird-Woodpecker feud from Ft. Bend County (1890–1906) with seven fatalities, the Baylor-Brann feud of McClennan County (1895–1898) that ended with four deaths, and the Wet-Dry feud in Waller County (1905) that resulted in four killings. Often, these feuds involved entire communities that supported one faction or the other. The scale and duration of the violence notwithstanding, the presence of these feuds in the late nineteenth century and the level of community involvement indicates that residents supported these extralegal methods of violence to an extent. In fact, state authorities often monitored the feuds and got involved only when the violence escalated to what they deemed a problematic level.[40]

Perhaps the most telling indication of how strongly the culture of violence pervaded Texas is in the example of lynching. Texans lynched more people than almost any other state in the country, including at least 376 African Americans, 39 whites, and 232 people of Mexican descent.[41] Similar to vigilante movements in many respects, lynch mobs involved organized groups, ranging in size from three to several hundred, that typically emerged in response to a perceived violation of communal norms or criminal activities.[42] Mobs in Texas targeted whites during the late nineteenth century, but by 1900, lynching became reserved almost solely for people of color.[43] Lynching, although met with occasional criticism and official repudiation, received widespread support in the state. Legal authorities, who were often actively involved in the killings, almost never held lynch mob members accountable for their participation in the extralegal killings. The widespread presence and acceptance of extralegal violence in conjunction with the support among Anglo Texans for the war against Native Americans indicated that a culture of violence remained pronounced in late-nineteenth-century Texas.[44]

In some respects, the violence of the late nineteenth century continued into the twentieth. While rates of lynching declined dramatically from 1900 to 1920, lynching remained comparatively high in the state when compared to others. Texas mobs lynched an average of five people every year between 1918 and 1927.[45] Texans lynched more people during the early twentieth century than did most other states. The killings of Mexicans and Mexican Americans in the Borderlands by Anglo communities, Texas Rangers and other legal authorities, and the American military reached a peak in the 1910s: estimates suggest that as many as five thousand Mexicans and Mexican Americans were killed.[46] Anglo

Texans frustrated with the new assertive nature of returning black World War I veterans participated in targeted violence against black communities during the Red Summer of 1919. Beginning on July 10, 1919, whites in Longview, Texas, attacked African American residents, killed one black man, and destroyed multiple black-owned properties over the course of several days.[47] Ku Klux Klan activity was also widespread into the 1920s. This "second coming" of the KKK in the 1920s resulted from several factors, including concerns over immigration, race relations, temperance, and an effort to preserve Victorian ideals. While the KKK presented itself as a respectable, law-abiding organization, the reality was that Klan members relied on violence and threats to impose their views on local communities across the state.[48]

Yet, the violence of the first two decades of the twentieth century concluded the most violent era of Texas history. The next several decades saw a general downward trend in occurrences and acceptance of extralegal violence. With the demise of the KKK and extralegal violence, there were many indications that the culture of violence that was so pervasive in the late nineteenth and early twentieth centuries was also receding. Rates of extralegal violence declined during the early twentieth century in response to a variety of factors. Most notably, the emergence of stronger state institutions, including regulatory agencies and law enforcement at the local level, negated the need for traditional, more violent methods of dispute resolution. In addition, the reliance on outside investors for economic growth and diversification led many state leaders and authorities to decry violence. Investors were notoriously wary of instability. The presence of vigilantes, community feuds, and lynch mobs presented a lawless, unstable image to investors. To quell those concerns, civic boosters and state and local authorities worked to limit and discredit extralegal violence.[49]

By the middle of the twentieth century, the decline in extralegal methods of violence coincided with an overall decrease in the murder rate (see fig. 2). During the mid-1930s, homicide rates in the state fluctuated between 15 and 20 homicides per 100,000 residents. Following a peak in 1936, the general trajectory of homicide rates was down (despite a slight rise in 1945 and 1946 as soldiers returned from World War II). By the mid-1960s, homicide rates fell by more than 63.8 percent. This

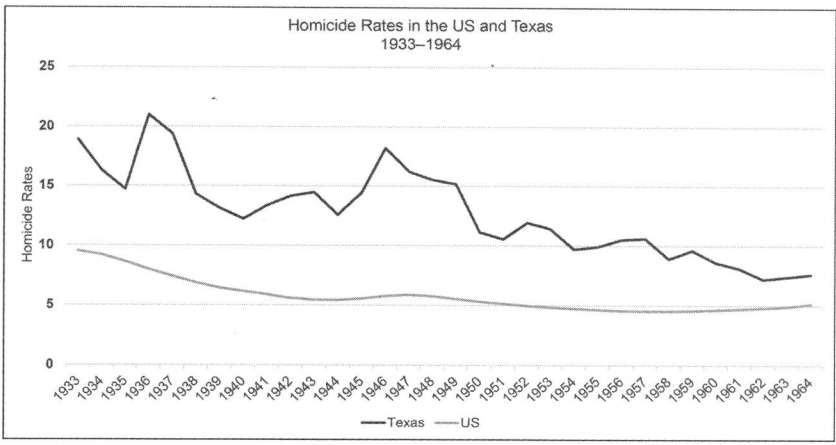

Figure 2. Texas vs. US homicide rates, 1933–1964.

sustained decrease mirrored national trends (see fig. 0.2). Several factors contributed to this decline, including the progress of the urban-industrial revolution across the United States; expansion of an increased faith in the institutions of government at the federal, state, and local levels; and the rise of the middle class.[50]

Although violence overall declined, Texas remained one of the more violent states in the country. From 1933 to 1964, the murder rate in Texas averaged 12.7 murders per 100,000 residents and ranked eighth highest in the country.[51] It was one of twelve states, including Alabama, Georgia, Tennessee, South Carolina, North Carolina, Florida, Arkansas, Virginia, Kentucky, Mississippi, and Louisiana, that averaged a double-digit murder rate during that period. Scholars of violence in the mid-twentieth century argued that southern culture promoted and encouraged violence even though larger forces pushed rates down overall. In 1969, Sheldon Hackney argued, "From the southern past arise the symbiosis of profuse hospitality and intense hostility . . . the paradox that southern heritage is at the same time one of grace and violence."[52] Two years later, Raymond D. Gastil echoed Hackney's arguments and claimed, "It is a predisposition to lethal violence in Southern regional culture that accounts for the greater part of the relative height of the American homicide rate."[53] With an average homicide rate of 12.7, Texans killed each other at more than double the rate of

Americans as a whole (the national homicide rate was 5.8).[54] While most of this violence resulted from homicides, much of it also related to the maintenance of the system of segregation, disenfranchisement, and second-class citizenship for African Americans, Latin Americans, and other nonwhite residents of the state.[55] A white mob lynched an African American man named Willie Vinson in Texarkana on July 13, 1942.[56] One year later, a white mob of nearly four thousand ransacked the black community in Beaumont. The mob seriously injured hundreds of black residents, destroyed hundreds of black homes, and killed twenty-one people.[57] Mobs threatened African American students who attempted to integrate schools in Mansfield and Texarkana in the mid-1950s and kidnapped and assaulted twenty-seven-year-old Felton Turner in response to a series of sit-ins on March 7, 1960.[58] Mexican American activists also faced the threat of violence in their attempts to break down barriers to equality. Law enforcement officers attacked several Mexican Americans in Crystal City in response to their activism.[59] While nowhere near as violent as the early twentieth century, violence remained part of life in Texas through 1965. Whether to maintain white supremacy, subdue labor protests, or in interpersonal disputes, Texans were more likely to lash out violently than were Americans in most other states.

By all appearances, a culture of violence has traditionally been a part of the Texas identity; yet, as powerful as the historical precedents are, few scholars have examined how this historical culture of violence shaped Texas history since 1965.[60] While the history and culture up to that point may have promoted and legitimized acts of violence, Texas in the post-1965 era underwent major changes that affected the state's culture and political, economic, and legal structures.[61] Economically, the state experienced a drastic expansion from what Randolph B. Campbell called a "semicolonial economy that depended on the production of a few raw materials—cotton, cattle, and oil," to a more diversified economy that "depends more heavily than ever on manufacturing, commerce, finance ... electronics and other high-tech industries, health-support enterprises, and service businesses."[62] Socially and politically, women, African Americans, Mexican Americans, Asian Americans, and other minority groups stood on much more equal footing with Anglo Texans than in the pre-1965 period. In addition, Texas cities expanded dramatically in the post-1965 era. Houston is the fourth-largest city in the nation, and San Antonio, Austin, Dallas, Ft. Worth, and El Paso all rank in the top twenty most populated cities in the United States.[63] The expansion of cities also coincided with a diversified population in the state. As of 2017, 41.2 percent of the population was white, 39.4 percent Hispanic or Latino/a, 11.7 percent African American, 4.8 percent Asian, and 1.6 percent two or more races.[64] Finally, and perhaps most important for our understanding of the ways in which citizens, politicians, and state authorities responded to instances of violence, the Texas criminal justice system expanded dramatically in the post-1965 era. Between 1965 and 2020, the Texas prison population grew by 1,200 percent, while sentences became longer and early releases less frequent. As of 2010, Texas ranked first in prison growth, for-profit imprisonment, supermax lockdown, adults under the supervision of the criminal justice system, and executions. In most respects, Texas has the most robust criminal justice apparatus of any state in the country.[65] While Anglo Texans in the late nineteenth and early twentieth centuries distrusted formal legal institutions and embraced extralegal methods of social control, since 1965, Texas has changed in myriad ways that could contribute to changing cultural values as it relates to violence, as well.

The essays in this volume explore trends in and reactions to different forms and locales of violence across the state from 1965 to 2020.[66] Coming from the perspectives of criminologists and historians, these essays, collectively, document two key trends regarding violence over the last fifty years. First, in almost all cases, rates of violence increased from the 1960s to the early 1990s. During this era, Texas became one of the most violent states in the United States, a country that has a homicide rate that far surpasses that of other industrialized nations. Second, rates of violence across the board saw a precipitous decline from the mid-1990s to 2019. These two significant trends appeared in overall homicides, intimate partner violence, anti-LGBTQ violence, racial violence, gang-related violence, and prison violence. Yet, a perpetual decline in violence is not a given. In fact, from 2020 to 2022, rates of violence spiked in the United States.[67]

Yet, throughout the rise and decline of violence in its myriad forms, nearly all of the authors found that a culture of violence undergirded each iteration of violence in the state. The factors related to the rise and decline of violence reflected changes in the economy, approaches to criminal justice, and a decline in the larger cultural embrace of different violent acts against different groups of people within the state. Despite the significant decline in violence from the 1990s to the late 2010s, a powerful cultural undercurrent lingers among segments of the Texas public that seems to justify or legitimize certain acts of violence in certain circumstances. It remains unknown how this cultural embrace of violence will shape Texan, and American, politics in the upcoming decades, especially as rates of violence, political divisions, and social and economic inequality increase.

To set the baseline for the rest of the volume, in chapter 1, "Homicide in Modern Texas," Jeffrey Littlejohn provides a broad look at homicide trends. Littlejohn demonstrates how homicides in Texas, while low in the late 1960s, experienced a spike in the 1970s, 1980s, and early 1990s. He attributes this spike to a "complex and evolving culture of violence" that "contributed to a surge in murders during key periods of racial and class conflict in the Lone Star State." Yet, as markedly as rates rose, from the mid-1990s to 2018, there was a precipitous decline. Littlejohn suggests that the "growth and efficiency of law enforcement, changes in popular culture, and the availability of new treatments for depression and psychiatric disorders led to the decline." Despite this rise and fall, Littlejohn maintains that a culture of violence, at least from the perspective of homicides, is still robust in Texas, as homicides still far surpass the rates of other industrialized nations.

While Littlejohn explored homicides as a whole, the rest of the essays in the collection take up specific forms or locales of violence. In chapter 2, "Intimate Partner Violence in Texas," Ashley Baggett examines the culture of violence that legitimized intimate partner violence and the efforts of activists to change that culture in modern Texas. A statistical analysis of intimate partner violence is limited by a lack of official records owing largely to the high rate of underreporting of this crime. Nonetheless, Baggett concludes that the efforts of activists to change the culture of violence that enabled intimate partner violence to become so problematic and widespread in the 1960s has "arguably [led to] a decline in rates of intimate partner violence. Despite the nation's and the state's progress over the last fifty years, abuse continues, with one in three women and one in four men experiencing physical violence by an intimate partner." She demonstrates how complex the culture of violence is surrounding domestic violence and examines the barriers that activists encountered in their struggle to dismantle that culture up through the twenty-first century.

In chapter 3, "Fighting the Killing Trail: LGBTQ Activism and the Hate Crime Epidemic in Texas," Christopher Haight examines the culture that promoted anti-LGBTQ violence in Texas up through the 1990s and the efforts of activists to dismantle it. Haight argues that a series of murders of LGBTQ Texans in the 1990s demonstrated to many LGBTQ activists in the state that there was "an oppressively homophobic culture, government, and legal system." Throughout the 1980s and 1990s, "the Lone Star State has been the center of some of the most notorious and symbolically important antigay hate crime cases in the country," he argues. He also documents an important shift in the tactics used by anti-LGBTQ violence activists from concerns over state violence against the LGBTQ community in the 1980s to an emphasis on using the state, via laws and police, for protection from violence in the 1990s and 2000s. While Haight demonstrates several successes the anti-LGBTQ violence activists experienced and that gay and lesbian Texans are more accepted in today's society than they were in the 1990s, he ends his chapter on a somber note, suggesting that despite these successes, the culture that supported anti-LGBTQ violence in the 1980s and 1990s has not completely disappeared, and the shortcomings of the Texas criminal justice system where it concerns LGBTQ crime victims are now becoming more evident to many activists.

According to Betsy Friauf and Michael Phillips in chapter 4, "'Those Boys Didn't Learn to Hate Here': Racial Violence in Texas since 1965,'" the history of racial violence in Texas follows a trajectory similar to that of anti-LGBTQ violence. Friauf and Phillips argue that racial violence in the last several decades of the twentieth century largely emerged out of police violence against people and communities of color. The first major push to undermine the culture of violence that supported police abuse and killing of racial minorities focused on changing police culture and the acceptance of police violence by the larger (white) Texas public. Yet, during the late 1990s, activists changed their focus and turned *to* the state to protect communities from violence. Friauf and Phillips express frustration at the lack of consistency in reporting instances of racial violence and hate crimes that make it impossible to accurately track rates. Nonetheless, the available evidence suggests to them that in the last two decades, instances of hate crime and racial violence stem mostly from racism or xenophobia and encompass acts of violence against African Americans, Muslims, and Latino/a Texans. While Friauf and Phillips assume that rates are declining, they argue that instances of racial violence will continue because "Texas today remains poised at the intersection of serious racial and economic inequality, elements providing the soil from which racial brutality has grown." Thus, while the overall rates of violence in the state declined, racial animosity and violence continue to plague the state, related in part, argue Friauf and Phillips, to a culture of violence that, except in rare instances such as the killing of James Byrd Jr., "ignores hate crimes as a serious threat."

In chapter 5, "Gang Violence in Texas: Urban Dynamics over Time," Mika Tapia's examination of gang violence details a rise in this crime from the 1960s to the early 1990s, followed by a noticeable decline, which echoes the trends seen in other forms of violence in the state. The sharp rise in gang-related violence, according to Tapia, occurred in response to "the increased demand for drugs in the United States, competition over territory and drug markets, the availability of more lethal weaponry, and mass incarceration associated with the war on drugs." Interestingly, though, gang-related violence declined "as drug markets became more regulated by the gangs themselves and reliance on and support for violence dissipated among those gangs that estwablished control over those drug markets." Violence, in other words, was bad for business. As gangs established control over drug markets, they worked to limit the amount of violence to increase the flow of money and illicit drugs. In term of a culture of violence within the gangs, the conclusions are mixed. While there is a certain amount of support and encouragement of different forms of violence in all gangs, Tapia argues that some gangs, especially Latino gangs, are less accepting of violence than others. Nonetheless, there is an overall culture within all gangs that supports and encourages a certain level of violence despite the economic motivations that work to limit it.

Building on the arguments made by Tapia concerning gang-related violence, Mitchel P. Roth, in chapter 6, "Violence in Texas Prisons," explores violent trends within prisons across the state. He, too, found a rise in violence from the 1960s to the 1990s, followed by a period of decline. The rise in prison violence was predictable, he suggests, as the number of inmates rose precipitously during the decades-long war on drugs and war on crime. He states, "In the mid-1960s, observers noticed that a surge in prison population combined with desegregation" contributed to a spike in violence as "a new generation of inmates . . . increasingly challenged the status quo in prisons across the nation." During the 1990s, the decline of violence within prison walls occurred, according to Roth, because the state hired more guards and trained them more effectively, prison administrators and guards better understood the nuances of prison gangs and worked to segregate gangs from one another, and prison guards' use of force to impose control on inmates increased along with the prison population. Despite the decline of violence, prisons still exhibit a culture of violence as both guards and gangs continue to rely on violence to impose order and control among and between gangs. Roth concludes, "In a counterintuitive way, violence is utilized to limit violence. Thus, while rates of prison violence seem to be lower in the twenty-first century than in the last two decades of the twentieth, a culture of violence still seems to predominate inside prison walls."

As explored in chapter 7, "Beyond the Gun: A Brief Examination of Mass Shootings in Texas, the real outlier to the trends seen in other forms of violence is mass shootings." While most Americans understand violence through these more sensationalized acts of violence, mass shootings followed the opposite trend of all other forms of violence. Kenneth Howell demonstrates that, although other forms of violence surged in the 1960s, 1970s, and 1980s, mass shootings were less frequent. The trends remained relatively steady throughout the last half of the twentieth century. Yet, as other forms of violence declined, mass shootings surged in the state from 2010 to 2020. Moreover, unlike other forms of violence, Howell argues the causes of mass shootings are not directly related to a larger cultural acceptance of violence but instead might be indirectly related to a prevalent gun culture and more directly associated with mental health; economic issues; domestic violence; and political, racial, and economic divisions within the state and country. Howell demonstrates that mass shooters face legal punishment or are killed (or kill themselves) before legal processes unfold. Moreover, state officials typically pass legislation designed to limit the chances of mass shootings recurring. While the actions, or seeming inaction, of lawmakers may be flawed in some ways, Howell suggests that their efforts indicate that a culture of violence that supports these acts of violence is not present.

As this volume demonstrates, our larger perceptions of violence do not always mesh with the realities on the ground. While many people believe we are living in one of the most violent eras, that is far from the truth. The first two decades of the twenty-first century have been some of the least violent years in American history. Yet, while some forms of violence have decreased, other, and in this case more publicized, acts of violence have increased.

The rates and frequency of violence change in response to larger economic and political developments. Despite the sustained decline in rates of violence from the 1990s to the late 2010s, this collection suggests that, although it is not as pervasive as it once was, in some instances, a culture of violence remains. This is important to remember because, as institutions can shape culture, our institutions are shaped by the culture from which they emerge. While economic equity, more robust mental health treatment options, and criminal justice and political reforms can help to reduce violence, the reality remains that Texas, and the United States as a whole, is more violent than most developed countries around the world. Moreover, from 2020 to 2022, rates of violence in the United States increased. While it is unclear if this spike will lead to a sustained rise in violence, it suggests that a greater understanding of the underlying causes of violence and cultural acceptance of it is necessary.[68] Any attempts to address violence must include changes to the larger structural and institutional inequalities and inequities that exist in Texan and American society, new approaches to criminal justice, and changes to culture as a whole to disavow and delegitimize acts of violence.

This book provides a large overview of the myriad forms of violence present in the state over the last several decades and of how communities and governmental institutions respond to those forms of violence, and it offers insight into the underlying causes of different forms of violence. As this modern era in Texas, and in the United States more broadly, receives increased scholarly attention in the coming years, we hope this volume inspires heightened interest in these topics, leads to more in-depth analysis of the period and trends, and spurs discussions on what we, collectively, can do to mitigate violence in our society.

Notes

1. Britteny Martin et al., "'Overwhelming Grief': 8 Students, 2 Teachers Killed in Texas High School Shooting," *Washington Post,* May 20, 2018, https://www .washingtonpost.com/news/post-nation/wp/2018/05/19/ten-killed-in-texas-high -school-shooting-were-mostly-students-police-say-suspect-confessed.

2. Saeed Ahmed and Christina Walker, "There Has Been, on Average, 1 School Shooting Every Week This Year," CNN, May 25, 2018, 11:05 a.m. EDT, https://www .cnn.com/2018/03/02/us/school-shootings-2018-list-trnd/index.html.

3. Kyle Swensen, "Oliver North Blames School Shootings On 'Culture of Violence,'" *Washington Post,* May 21, 2018, https://www.washingtonpost.com/news/morning-mix/ wp/2018/05/21/oliver-north-blames-school-shootings-on-culture-of-violence-he-was- a-pitchman-for-a-violent-video-game/?utm_term=.b059229cb315.

4. Nicholas Thompson, "America's Culture of Violence," *New Yorker,* December 15, 2012; Ana Nogales, "We Live in a Culture of Violence," *Psychology Today,* January 31, 2018.

5. Barry Latzer, *The Rise and Fall of Violent Crime in America* (New York: Encounter Books, 2016), 19.

6. For more on the decline in rates of and the culture of violence, see Norbert Elias, *The Civilizing Process: The History of Manners* (1939; reprint, New York, 1978); Roger Lane, *Violent Death in the City: Suicide, Accident, and Murder in Nineteenth-Century Philadelphia* (Cambridge: Harvard University Press, 1979); Eric H. Monkkonen, *Murder in New York City* (Berkeley: University of California Press, 2001); Jeffrey S. Adler, *First in Violence, Deepest in Dirt: Homicide in Chicago, 1875–1920* (Cambridge: Harvard University Press, 2006); Pieter Spierenburg, *A History of Murder: Personal Violence in Europe from the Middle Ages to the Present* (Cambridge: Polity Press, 2008); Steven Pinker, *The Better Angels of Our Nature: Why Violence Has Declined* (New York: Penguin Books, 2011). A number of recently published articles articulate the idea that the United States supports a culture of violence. For examples, see Thompson, "America's Culture of Violence"; Eric Schnurer, "Change Our Violence Culture," *U. S. News and World Report,* October 16, 2017; Nogales, "We Live in a Culture of Violence."

7. The editors came to this definition by blending the idea of "cultural violence" as articulated by Johan Galtung in "Cultural Violence," *Journal of Peace Research* 27, no. 3 (1990), 291–305; and David Matsumoto's definition of culture in *Culture and Psychology* (Pacific Grove, CA: Brooks/Cole, 1996), 16. For more on the notion of a culture of violence, see Matthew Jennings, *New Worlds of Violence: Cultures and Conquests in the Early American Southeast* (Knoxville: University of Tennessee Press, 2011).

8. For examples, see W. Eugene Hollon, *Frontier Violence: Another Look* (New York: Oxford University Press, 1974), 36–55; Richard Maxwell Brown, *Strain of Violence: Historical Studies of American Violence and Vigilantism* (New York: Oxford University Press, 1975), 236–300; William Carrigan, *The Making of a Lynching Culture: Violence and Vigilantism in Central Texas, 1836–1916* (Urbana: University of Illinois Press, 2004); Monica Muñoz Martinez, *The Injustice Never Leaves You: Anti-Mexican Violence in Texas* (Cambridge: Harvard University Press, 2018).

9. Robert Perkinson, *Texas Tough: The Rise of America's Prison Empire* (New York: Metropolitan Books, 2010), 5.

10. Roger Lane, *Murder in America: A History* (Columbus: Ohio State University Press, 1997), 268–303; Randolph Roth, *American Homicide* (Cambridge, MA: Harvard University Press, 2009), 452–68; David T. Courtwright, *Violent Land: Single Men and Social Disorder from the Frontier to the Inner City* (Cambridge, MA: Harvard University Press, 1996), 198–246; Latzer, *Rise and Fall of Violent Crime*, 103–70.

11. For more on the Caddo, see Cecile Elkins Carter, *Caddo Indians: Where We Come From* (Norman: University of Oklahoma Press), 1995; Steve Black et al., "Caddo Fundamentals," Texas Beyond History (web site), accessed September 18, 2019, https://texasbeyondhistory.net/tejas/fundamentals/miss.html.

12. Elizabeth A. H. John, *Storms Brewed in Other Men's Worlds: The Confrontation of Indians, Spanish, and French in the Southwest, 1540–1795* (Lincoln: University of Nebraska Press, 1975), 166–67.

13. Kenneth W. Howell et al., *Beyond Myths and Legends: A Narrative History of Texas,* 5th ed. (Wheaton, IL: Abigail Press, 2017), 28–30.

14. For more on Cabeza de Vaca's journey, see Andrés Reséndez, *A Land So Strange: The Extraordinary Tale of a Shipwrecked Spaniard Who Walked Across America in the Sixteenth Century* (New York: BasicBooks, 2007).

15. Howell et al., *Beyond Myths and Legends,* 34–35.

16. For more on Spanish Texas, see Randolph B. Campbell, *Gone to Texas: A History of the Lone Star State* (New York: Oxford University Press, 2003), 49–99; Donald Chipman and Harriet Denise Joseph, *Spanish Texas: 1519–1821,* 2nd ed. (Austin: University of Texas Press, 2010).

17. Pekka Hamalainen, *The Comanche Empire* (New Haven: Yale University Press, 2008), 1.

18. Hamalainen, *Comanche Empire,* 1.

19. Hamalainen, 279–80.

20. Howell et al., *Beyond Myths and Legends,* 16.

21. Jennings, *New Worlds of Violence*, xxi.

22. Campbell, *Gone to Texas*, 128–58; 187–89; 239–67.

23. Laura Lyons McLemore, "Early Historians and the Shaping of Texas Memory," in *Lone Star Pasts: Memory and History in Texas*, ed. Gregg Cantrell and Elizabeth Hayes Turner (College Station: Texas A&M University Press, 2007), 15–38.

24. Greg Cantrell, "The Bones of Stephen F. Austin: History and Memory in Progressive-Era Texas," and Don Graham, "Mission Statement: The Alamo and the Fallacy of Historical Accuracy in Epic Filmmaking," in Cantrell and Turner, *Lone Star Pasts*, 39–74; 242–69.

25. David W. Blight, *Race and Reunion: The Civil War in American Memory* (Cambridge, MA: Harvard University Press, 2001); Walter L. Buenger, *The Path to a Modern South: Northeast Texas between Reconstruction and the Great Depression* (Austin: University of Texas Press, 200 I), xxiv, 104, 123–27; Bobby, Blanchard, "Texas Has More than 180 Public Symbols of the Confederacy," *Texas Tribune*, August 21, 2017, https://www.texastribune.org/2017/08/21/texas-has-second-most-public-symbols-confederacy-nation.

26. Edward L. Ayers, *Vengeance and Justice: Crime and Punishment in the 19th-Century American South* (New York: Oxford University Press, 1984), 13.

27. Bertram Wyatt-Brown, *Southern Honor: Ethics & Behavior in the Old South* (New York: Oxford University Press, 1983; Lane, *Murder in America*, 127.

28. Randolph B. Campbell, *An Empire for Slavery: The Peculiar Institution in Texas, 1821–1861* (Baton Rouge, Louisiana State University Press, 1991).

29. Ayers, *Vengeance and Justice*, 26–27.

30. Ayers, 34–72; Donald R. Walker, "Texas State Penitentiary at Huntsville," *Handbook of Texas Online*, July 1, 1995, http://www.tshaonline.org/handbook/online/articles/jjt01.

31. Michael S. Hindus, *Prison and Plantation: Crime, Justice, and Authority in Massachusetts and South Carolina, 1767–1878* (Chapel Hill: University of North Carolina Press, 1980); Ayers, 9; Lawrence M. Friedman, *Crime and Punishment in American History* (New York: Basic Books, 1993), 81–82; Randall Kennedy, *Race, Crime, and the Law* (New York: Vintage Books, 1991), 30–34; Campbell, *Gone to Texas*, 224.

32. Carrigan, *Making of a Lynching Culture*; Brown, *Strain of Violence*, 236–300.

33. Carrigan, 8.

34. Kenneth W. Howell, ed., "Preface," in *Still the Arena of Civil War: Violence and Turmoil in Reconstruction Texas, 1865–1874* (Denton: University of North Texas Press, 2012), ix.

35. Howell, "Introduction: The Elusive Story of Violence in Reconstruction Texas, 1865–1874," in *Still the Arena of Civil War*, 24.

36. Howell, *Still the Arena of Civil War*; James Smallwood, Barry A Crouch, and Larry Peacock, *Murder and Mayhem: The War of Reconstruction in Texas* (College Station: Texas A&M University Press, 2003). Charles Ramsdell described Ku Klux Klan and terrorist violence in Texas during Reconstruction in very positive ways. He believed that those groups represented upstanding citizens who banded together

to save the South from the abuses of the Radical Republicans. Ramsdell represents the Dunning School of Reconstruction history that shaped historiographical views of the era for much of the early twentieth century. See Ramsdell, *Reconstruction in Texas* (New York: Columbia University Press, 1910).

37. Hamalainen, *Comanche Empire*, 321–41; Brown, *Strain of Violence*, 243–46.

38. Robert P. Ingalls, "Vigilantism," in *Violence*, ed. Amy Louise Wood (Chapel Hill: University of North Carolina Press, 2011), 185.

39. Brown, *Strain of Violence*, 246–51.

40. Brown, 251–60.

41. The lynching statistics extend slightly before and beyond the 1860 to 1900 timeframe. See William D. Carrigan and Clive Webb, *Forgotten Dead: Mob Violence against Mexicans in the United States, 1848–1928* (New York: Oxford University Press, 2013), 6; Equal Justice Initiative, *Lynching in America: Confronting the Legacy of Racial Terror* (Montgomery, AL: Equal Justice Initiative, 2015), 40; David L. Chapman, "Lynching in Texas" (master's thesis, Texas Tech University, 1973), 94–96.

42. W. Fitzhugh Brundage, *Lynching in the New South: Georgia and Virginia, 1880–1930* (Urbana: University of Illinois Press, 1993), 17–48.

43. Carrigan, *Making of a Lynching Culture*, 132–61.

44. Carrigan, 8.

45. Walter White, *Rope and Faggot: A Biography of Judge Lynch* (New York: Alfred A. Knopf, Inc., 1929), 20–22; W. Eugene Hollon, *Frontier Violence: Another Look* (New York: Oxford University Press, 1974), 51.

46. Nicholas Villanueva Jr., *The Lynching of Mexicans in the Texas Borderlands* (Albuquerque: University of New Mexico Press, 2017), 167; Martinez, *Injustice Never Leaves You*, 7; Carrigan and Webb, *Forgotten Dead*, 84–88.

47. William M. Tuttle Jr., "Violence in a 'Heathen' Land: The Longview Race Riot of 1919," *Phylon* 33, no. 4 (4th Qtr. 1972), 324–33; Kenneth R. Durham, "The Longview Race Riot of 1919," *East Texas Historical Journal* 18, no. 2 (1980), 13–24.

48. Brandon T. Jett, "'Let Us Be Law Abiding Citizens': Mob Violence and the Local Response in Harrison County, Texas, 1890–1925," *East Texas Historical Journal* 54, no. 2 (Fall 2016): 40–46; David M. Chalmers, *Hooded Americanism: The History of the Ku Klux Klan* (New York: New Viewpoints, 1981), 39–48.

49. Michael J. Pfeifer, *Rough Justice: Lynching and American Society, 1874–1947* (Urbana: University of Illinois Press, 2004); Dwight W. Watson, "'In the Name of Progress and Decency': The Response of Houston's Civic Leaders to the Lynching of Robert Powell in 1928," *Houston Review* 1, no. 2 (1995), 26–30; Brandon T. Jett, "Paris Is Burning: Lynching and Racial Violence in Lamar County, Texas, 1890–1920," *East Texas Historical Journal* 51, no. 2 (Fall 2013), 40–63; Brandon T. Jett, "'Detrimental to the Interests of the City:' Lynching and the Local Response in Bowie County, 1886–1922," *Journal of South Texas* 28, no. 1 (Spring 2015), 30–45; Jett, "'Let Us Be Law Abiding Citizens.'"

50. Monkkonen, *Murder in New York City*, 22; Lane, *Murder in America*, 215; Roth, *American Homicide*, 440–50; Latzer, *Rise and Fall of Violent Crime*, 1–102.

51. This data is pulled from the FBI Uniform Crime Reports.

52. Sheldon Hackney, "Southern Violence," *American Historical Review* 74, no. 3 (February 1969), 925.

53. Raymond D. Gastil, "Homicide and a Regional Culture of Violence," *American Sociological Review* 36, no. 3 (June 1971), 412.

54. This data is pulled from my own databases compiled with data from the FBI Uniform Crime Reports, Vital Statistics, and secondary literature.

55. For more on the broader movements for civil rights in the state, see Brian D. Behnken, *Fighting Their Own Battles: Mexican Americans, African Americans, and the Struggle for Civil Rights in Texas* (Chapel Hill: University of North Carolina Press, 2011); Max Krochmal, *Blue Texas: The Making of a Multiracial Democratic Coalition in the Civil Rights Era* (Chapel Hill: University of North Carolina Press, 2016).

56. Clifford R. Caldwell and Ron DeLord, *Eternity at the End of a Rope: Executions, Lynchings and Vigilante Justice in Texas, 1819–1923* (Santa Fe, NM: Sunstone Press, 2015), 593.

57. James A. Burran, "Violence in an 'Arsenal of Democracy': The Beaumont Race Riot, 1943," *East Texas Historical Journal* 14, no 1 (1976), 39–52; James S. Olson, "Beaumont Riot of 1943," *Handbook of Texas Online,* published November 1, 1994, updated September 30, 2020, https://www.tshaonline.org/handbook/entries/beaumont-riot-of-1943.

58. "Many Schools Integrate Peacefully, but Not All Try," *Texas Observer,* September 12, 1956; Behnken, *Fighting Their Own Battles,* 75.

59. Behnken, 90.

60. Brown, *Strain of Violence;* Richard Maxwell Brown, *No Duty to Retreat: Violence and Values in American History and Society* (Norman: University of Oklahoma Press, 1991); William Carrigan, *The Making of a Lynching Culture: Violence and Vigilantism in Central Texas, 1836–1916* (Urbana: University of Illinois Press, 2007); Henry P. Lundsgaarde, *Murder in Space City: A Cultural Analysis of Houston Homicide Patterns* (New York: Oxford University Press, 1977).

61. For overviews of various changes in Texas since the mid-1960s, see Campbell, *Gone to Texas,* 438–71; Howell et al., *Beyond Myths and Legends,* 451–531.

62. Campbell, 438.

63. "The 30 Most Populous Cities," National League of Cities, accessed September 25, 2019, https://www.politifact.com/largestcities/.

64. "Resident Population of Texas in 2017, by Race and Ethnicity," Statista, accessed September 25, 2019, https://www.statista.com/statistics/306044/texas-population-ethnicity-race.

65. Perkinson, *Texas Tough,* 6.

66. Violence has occurred in many forms over the course of Texas' history.

Instead of choosing one form, we compiled essays exploring multiple forms of violence with an eye toward understanding the cultural and institutional responses to them. This approach allows for a fuller understanding of the complicated nature of violence over time.

67. There was a spike in violence during 2020 for several reasons that researchers are still grappling with. Even with that spike, rates of homicides and violence in the United States remain well below where those rates were in the early 1990s. It is also not clear if the spike in 2020 will lead to a sustained rise in violence over several years or something more short-term. For more on violence in 2020, 2021, and 2022, see Ames Grawert and Noah Kim, "Myths and Realities: Understanding Recent Trends in Violent Crime, "Brennan Center for Justice, July 12, 2022, https://www.brennancenter.org/our-work/research-reports/myths-and-realities-understanding-recent-trends-violent-crime.

68. For more on violence in 2020, 2021, and 2022, see Ames Grawert and Noah Kim, "Myths and Realities: Understanding Recent Trends in Violent Crime, "Brennan Center for Justice, July 12, 2022, https://www.brennancenter.org/our-work/research-reports/myths-and-realities-understanding-recent-trends-violent-crime.

1

HOMICIDE IN MODERN TEXAS

Jeffrey L. Littlejohn

On Friday, July 2, 1982, Barbara L. Smith and her son, Steven Mark Reynolds, hurriedly prepared to leave their home at 7827 Idlewood Lane in Dallas, Texas. The thirty-nine-year-old mother had been in an ongoing domestic dispute with her second husband, Kenneth Eugene Smith, and she hoped that separating from him might prevent any additional conflict. As Barbara and her son packed their bags, however, Ken returned home and interrupted them. An argument quickly ensued, and Barbara sent her fifteen-year-old son out of the house. The teenager later told investigators that "his parents were in the bedroom arguing when he heard a gunshot." Dallas police quickly arrived on the scene, and Barbara was pronounced dead at 12:15 a.m. Homicide detectives found that Ken had drawn a firearm on his wife, shot her in the neck, and then turned the gun on himself. Although his wound proved serious, it was not fatal.[1]

Ken Smith faced swift prosecution for the alleged murder of his wife. On July 10, eight days after the incident, his case was assigned to Criminal District Court Five in Dallas County. At the advice of his attorneys, Smith pled not guilty to the charges against him. Investigators continued to gather evidence, and prosecutors took the case to trial on December 10, 1982. After hearing from family members, psychiatric doctors, and police investigators, the jury found Smith guilty of murder and sentenced him to 120 days in jail and ten years of probation. Shortly after this decision, Smith posted a twenty-five-hundred-dollar bond, and his attorneys appealed his case. In April 1985, Smith received a new sentence that limited his punishment to ten years of probation, and in October 1994 he was released from any further responsibility in Barbara Smith's death.[2]

I was eight years old when my aunt Barbara was murdered, but my parents shielded me from the gruesome details of her death. Even if they had chosen to share the story with me, Barbara's murder would have made little sense. Popular culture and my own fears led me to believe that homicide was a crime most often committed by the type of evil characters who were portrayed on television shows and in Hollywood movies. I certainly did not understand that the majority of murders in the United States were committed by adults who knew their victims, either as family members, neighbors, or acquaintances. Nor did I understand that aunt Barbara was killed during one of the most violent periods in recent history. In 1982, Texas ranked second among the most homicidal states in America, with a murder rate that had skyrocketed from 7.5 victims per 100,000 people in 1965 to 16.1 victims per 100,000 people in 1982.[3] Although this dramatic rise in the murder rate held little interest for me in the 1980s, today I understand that it contributed to the passage of draconian legal reforms, the militarization of urban police forces, the federal war on drugs, and the current state of mass incarceration.[4] Why did the homicide rate in the Lone Star State rise so precipitously between 1965 and 1982? And, why, after that period, did it begin a slow but steady decline to the rate of 4.6 victims per 100,000 people in 2018?[5] This chapter argues that a complex and evolving culture of violence in Texas contributed to a surge in murders during key periods of racial and class conflict in the Lone Star State. Those murders, in turn, declined due to a variety of factors, including the growth and efficiency of law enforcement, changes in popular culture, and the availability of new treatments for depression and psychiatric disorders.

Police officers, policymakers, and social scientists have long been interested in the homicide rate. Because murder is generally considered the most heinous of crimes, each known episode is recorded in multiple databases, including the Federal Bureau of Investigation's Uniform Crime Reporting Program and the Texas Department of Public Safety's yearly Crime in Texas reports. Although the statistics presented in these and other databases may contain minor discrepancies, all reports define homicide as the willful killing of one human being by another. Deaths that result from fights, arguments, assaults, or the commission of a crime are included by the Uniform Crime Reporting Program as homicides. Failed attempts to kill another person, on the other hand, are categorized as aggravated assaults and not as murders. Likewise, suicides, accidental deaths, and justifiable homicides are excluded from statistics on murder.[6]

In Texas, the high frequency of homicide has often been traced back to the violent culture that first developed during the nineteenth century. As Anglo Americans moved with enslaved African Americans from Tennessee, Alabama, and other southern states into Texas, they carried firearms with them to tame the wilderness and maintain their control. The ownership of guns and knives not only was acceptable but was virtually required for Anglo Texans who sought to provide food for their families, manage enslaved African Americans, and defend newly claimed property from Native Americans. In this borderland space, a "primal" concept of honor served as the "keystone in the arch of social order," as Bertram Wyatt-Brown has written.[7] A man's reputation for strength and resolve became paramount, and any criticism or slight had to be met with force. "Self-respect, as the Southerners understand it, has always demanded much fighting," historian Edward L. Ayers reminds us. White Southerners' "often-repeated explanation of why they killed each other with such frequency and regularity . . . [was that] they did it for honor's sake."[8]

Of course, white migrants to Texas did not envision a multiracial or multiethnic republic in the Southwest. On the contrary, they viewed Native Americans as heathen savages, African Americans as chattel property, and Tejanos (Mexican Texans) as the inferior mix of Spaniards, Africans, and Indians.[9] As promoters of these racial stereotypes, Anglo Texans developed a culture of violence that stressed their own superiority and independence, backed, whenever necessary, by armed force.[10] As W. J. Cash, the great analyst of Southern culture wrote, they became consumed with the "bald, immediate, unsupported assertion of the ego, which placed . . . stress on the inviolability of personal whim, and which was full of the chip-on-shoulder swagger and brag of a boy." In brief, Cash wrote, the essence of Anglo supremacy "was the boast, voiced or not, on the part of every Southerner, that he would knock the hell out of whoever dared to cross him."[11]

Texans have actively participated in a culture of violence for much of the last 150 years, but two key events in the state ushered in a new era of homicidal violence in the 1960s.[12] The first and most infamous occurred on November 22, 1963, when Lee Harvey Oswald, a former Marine sharpshooter and defector to the Soviet Union, shot and killed President John F. Kennedy as his motorcade made its way through Dealey Plaza in Dallas, Texas. Police officers in Dallas quickly focused their attention on Oswald, who had been working on the sixth floor of the Texas School Book Depository during the president's procession. When officer J. D. Tippit confronted Oswald on a side street a short distance from Dealey Plaza, the suspect shot and killed Tippit before escaping into a nearby theater. Once discovered, Oswald was arrested and charged with the murder of President Kennedy. Two days later, however, Jack Ruby, a Dallas nightclub owner, fatally shot Oswald on live television as he was being escorted through the basement of Dallas Police Department headquarters. "When the assassin is assassinated on television," Todd Gitlin, a student activist, later said, it "is not only appalling, it's also uncanny. Being witnesses in this odd way via television, you are an extra in this . . . historical drama, and you are therefore implicated in it."[13] Josiah Thompson, a private investigator at the time, agreed: "The Kennedy assassination was a kind of tectonic shift, and we knew it at the time. Something had shifted under our feet. And we knew during that weekend and certainly within days of that weekend in November 1963, that things would never be the same again."[14]

Three years after the Kennedy assassination, a second tragic act of homicidal violence took place in Texas. This time, Austin served as the scene of the crime. There, on August 1, 1966, Charles Whitman, a former Marine and student at the University of Texas, went on an unprecedented killing spree. Whitman began his murderous rampage by stabbing his mother and wife to death. Then, he took a Marine Corp footlocker loaded with hundreds of rounds of ammunition and seven guns to the observation deck of the iconic 307-foot tower on the campus at the University of Texas. From his perch atop the tower, Whitman opened fire on students, faculty, and local residents in the surrounding area. Over the next hour and a half, he shot and killed sixteen people and wounded thirty-one others. His murder spree did not end until two Austin Police Department patrolmen reached the observation deck and shot Whitman dead. At the time, the incident was the deadliest mass shooting in US history.[15]

Taken together, these two acts of public violence helped launch what historian Roger Lane has called an "anxious decade" full of "turbulence, bloodshed, and confusion."[16] On the national stage, the murder rate doubled between 1965 and 1980, rising from 5.1 to 10.2 per 100,000 people. Cultural conflicts, urban riots, student demonstrations, Vietnam protests, and the Watergate scandal were all implicated as possible reasons for the upsurge in violence. At the same time, in Texas, the homicide rate increased by more than 125 percent, jumping from 7.5 to 16.9 per 100,000 people. Although the Lone Star State had always been among the top twelve most violent areas in America, by 1980 it was the second-most homicidal state in the nation.[17]

The murder rate in Texas exceeded the national average during the 1960s and 1970s for a variety of complicated reasons. Foremost may have been the culture of violence that existed in the state. Long a bastion of gun-toting cowboys and wildcat oil drillers, Texas had a reputation for strong men, such as Ethan Edwards, the hero in John Ford's film *The Searchers* (1956). Hyper-masculine and self-reliant, Edwards is a Confederate veteran who spends five years searching for his abducted niece, Debbie. When he finds her living with a Comanche chief named Scar, Edwards insists that she return home with him. When Debbie refuses, he threatens to shoot her. Instead, he later kills and scalps Scar, then takes Debbie home to Texas.[18]

Texans celebrated men like Edwards. Their strength, grit, and tenacity proved their superiority to other men. And, if they were misogynistic, racist bullies, then so be it. They were Texans. They played high school, college, and professional football like gladiators in ancient Rome. They rode bulls, wrestled steers, and roped calves in that sport called rodeo. Violence was a way of life for Texas men. They made their point, like their president, Lyndon Johnson, by leaning into lesser men and giving them the treatment. Their heroes were wild and untamed, like Warren Betty's Clyde Barrow in the 1967 film *Bonnie and Clyde*. Dangerous and armed, they shook up the boredom of everyday life and added a bit of excitement to daily existence. And when they went too far, lawmen like Frank Hamer, the feared Texas Ranger, were there to handle them.[19]

The popular culture of violence in Texas explained only so much, however. When Texans at the time debated the unprecedented rise in homicide rates between 1965 and 1980, they broke down into two essential positions. First, conservative commentators argued that the homicide rate in Texas had risen because the US Supreme Court and liberal Democratic politicians had "handcuffed" the police, curtailed capital punishment, and excused radical actions by civil rights demonstrators and student protesters. Crime was seen as "a problem of permissiveness and moral laxity,"[20] historian Sean Cunningham has written. Conservatives did not believe that federal antipoverty programs and public education could reduce crime rates, and they viewed liberals who made such arguments as naïve do-gooders. As advocates of strict law and order, conservatives focused their initial complaints on a set of US Supreme Court decisions between 1961 and 1966 that applied constitutional protections in the Fourth, Fifth, and Sixth Amendments to the states through the Fourteenth Amendment in a judicial process known as selective incorporation. In practice, this meant that the court ruled in *Mapp v. Ohio* (1961) that evidence secured through unwarranted searches and seizures was inadmissible in state courts. Likewise, in *Gideon v. Wainwright* (1963), the court found that the Sixth Amendment's guarantee of a right to counsel applied to defendants in state courts. Then, in *Griffin v. California* (1965), the justices ruled that the Fifth Amendment prohibited a prosecutor or judge from disparaging a defendant's refusal to testify in his or her own defense. And, finally, in *Miranda v. Arizona* (1966), the court found that the Fifth Amendment required police officers to advise suspects of their right to remain silent and their right to obtain an attorney during interrogations while in police custody. Taken together, these four decisions established a "single, national, and high set of standards for criminal proceedings across the whole of the country."[21]

Despite widespread support for the Supreme Court's decisions on criminal proceedings, conservatives such as Senator John Tower of Texas lambasted them as "a sacrifice of the rights of society in favor of those of the individual." For example, Tower said, there "can be little doubt that the standard imposed upon the law enforcement officer by virtue of the *Miranda* case results in the virtual elimination of the use of confessions." As a result, he said, "Criminals of the most despicable sort have been set free to endanger our society." In fact, Tower joined with other Southern conservatives, including Sam Ervin of North Carolina, Harry Byrd of Virginia, and Strom Thurmond of South Carolina, to support a constitutional amendment that would have overridden the court's decision in the *Miranda* case and allowed for the resumption of so-called "voluntary" confessions. "The vital question which has been raised by the combination of the recent trend of Supreme Court decisions and the ever-increasing rate of crime," Tower told a crowd in 1967, "is whether the law enforcement agencies of this nation can effectively discharge their responsibilities without a change in the existing constitutional provisions. At this time in our nation's history when the need for law enforcement has heightened, we cannot turn to the Supreme Court for guidance. Therefore, we must, for the good of our society, bring about a resurgence of police powers . . . through ratification of the proposed amendment to the United States Constitution."[22]

Although no amendment on voluntary confessions was ever ratified, conservative critics of the Supreme Court proved more successful on another front: capital punishment. The death penalty had been used to punish convicted murderers in Texas since the early nineteenth century when the territory belonged to Mexico. Between 1819 and 1923, Texans carried out executions at the county level by hanging convicted criminals. Then, following a wave of infamous lynchings, legislators moved all executions to the state penitentiary in Huntsville, where a new electric chair was installed.[23] Between February 1924 and July 1964, the state carried out 361 executions by electrocution. Judicial challenges to capital punishment in the mid-1960s resulted in a de facto moratorium on executions, however, and in June 1972, the US Supreme Court issued a 5 to 4 decision in *Furman v. Georgia,* ruling that capital punishment as then practiced was unconstitutional. "The Court's majority concluded that jurors were not being given effective sentencing guidelines for their deliberations, resulting in a situation in which death was being 'wantonly and freakishly' imposed."[24] In Texas at the time, forty-seven men sat on death row. The state's Democratic governor, Preston Smith, commuted all of those death sentences to life in prison, and death row was therefore cleared in March 1973. In fact, the state's next execution did not take place until December 7, 1982, almost a decade later, and even then, executions remained rare with just one in 1982 and none in 1983. Thus, in the nearly twenty-year period from August 1, 1964 to January 1, 1984, Texas executed only one person.[25]

Texas conservatives needed no help linking the twenty-year break in executions with the rise in the state's violent crime and homicide rate. The matter seemed obvious and commonsensical. After the death penalty ceased to be applied in horrific murder and rape cases, they argued, the homicide rate naturally went up. Indeed, four short months after the Supreme Court's *Furman* decision, Governor Smith expanded his call for a special session of the state legislature so that Texas representatives and senators could consider new laws to restore the state's death penalty for "heinous crimes." Although that year's bill was sidelined because of a legislative technicality, lawmakers passed House Bill 200 the following year. It became effective on June 14, 1973, reinstating capital punishment in Texas for certain categories of homicide. This revision to the Texas code received approval from the US Supreme Court in *Jurek v. Texas* (1976), and the following year, the state adopted lethal injection as its new form of execution.[26]

National polls indicated that Texas legislators had done the right, or at least the popular, thing. In November 1972, a nationwide Gallup poll showed the "highest level of support for capital punishment in two decades," with 57 percent of respondents in favor of the procedure. But, that number paled in comparison with the 77 percent of Texans who, in a November 1978 state crime poll, said that the death penalty was the proper punishment for criminals convicted of murder.[27] This widespread support for capital punishment soon made Huntsville, Texas, the "execution capital of the world." Since the reintroduction of the death penalty in 1976, Texas has put to death roughly "37.3 percent (540 of 1,446) of the persons executed in the US."[28]

Liberal critics of capital punishment challenged conservative arguments, suggesting that rightwing commentators had exaggerated the significance of the death penalty as a deterrent force. In 1969, for example, Rupert Koeninger, a professor of sociology at Texas Southern University, published a widely read article, "Capital Punishment in Texas, 1924–1968." The piece examined the trial and disposition of 460 of 483 cases in which a defendant was sentenced to death during the period (final disposition in twenty-three cases had not been made). Koeninger's findings proved shocking. He showed, first of all, that African Americans accounted for 58.4 percent of those charged with capital crimes, although they made up just 15 percent of the state's population. Likewise, Koeninger demonstrated that 118 of the 460 convicted criminals had less than three years of schooling and were functionally "illiterate," while an additional 304 had less than a high school education. Put simply, the vast majority of those who had been executed or placed on death row were poor and uneducated. Making matters worse, only 30 percent of the accused had court-appointed attorneys, and as a result, many of them offered weak or nonsensical defense arguments, including drunkenness. Koeninger found this last point to be particularly disturbing and argued that many death penalty trials had been handled in a hasty manner, unsuited to the seriousness of the situation. In most cases, he said, the "period between arrest and final disposition was [just] a year or eighteen months."[29]

Koeninger obviously opposed the resumption of the death penalty in Texas and argued that it had not accomplished what its advocates hoped it would. During the twenty-one-year period from 1946 to 1967, he wrote, capital punishment had done nothing to deter murder in Texas. Rather, the homicide rate had continuously fluctuated between a high of 11.1 and a low of 7.2 per 100,000 people. There existed no evidence of a causal relationship between the number of people executed and the rise or decline in the homicide rate. In fact, Texas ranked ninth among the fifty states in the murder rate in 1966 and sixth in 1967. Moreover, it could not even be said that capital punishment assured the safety of law enforcement officers given that thirty-five of them were murdered between 1924 and 1965. As a result, Koeninger wrote that his findings warranted "the conclusions that execution has not reduced homicides in Texas, has not insured the safety of law enforcement officers, and is applied disproportionately to the Negro, young, poor, and ignorant."[30]

Since Koeninger's work appeared in 1969, numerous scholars have examined the effect that capital punishment has on homicide, but no general consensus on the subject has emerged.[31] Historian Roger Lane has argued that the entire issue is a red herring that diverts attention from the true causes of homicidal violence. In his book *Murder in America,* Lane argues that rising violence in the United States during the 1960s and 1970s was "part of an international shift" from the industrial to the postindustrial age. Although different countries entered the new era at different times, "once the decay of the urban industrial revolution" set in, cities such as Houston, Detroit, and Memphis were plagued by violence. The public education systems, routinized corporate discipline, and stringent moral lessons of the industrial era "came to seem irrelevant and the institutions of social control simply tyrannical." The material abundance that had once justified staying out of trouble and obeying the police no longer trickled down to the people living at the bottom of the social order. And so, with alcohol and drugs widely available, and with time on their hands, "a growing number of young men in the postindustrial age drifted into impulsively violent criminal behavior." As a result, homicide rates rose, especially in urban areas, and states were forced to create more rigid criminal justice systems to deal with law breakers.[32]

The clarity and simplicity of Lane's argument certainly make it appealing, but it fails to address the contingent historical realities that existed in different locations throughout the 1960s and 1970s. Historian Randolph Roth offers a far more comprehensive and satisfying analysis of the murder rate in his book *American Homicide.* He argues that "homicide rates among adults are not determined by proximate causes such as poverty, drugs, unemployment, alcohol, race, or ethnicity." Rather, he says, the homicide rate is determined "by factors that seem . . . impossibly remote, like the feelings that people have toward their government, the degree to which they identify with members of their own communities, and the opportunities they have to earn respect without resorting to violence."[33] Roth relates these three analytical factors directly to the lived experience of people in various communities throughout the United States. In Texas, for example, he shows how indignation over the Vietnam War, frustration about the lack of good-paying jobs, disgust with the Watergate scandal, and rancor over the civil rights movement led to an increase in the homicide rate.

One good example to consider is the rise in urban upheavals during the 1960s and 1970s. Following the passage of the Civil Rights Act of 1964 and the Voting Rights Act of 1965, many Anglo Texans believed that the federal government had gone far enough, indeed too far, to ensure African American and Hispanic inclusion in the broader national society. Yet, African American and Hispanic Texans felt these new laws were simply a remedy for long-existing discrimination that had prohibited them from participating in the social, political, and economic progress that Anglo Americans had experienced since World War II. These divergent views contributed to a culture of distrust and hostility in Texas, which erupted in 1966 and 1967 in two major confrontations. The first clash resulted when, in the summer of 1966, a group of Hispanic farmworkers from the Rio Grande Valley staged a march to the state capital in Austin to secure support for unionization and farmworkers' rights. Feeling that enough had already been done for Hispanic workers, governor John Connally and his attorney general, Waggoner Carr, ordered the Texas Highway Patrol and Texas Rangers to disperse the marchers, who were accused of disrupting traffic on State Highway 10. A violent confrontation ensued, and the farmworkers were forced to retreat. As a result, Connally and Carr, who was running for the US Senate against John Tower, lost their support in the Tejano community.[34]

A second and more dangerous confrontation erupted in Houston in May 1967. At the time, mayor Louie Welch, police chief Herman Short, and officers with the Houston Police Department had launched a surveillance program on the campus of Texas Southern University (TSU). Founded in 1947, the school was one of the Lone Star State's last attempts to prevent the desegregation of higher education in Texas. Located in a lower-middle-class African American neighborhood called Third Ward, TSU's campus infrastructure, library collections, and academic resources were underfunded and compared poorly to those at the University of Texas at Austin. Nevertheless, TSU students proved to be civically engaged and participated in local demonstrations against police brutality, inadequate housing, and unfair business practices in Houston. In May 1967, several TSU students joined environmental activists in sit-in protests at the Holmes Road Dump, where an eleven-year-old boy named Victor George had drowned in a garbage-filled pond early in the month. During two days of protest, dozens of activists were manhandled and arrested by Houston police. Then, on the night of May 16, when officers apprehended a TSU student on campus for discussing police brutality at the dump protest, outraged students began throwing rocks and shouting at police. In response, police chief Short assembled a large riot squad, closed the TSU campus, and marched his forces to Lanier Hall, where students had barricaded themselves in for defense. The volatile combination of student angst and police bravado exploded when an unknown party fired a gunshot. Police reacted by shooting almost five thousand rounds of ammunition into the dormitory, and a young officer, Louis R. Kuba, was killed. Police responded to Kuba's death, which later reports proved to have been the result of ricocheting friendly fire, by storming the dorm and arresting 488 students, most of whom had nothing to do with the protests.[35]

The TSU and farmworker confrontations with police revealed how little faith African Americans and Tejanos had in the Texas government and law enforcement. In fact, at least eight further urban disorders took place in Texas between 1967 and 1971. Four occurred, as historian Peter Levy has shown, in Dallas, Tyler, Prairie View, and San Antonio in 1968.[36] Federal officials became so concerned about urban disorders during the period that President Lyndon Johnson established two separate commissions to investigate the causes of the violence. The National Advisory Commission on Civil Disorders (Kerner Commission) was set up in July 1967, and the National Commission on the Causes and Prevention of Violence (Eisenhower Commission) was established in June 1968. Although the two groups issued different reports, their general findings proved to be very similar.[37]

The Kerner Commission found, for example, that state and federal governments had failed to address glaring housing, education, and cultural needs in America's cities. The commission's report warned, "Our nation is moving toward two societies, one black, one white—separate and unequal." It suggested that white racism was one of the principal causes of urban violence and called on the federal government to create new jobs, housing, and public policies that would provide opportunities for African Americans and other racial and ethnic minorities in urban areas. Issued on February 29, 1968, the report was largely ignored by President Johnson until the assassinations of civil rights leader Reverend Martin Luther King Jr. and Democratic presidential candidate Robert Kennedy. In the wake of these tragedies, Johnson created the Eisenhower Commission, which issued its final report in December 1969. Like the Kerner Commission, the Eisenhower group argued that the most important issues facing urban communities were the lack of employment and educational opportunities in many neighborhoods. The commission's report included many haunting assessments, including one that placed the lack of inner-city opportunity within the larger framework of America's meritocratic culture that celebrated financial success. "To be a young, poor male; to be undereducated and without means of escape from an oppressive urban environment; to want what the society claims is available (but mostly to others); to see around oneself illegitimate and often violent methods being used to achieve material success; and to observe others using these means with impunity—all this is to be burdened with an enormous set of influences that pull many toward crime and delinquency. To be also a Negro, Mexican or Puerto Rican American and subject to discrimination and segregation adds considerably to the pull of these other criminogenic forces."[38]

As the federal government's own commissions reported, many African Americans, Tejanos, and other minorities felt isolated and abandoned. Polling from 1974 showed that the proportion of African Americans who trusted the government had reached an all-time low of 18 percent.[39] This dissatisfaction certainly helped to explain why urban disturbances had broken out in places like Watts, Houston, Detroit, and Chicago, but it also contributed to an understanding of rising homicide rates during the 1970s. As Roth has written, "The anger, alienation, and disillusionment of young black men were channeled into violent crimes such as robberies, rapes, and murders. A few incidents were racially motivated. . . . There were very few such killings, however. Most black murderers, robbers, and rapists selected their victims without regard to race. They felt so disconnected, disempowered, and disrespected that they were willing to attack anyone, friend or stranger, who crossed them or presented a target of opportunity. For that reason, most of their victims were black."[40] Indeed, black men in Texas proved to be the most likely victims of homicide. In 1980, for example, African American men between the ages of thirty and thirty-nine stood a 1 in 678 chance of being murdered, while white men in the same age category stood a 1 in 4,815 chance.[41]

Despite the obvious plight of African Americans in Texas, many Anglos in the state found the federal government's continuing efforts to counteract discrimination and assist racial and ethnic minorities to be offensive and counterproductive. As a result, white anger during the 1970s skyrocketed, as opponents of crosstown busing, affirmative action, and welfare assistance formed themselves into a potent conservative force that President Richard Nixon described as the "silent majority." These white voters found the counterculture and student movements of the 1960s to be gross displays of youthful arrogance and naiveite, and when Nixon, their chosen leader, failed to win the Vietnam War and succumbed to his own scandals and excesses, that was the last straw. Presidents Gerald Ford and Jimmy Carter were brought in to clean up the mess, but they both faced serious domestic and foreign issues that made it difficult to achieve anything like the successes of World War II or the early Cold War. Deficit spending on the long-running Vietnam War and increasing oil prices around the world brought on "stagflation," with high inflation, high unemployment, and slow economic growth. The press and President Carter agreed, America's "national malaise" had made people critical of government and polarized the nation. As Roth has shown, the "proportion of whites who trusted the government fell from 38 percent in 1974 to 25 percent in 1980, and the homicide rate for whites rose from 5.8 per 100,000 persons per year to 7.0 per 100,000, nearly three times what it had been in 1963." In conservative Texas, the homicide rate proved even worse for whites, rising to 17.16 per 100,000 in 1980.[42]

With the dawn of the 1980s, homicide statistics in Texas began to exhibit two interesting and seemingly contradictory trends. On one hand, the murder rate dropped significantly over the course of the decade from 16.9 to 11.9 per 100,000 people, signaling a substantial decline in the number of murder victims. This encouraging development masked a deeper, darker reality, however, for despite the decline, Texas simultaneously ranked as the first-, second-, or third-most homicidal state in the nation, placing at the top of the list each year from 1983 to 1986. Further complicating matters, the homicide rate jumped back up in 1990 and 1991, reaching 15.3 per 100,000 people. In fact, 1991 remains the deadliest year on record in Texas for homicides, with 2,652 victims, including the twenty-three people killed by George Hennard at Luby's Cafeteria in Killeen.[43]

Social scientists have highlighted five key ingredients in the Texas homicide narrative from the 1980s: urban growth, economic volatility, political instability, drug trafficking, and widespread access to firearms. The first element in the story proved to be the tremendous growth that Texas experienced from 1970 to 1980. During that period, as job seekers from the Midwest and New England moved to the Sunbelt, the Lone Star State's population climbed from 11,196,730 to 14,229,191, a gain of 28 percent. Much of that growth occurred in cities, where local governments struggled to build infrastructure for thousands of new residents every month. Houston, for example, grew by 29 percent during the decade, reaching a population of 1.6 million. Likewise, Dallas grew to 1 million residents by 1990 and San Antonio crept ever closer to the 1 million mark as well.[44]

Migrants came to Texas at the dawn of the 1980s for a variety of reasons. Many were trying to escape the lackluster economic situations in their home states. In the four years between 1979 and 1982, for example, the nation "suffered a loss of $26 million in gross national product and 200,000 jobs." In Texas, however, the oil boom during the same period led to an increase of "$43 million in output and . . . 800,000 jobs."[45] This economic surge made Texas one of the most popular places in America. The romantic western movie *Urban Cowboy* won a nationwide following in 1980, as its two main characters, Bud and Sissy, danced at Gilley's honky-tonk and made a life for themselves during the Houston oil boom. At the same time, the weekly primetime soap opera *Dallas* proved to be one of the most popular shows on television, with thousands of people tuning in to find out what would happen next to J. R. and the Ewings.[46]

Yet, the oil boom did not go on forever. In 1982, a glut in production led to a global price reduction, which cost Texas roughly 200,000 jobs. Then, four years later, things took a much sharper turn for the worse. Oil prices "suffered a dramatic fall in 1986, from more than $30 a barrel to less than $10. . . . The collapse of the oil industry rippled through the entire economy, destroying public confidence, bankrupting businesses, and throwing workers out of their jobs by the thousands." Further complicating this scenario was that Texas had largely deregulated the operation of local savings and loan organizations (S&Ls), which had, in turn, loaned huge amounts of money for speculative real estate and land deals. When the oil market imploded, developers and real estate speculators left the S&Ls holding titles to vast amounts of worthless property. By October 1987, "the combined value of all the state's S&Ls was a minus $5.1 billion."[47]

As Texans experienced these fluctuations in the economy, violent crime exploded across the state. In 1983, for example, seven of the top twenty most homicidal cities in America were located in Texas. Odessa, a booming city of ninety thousand people in the oil-rich Permian Basin of West Texas, took first place nationwide, with 29.8 homicides per 100,000 people. Three other Texas cities—Houston, Longview-Marshall, and San Antonio—were in the top ten, with Midland, Waco, and Dallas-Fort Worth rounding out the set. Some police chiefs and criminologists blamed the oil boom for the rise in homicide. "When the oil field went dry, a lot of people started leaving [Odessa]," officer Mike McKnight, a spokesman for the city's police department, told the *New York Times*. "A lot stayed and got mad." Other officers, like Lieutenant Jack Summey, chief of the homicide division in San Antonio, said it was the "handguns and knives." "They occur in and around the bar areas in the low-income neighborhoods," Summey said. In Longview, police chief James McLaughlin told reporters, "Basically, if you get along with your spouse and don't go honky-tonking around at night, you'll have no problems."[48]

Gun violence, drugs, and homicide became major issues in the 1988 presidential election between Republican Vice President George H. W. Bush of Texas and Democratic Governor Michael Dukakis of Massachusetts. As a former director of the Central Intelligence Agency and the leader of the Reagan administration's war on drugs, Bush ridiculed Dukakis for being a leftwing extremist who was soft on crime. Specifically, Bush highlighted Dukakis's support for a prison furlough program that allowed convicted murderer Willie Horton to receive a weekend pass from prison. While out on furlough, Horton committed an assault and rape in Maryland before he could be rearrested in that state and convicted of the crimes he committed. A political action committee supporting Bush ran an advertisement called Weekend Passes, which featured a mugshot of Horton, and the Bush campaign then put out a spot of their own that charged Dukakis with presiding over a "revolving door" that allowed dangerous convicted felons to leave prison.[49]

Dukakis countered with claims of his own against Bush. In September, the Massachusetts governor traveled to Dallas to appear with his vice-presidential running mate, US Senator Lloyd Bentsen of Texas. In a press conference at the Fairmont Hotel, Dukakis complained that Bush's tenure as leader of the war on drugs was a "failure," which had allowed drug use and drug-related crimes to rise higher than ever. Ron DeLord, president of the Combined Law Enforcement Association of Texas, supported Dukakis, claiming that Bush "walks loudly but carries no stick" in the war on crime. Specifically, DeLord argued that law enforcement agencies across Texas were suffering from a lack of funding, personnel, and equipment, while Bush's anticrime program called simply for a federal death penalty to be instituted. "Well, fellows," DeLord said, "we've had the death penalty in Texas for probably 200 years. We probably execute more people than any nation in the world. We have 300 people on Death Row. We have the highest crime rate in the country, with the highest homicide rate for police officers in the nation. So obviously, it won't solve the nation's problems, because it sure hasn't solved our problems."[50]

On February 27, 1993, reporters Mark England and Darlene McCormick launched a provocative newspaper series titled "The Sinful Messiah" in the *Waco Tribune-Herald*. Their initial article recounted numerous allegations of physical and sexual abuse against David Koresh, the leader of the Branch Davidians religious group headquartered at Mount Carmel Center near Axtel, Texas. The reporters presented evidence that Koresh had married several of the community's female residents, some as young as twelve or thirteen years old, and that he had fathered at least a dozen children at Mount Carmel. Disturbed by the allegations they had received, England and McCormick called on local officials to investigate Koresh and to protect the children in the community.[51]

State and federal law enforcement officials had already begun an examination of the Branch Davidians when "The Sinful Messiah" went to press. The Bureau of Alcohol, Tobacco, and Firearms (ATF) believed that, in addition to the allegations of sexual abuse and misconduct, the group was also stockpiling illegal firearms and ammunition. As a result, on February 28, the ATF attempted to execute a search warrant at Mount Carmel, but Koresh and the Branch Davidians resisted. A fierce gun battle ensued, resulting in the deaths of six Branch Davidians and four government officials. The Federal Bureau of Investigation (FBI) then took control of the situation, launching a fifty-one-day siege that ended with a failed assault on the compound and a raging fire that destroyed Mount Carmel Center. Seventy-six Branch Davidians were killed, including twenty children and David Koresh.[52]

The FBI's raid on the Branch Davidians' compound took place roughly six months after a similar law enforcement debacle at Ruby Ridge, Idaho, in which a US Marshall, a fourteen-year-old boy, and a forty-three-year-old woman were killed during an eleven-day siege. Taken together, the two events led to a national discussion about guns, homicide, and the role of the law enforcement officials. The new Democratic president, Bill Clinton, and his attorney general, Janet Reno, served as key figures in the debate. In Congress, the chairman of the US House Judiciary Committee, Jack Brooks of Beaumont, Texas, emerged as the point man in a campaign to pass a new omnibus crime bill that would address many of the issues raised by Waco and Ruby Ridge.[53]

Working with Senator Joe Biden of Delaware, Brooks and his allies passed the Violent Crime Control and Law Enforcement Act, which was signed into law by President Clinton in August 1994. Hundreds of pages in length, the act proved to be the largest crime bill ever passed by Congress. It expanded federal, state, and local law enforcement, providing for 100,000 new police officers, $10 billion in funding for new prisons, and $6 billion for drug, alcohol, and crime prevention programs. The new law expanded the list of crimes that could be punished by the federal death penalty and added new statutory crimes in the fields of immigration, hate crime, sex crime, and gang activity. Most controversially, the bill also included a federal ban on assault weapons and prohibited many new classes of convicted individuals from possessing firearms.[54]

The national press and politicians of both parties expressed support for the new crime bill. Republicans hailed it as a needed remedy to the drug epidemic and homicidal violence then plaguing the nation. And Democrats claimed it as a great victory because they "were able to wrest the crime issue from the Republicans and make it their own."[55] Jack Brooks called it "good legislation." "It's strong," he said. "Going to put violent criminals in the clink where they belong. It's [also] going to have a lot of innovative operations in it that give us a chance to save people so we don't have to put them in jail."[56] Over the long term, supporters of the bill have claimed that it led to sharp reductions in violent crimes and homicide in Texas. Between 1994 and 2018, they say, the murder rate in Texas has declined almost every year, dropping from 12.7 to 4.6 per 100,000 people.[57]

Despite the widespread popularity of the 1994 crime bill, critics of the act, such as Michelle Alexander, have argued that it "escalated the drug war" and led to a system of mass incarceration that "emerged as a stunningly comprehensive and well-disguised system of racialized social control."[58] Alexander's book *The New Jim Crow* presents a controversial but well-documented argument that the modern criminal justice system in the United States is functioning as a racial caste system. The new system had its origins in the war on drugs, which President Reagan launched in 1982. Built upon a media campaign that saturated the public with images of "black crack whores," "crack dealers," and "crack babies," the media effort "confirmed the worst racial stereotypes about black inner-city residents."[59] In 1986 and 1988, additional antidrug acts were passed, the result being that the incarcerated population in

America grew from roughly 350,000 in 1970 to more than 2 million in 2010. As Alexander writes, "The United States now boasts an incarceration rate that is six to ten times greater than that of other industrialized nations, . . . and no other country in the world incarcerates such an astonishing percentage of its racial or ethnic minorities."[60]

In August 2000, professional analysis by the Justice Policy Institute of Washington, DC, indicated that the "Texas prison system grew faster than any other in the country" during the 1990s. "One out of every 20 adults in the state" was under the "watch of the criminal justice system" at the time. Some were inmates, others were probationers or parolees. "If Texas was a country," the report said, "it would have the highest incarceration rate in the world, easily surpassing that of the United States and Russia, the next two finishers, and would be seven times that of the next biggest prison system in China." In addition, the report found that "blacks in Texas are incarcerated at seven times the rate of whites, and nearly one in three young African American men in Texas is under some form of criminal justice control." A spokesman for the Republican governor and future US president, George W. Bush, said at the time that "Texas was right to develop strong laws for dealing with criminal activities and strong laws covering juvenile crime to let them know that there are consequences for their behavior." But state Senator Rodney Ellis, a Democrat from Houston, said that he welcomed the critical analysis and lamented what the "graphic statistics" represented.[61]

The incarceration of thousands of African American, Hispanic, and Anglo men and women in Texas may have reduced the homicide rate during the 1990s and 2000s. But philosopher and social scientist Steven Pinker presents a more nuanced take on the reduction of violence in his prize-winning 2011 book, *The Better Angels of Our Nature: Why Violence Has Declined*. In subtle, brilliant prose, he argues that violence across the world has declined significantly over millennia and that we are likely living in the most peaceful time in world history. "The way to explain the decline of violence," Pinker argues, "is to identify the changes in our cultural and material milieu that have given our peaceable motives the upper hand."[62] He then examines a number of interpretations about the decline in violence and homicide. Pinker rejects the argument—put forward in *Freakonomics*—that the Supreme Court's legalization of abortion in *Roe v. Wade* (1973) led to a decline in the homicide rate because "begrudging or unfit mothers" had abortions rather than raising unwanted children who might have grown up to be criminals.[63] In place of this popular but troubling hypothesis, Pinker focuses on several social and cultural factors, including (1) the growth and effectiveness of the state; (2) changes in popular culture that emphasize the rights of women, racial and ethnic minorities, and LGBTQI Americans; and (3) the treatment of depression and psychological disorders that have historically led to violent acts.[64] These forces, rather than simple incarceration and punishment, have likely pushed the homicide rate in Texas, the United States, and the world down over the past few decades, thankfully yielding a more human, less violent world for us all.

Yet, despite the decline from the 1990s to 2018, Texas remains a dangerous place with a complex culture of violence. The homicide rate in Texas still far surpasses that of other states in the United States and even that of industrialized countries around the world. For example, in 2017, Texas logged a homicide rate of 5.0 per 100,000, while the United Kingdom's homicide rate was 1.2. The video game industry in recent years has certainly contributed to the culture of violence with games such as Grand Theft Auto, Red Dead Redemption, Call of Duty, and Fortnite. These so-called first-person shooters immerse players in a hostile environment in which they must hunt and kill other players to win. A similar trend may be seen in popular movies about Texas. Take, for example, the Coen Brother's 2007 thriller *No Country for Old Men*, which was based on Cormac McCarthy's novel of the same name. Set on the southern border of Texas, the film focuses on the exploits of Anton Chigurh, a merciless criminal, who uses a bolt pistol to kill anyone who gets in his way. The film won four academy awards, including Best Picture and Best Director, and helped confirm in many people's minds the treacherous nature of living in Texas. Indeed, the election and presidency of Donald Trump also contributed to acts of violence in the Lone Star State. In August 2019, for example, Patrick Crusius, a twenty-one-year-old man from Allen, Texas, entered a Walmart store in El Paso and shot twenty-three people to death in an act of domestic terrorism aimed at Latinos.[65] Although Crusius claimed his ideology predated Trump and his presidential campaign, reports suggest that

Trump's views on immigration and his repeated his anti-immigrant declarations on television have brought the more radical ideologies of people like Crusius out of the fringes of political discourse and more into the mainstream.[66] In addition, it seems that distrust in government leadership during the coronavirus pandemic made matters worse. As the *Wall Street Journal* reported, US cities were hit by double-digit increases in the homicide rate in 2020. Houston and Dallas remain the deadliest places in the state, but Austin, Fort Worth, and San Antonio have seen their homicide rates skyrocket as frustration with the pandemic lockdown, business failures, spiking unemployment, and inept federal leadership spark desperate acts of violence by desperate people.[67]

Notes

1. "Wife Killed, Husband Shot in Domestic Quarrel," *Dallas Morning News,* July 3, 1982, 31; Jeffrey L. Littlejohn interview with Ronnie L. Littlejohn, July 11, 2019.

2. Dallas County Felony and Misdemeanor Courts Case Information, Judicial Case ID: F-8287680, accessed April 6, 2020, https://www.dallascounty.org/criminalBackgroundSearch/.

3. "Texas Crime Rates, 1960–2018," Compiled by the Disaster Center from the Federal Bureau of Investigation's Uniform Crime Reporting Program, http://www.disastercenter.com/crime/txcrime.htm.

4. Michelle Alexander, *The New Jim Crow: Mass Incarceration in the Age of Colorblindness* (New York: New Press, 2010); Marie Gottschalk, "America Needs a Third Reconstruction: The Problem of Mass Incarceration Is a Problem of High Inequality," *The Atlantic* (September 18, 2015).

5. Disaster Center, "Texas Crime Rates, 1960–2018," accessed April 6, 2020, http://www.disastercenter.com/crime/txcrime.htm.

6. The Crime in Texas reports for each year between 1965 and 2018 are available in published form. Reports from 1999 to 2018 are available online at https://www.dps.texas.gov/administration/crime_records/pages/crimestatistics.htm. Enter "Crime in Texas [YEAR] report" in the Search bar to find the report you are interested in.

7. Bertram Wyatt-Brown, *Southern Honor: Ethics and Behavior in the Old South* (New York: Oxford University Press, 1982), 21.

8. Edward L. Ayers, *Vengeance and Justice: Capital Punishment in the 19th-Century American South* (New York: Oxford University Press, 1984), 12.

9. Neil Foley, *The White Scourge: Mexicans, Blacks, and Poor Whites in Texas Cotton Culture* (Berkeley: University of California Press, 1997), 17–39.

10. Many migrants to Texas had to be totally self-sufficient. As a result, they had

to know how to carry and use a gun and knife. Senseless brawls, gang uprisings, and domestic disturbances often ended in homicides when firearms were involved. Raymond D. Gastil, "Homicide and Regional Culture of Violence," *American Sociological Review* 36 (1971): 414–15.

11. W. J. Cash, *The Mind of the South* (New York: Random House, 1941; Vintage, reprint, 1960), 44.

12. For more on the long-existing culture of violence in Texas, see Gary Clayton Anderson, *The Conquest of Texas: Ethnic Cleansing in the Promised Land, 1820–1875* (Norman: University of Oklahoma Press, 2005); William Carrigan, *The Making of a Lynching Culture: Violence and Vigilantism in Central Texas, 1836–1916* (Champaign: University of Illinois Press, 2004); Monica Munoz Martinez, *The Injustice Never Leaves You: Anti-Mexican Violence in Texas* (Cambridge: Harvard University Press, 2018); Doug J. Swanson, *Cult of Glory: The Bold and Brutal History of the Texas Rangers* (New York: Viking, 2020); David T. Courtwright, *Violent Land: Single Men and Social Disorder from the Frontier to the Inner City* (Cambridge, MA: Harvard University Press, 1996). Robert Perkinson, *Texas Tough: The Rise of America's Prison Empire* (New York: Metropolitan Books, 2010); Jeffrey I. Littlejohn with Charles H. Ford, Jami Horne, and Briana Weaver, "The Cabiness Family Lynching: Race, War, and Memory in Walker County, Texas," *Southwestern Historical Quarterly* 122, no. 1 (July 2018): 1–30.

13. Todd Gitlin quoted in *Oswald's Ghost,* directed by Robert Stone (Robert Stone Productions for American Experience in association with the British Broadcasting Corporation, 2007).

14. Josiah Thompson quoted in *Oswald's Ghost.*

15. Sean P. Cunningham, *Cowboy Conservatism: Texas and the Rise of the Modern Right* (Lexington: University Press of Kentucky, 2010), 71.

16. Roger Lane, *Murder in America: A History* (Columbus: Ohio State University Press, 1997), 296, 269.

17. Disaster Center, "Texas Crime Rates."

18. Roger Ebert, "The Searchers," review of *The Searchers,* directed by John Ford, November 25, 2001, https://www.rogerebert.com/reviews/great-movie-the-searchers-1956.

19. Roger Ebert, "Bonnie and Clyde," review of *Bonnie and Clyde,* directed by Arthur Penn, September 25, 1967, https://www.rogerebert.com/reviews/bonnie-and-clyde-1967.

20. Cunningham, *Cowboy Conservatism,* 70.

21. Lane, *Murder in America,* 289.

22. John G. Tower, "A Constitutional Amendment to Restore the Power of the Police" (speech),1967, Senator John G. Tower Collection (https://texashistory.unt.edu/ark:/67531/metapth612188), University of North Texas Libraries, The Portal to Texas History, https://texashistory.unt.edu; crediting Southwestern University. For the proposed amendment, see *A Proposed Constitutional Amendment Relating to the*

Power of Courts of the United States to Admit Voluntary Confessions of Guilt in Criminal Cases, S.J. Res. 22, Cong. Rec. 113, Part I (January 10, 1967, to January 24, 1967), 90th Cong., 1st Sess., 1173–1177.

23. James W. Marquart, Sheldon Ekland-Olson, and Jonathan R. Sorensen, *The Rope, the Chair, and the Needle: Capital Punishment in Texas, 1923–1990* (Austin: University of Texas Press, 1994), 13.

24. Marquart et al., *The Rope,* 123.

25. Jon Sorensen and Rocky Leann Pilgrim, *Lethal Injection: Capital Punishment in Texas during the Modern Era* (Austin: University of Texas Press, 2006).

26. Sorensen and Pilgrim, *Lethal Injection.*

27. "Insurance Compromise Seen," *Kilgore News,* October 13, 1972, 1; Dick Stanley, "History of Texas Marked by Debate about Executions," *Austin American-Statesman,* December 7, 1982, 14; "Views on Crime," *Tyler Morning Telegraph,* November 28, 1978, 14; "Death Penalty Bill Blocked in Senate," *Victoria Advocate,* October 18, 1972, 8; "Poll: Texans Favor Capital Punishment," *El Paso Times,* September 11, 1980, 6.

28. Cal Jillson, *Lone Star Tarnished: A Critical Look at Texas Politics and Public Policy* (New York: Routledge, Taylor and Francis Group, 2018), 196.

29. Rupert Koeninger, "Capital Punishment in Texas, 1924–1968," *Crime and Delinquency* 15, no. 1 (January 1969): 132–41.

30. Koeninger, "Capital Punishment in Texas," 132–41.

31. Scholars such as Hashem Dezhbakhsh and Joanna M. Shepherd argue that capital punishment does have a deterrent effect. Shepherd, in particular, "uses monthly murder and execution data [to] measure deterrence more precisely than the annual data of most capital punishment studies." She argued in congressional testimony that "modern studies have consistently shown that capital punishment has a strong deterrent effect, with each execution deterring between 3 and 19 murders." Likewise, Nai Mocan, another leading scholar in the field, told the Associated Press that "science does really draw a conclusion.... There is no question about it. The conclusion is there is a deterrent effect." On the other hand, scholars Patrick T. Brandt and Tomislav V. Kovandzic of the University of Texas at Dallas, argue that executions in Texas have not deterred homicides.

32. Lane, *Murder in America,* 299.

33. Randolph Roth, *American Homicide* (Cambridge, MA: Harvard University Press, 2009), 3.

34. Cunningham, *Cowboy Conservatism,* 75.

35. Wesley G. Phelps, *A People's War on Poverty: Urban Politics and Grassroots Activists in Houston* (Athens: University of Georgia Press, 2014), 89–117.

36. Peter B. Levy, *The Great Uprising: Race Riots in Urban American during the 1960s* (New York: Cambridge University Press, 2018).

37. Jane A. Baskin et al., *The Long, Hot Summer? An Analysis of Summer Disorders, 1967–1971* (Waltham, MA: Lemberg Center for the Study of Violence at Brandeis University, 1972), 1.

38. Steven M. Gillon, *Separate and Unequal: The Kerner Commission and the Unraveling of American Liberalism* (New York: Basic Books, 2018); National Commission on the Causes and Prevention of Violence, *To Establish Justice, To Insure Domestic Tranquility: The Final Report* (New York: Bantam Books, 1970).

39. Roth, *American Homicide,* 463.

40. Roth, 457–58.

41. Raymond H. C. Teske, Jr., ed., *Crime and Justice in Texas* (Huntsville, TX: Sam Houston Press, 1995), 24.

42. Roth, American Homicide, 460–65.

43. Disaster Center, "Texas Crime Rates"; Thomas C. Hayes, "Gunman Kills 22 and Himself in Texas Cafeteria," *New York Times,* October 17, 1991.

44. Randolph Campbell, *Gone to Texas: A History of the Lone Star State* (New York: Oxford University Press, 2003), 445.

45. Campbell, *Gone to Texas,* 444–45.

46. Campbell, 446.

47. Campbell, 447.

48. Wayne King, "7 Texas Cities are in Top 20 in Murder Per Capita," *New York Times,* September 17, 1983, 7.

49. John J. Pitney Jr., *After Reagan: Bush, Dukakis, and the 1988 Election* (Lawrence: University of Kansas Press, 2019).

50. Dave McNeely, "Dukakis Fires Away at Bush on Crime," *Austin American-Statesman,* September 30, 1988, A11.

51. Mark England and Darlene McCormick, "The Sinful Messiah," *Waco Tribune-Herald,* February 27, 1993, A1.

52. Dick J. Reavis, *The Ashes of Waco: An Investigation* (Syracuse, NY: Syracuse University Press, 1998).

53. Timothy McNulty and Brendan McNulty, The Meanest Man in Congress: Jack Brooks and the Making of an American Century (Montgomery, Alabama: NewSouth Books, 2019), 452–84.

54. David Masci, "30 Billion Anti-Crime Bill Heads to Clinton's Desk," Congressional Quarterly (August 27, 1994): 2488–93.

55. Michelle Alexander, *The New Jim Crow: Mass Incarceration in the Age of Colorblindness* (New York: New Press, 2012), 56.

56. McNulty and McNulty, *Meanest Man in Congress,* 477.

57. Disaster Center, "Texas Crime Rates."

58. Alexander, *New Jim Crow,* 4.

59. Alexander, 5.

60. Alexander, 7–8.

61. John Moritz, "Texas Prison Growth is Fastest," *Fort Wort Star-Telegram,* August 28, 2000, 1.

62. Steven Pinker, *The Better Angels of Our Nature: Why Violence Has Declined* (New York: Viking, 2011), xxiii.

63. Steven D. Levitt and Stephen J. Dubner, *Freakonomics: A Rogue Economist Explores the Hidden Side of Everything* (New York: William Morrow, 2009).

64. Pinker, *Better Angels,* xxvi.

65. Alfredo Corchado, Cassandra Jaramillo, and James Barragán, "'Every Day Is a Struggle': El Paso, One Year Later," *Dallas Morning News,* July 31, 2020.

66. Peter Baker and Michael D. Shear, "El Paso Shooting Suspect's Manifesto Echoes Trump's Language," *New York Times,* August 4, 2019; Lauren Villagran, "El Paso shooting suspect's hate-filled writing used similar language as Trump campaign," *El Paso Times,* August 6, 2019;

67. Jon Hilsenrath, "Homicide Spike Hits Most Large US Cities," *Wall Street Journal,* August 2, 220.

2

INTIMATE PARTNER VIOLENCE IN TEXAS

Ashley Baggett

In the race against domestic violence, we must sprint to stand still. Like the mythical hydra, the elimination of one violent situation only serves to enlighten us to two more.[1]

Intimate partner violence—the physical, sexual, emotional, and/or economic abuse by one partner in a current or former intimate relationship against another—is a multifaceted problem. Since the modern movement against intimate partner violence began in the 1970s, activists debated how best to end abuse, but no simple or single solution exists. However, experts succeeded in identifying several factors that contribute to intimate partner violence, and consistently, the community's social attitudes and beliefs are among the primary concerns. Views that prioritize family privacy over involving the legal system or that uphold stereotypical sex roles collectively create a culture of violence that enables abuse to continue. Important social and legal efforts have been made to address the causes of domestic violence. Texans, following national trends, helped to spearhead policy reform, including their role in founding the Texas-based National Domestic Violence Hotline and the National Center on Domestic and Sexual Violence (NCDSV). Texans even earned national awards for their role in the anti–intimate partner violence movement; for example, Deborah (Debby) G. Tucker won the National Network to End Domestic Violence's Standing in the Light of Justice Award in 2005. These efforts led to increased public awareness, better responses to the problem of abuse, and arguably a decline in rates of intimate partner violence from 1965 through 2019. Yet, early research suggests that rates of intimate partner violence increased during 2020 as a result of pandemic-related lockdowns "exacerbated factors typically associated with domestic violence, such as increased unemployment, stress associated with childcare and homeschooling, and increased financial insecurity, and that the increased use of alcohol and other substances as a coping strategy also may have elevated the threat."[2] Despite the nation's and the state's progress over the last fifty years, abuse continues: one in three women and one in four men have experienced physical violence by an intimate partner; the statistic does not even include other forms of violence, such as emotional, economic, or psychological abuse.[3] Moreover, a disturbing increase in the most lethal form of intimate partner violence—intimate partner homicide—has alarmed anti–intimate partner violence advocates both nationally and in Texas.[4] The struggle to end the culture of violence that perpetuates intimate partner violence continues.

Although a brief movement to end intimate partner violence began in the nineteenth century, a larger, more sustained movement emerged by the 1970s. It arose spontaneously on the grassroots level throughout the globe, but the origins of the modern anti–intimate partner violence movement are generally agreed to have begun in England. These pioneering efforts influenced the rest of the world, including efforts in Texas. The Chiswick Women's Aid established the first women's shelter in Chiswick, England, and the shelter served as a model for similar sanctuaries across the world. In 1974, Erin Prizzey authored the foundational work on abuse, *Scream Quietly or Our Neighbors Will Hear*. A year later, the United Nations (UN) named 1975 as International Women's Year (IWY) and held the World Conference of the IWY in Mexico City. The first of its kind, the conference brought together more than thirteen hundred delegates from 133 countries to discuss gender inequality. The UN called it "the world's largest consciousness raising session."[5] The most tangible result—the World Plan of Action—outlined a ten-year plan to improve the status of women. It called for countries to hold national conferences and address numerous issues women face, including "particular forms of violence and cruelty, both physical and mental, that are perpetuated against women."[6] Collectively, these efforts raised awareness about the global problem of intimate partner violence.

In the United States, activists in the women's movement of the 1960s and 1970s were already addressing a multitude of inequalities women faced, but following a growing international response to intimate partner violence, American activists began mobilizing on abuse.[7] No formal reporting system for intimate partner violence existed in the nation at the time, but national sources indicate a high rate of abuse. FBI statistics in 1977 called spousal abuse "the most underreported crime in the country."[8] Two influential American publications tore down the veil of family privacy, prompting action across the country. First, LGBTQ activist and feminist Del Martin published a groundbreaking book—*Battered Wives* (1975)—which drew attention to unequal power dynamics in marriage as well as solutions through legal and social changes. The following year, the four-year-old feminist publication *Ms.* dedicated its August issue to intimate partner violence. The cover featured a white woman with a dark black bruise under her eye with large print: "Battered Wives Help for the Secret Victim Next Door."[9] Along with examining the problem and resources, the issue contained an article by a former abuser who discussed why he abused his wife. He spoke of learned behavior and specifically condemned a culture that teaches men that violence toward women is acceptable. The issue broke barriers by shocking the public with powerful and raw depictions of intimate partner violence.

Organizers sought to address immediate needs of abuse victims by raising awareness and establishing shelters. The first Take Back the Night (TBTN) took place in Philadelphia in 1975 with a march and speak-out to protest violence against women, and early shelters emerged in St. Paul, Minnesota, Phoenix, Arizona, and Pasadena, California.[10] However, the National Organization for Women (NOW) spurred a more coordinated nationwide effort with establishment of the National Task Force on Battered Women.[11] The task force sought to address the problem of intimate partner violence and resulted in the Ann Arbor–Washtenaw chapter publishing several handbooks to aid activists nationwide in advocacy, crisis intervention, emergency shelters, and counseling.[12] These publications served as accessible blueprints for grassroots organizers, and activists across the country relied on the foundational knowledge provided in the manuals.

In Texas, as in most of the country, intimate partner homicide went largely unaddressed before the modern anti–intimate partner violence movement emerged. No recordkeeping on the problem of intimate partner violence existed. No emergency shelters or organized resources were available to victims. Any legal response largely lay in the willingness of police and courts to prosecute abusers under general assault and battery statutes, and given the dominant social view at the time that the family was private and beyond the reach of the law, an overwhelming majority of intimate partner violence incidents—80 percent—went unreported.[13] National trends influenced women's rights activists in Texas to organize and address abuse victims' needs. NOW chapters in Dallas and Houston formed their own task force in 1976.[14] Dallas activists collaborated with others in the community, including the YWCA, to establish the Dallas Violence Intervention Alliance (DVIA) within the same year. The DVIA offered critical services including referrals and a hotline.[15] In Austin, citizens met to discuss addressing the problem in their community, forming the Austin Coalition for Battered Women. The coalition held a one-day workshop in which 150 to 200 people attended, ranging from medical and legal experts to abuse survivors seeking help.[16] Although several solutions emerged, a consensus agreed that a shelter was the "only direct and viable solution to the problem of wife abuse."[17] With grants, land, and other aid, the coalition opened a temporary shelter called the Austin Center for Battered Women (ACBW) in June 1977.[18] It was the first shelter for abuse survivors in Texas during the twentieth century and, at the time, one of only approximately thirty nationwide.[19]

By the end of the first year of operation, the center served more than four hundred women and children, and the hotline received more than one thousand calls from individuals in the city of Austin alone.[20] The high demand for services and need for repairs required continued financial support. In an appeal for funding just two years later, Debby

Tucker, executive director of the ACBW, spoke of the most significant obstacles to organizing against intimate partner violence. Both involved social attitudes that enabled the problem: first, the mistaken belief that violence did not occur within a family, and second, "the hesitation by outsiders to interfere with the family dynamic."[21] Ultimately, these social views, "woven deeply into the matrix of society's norms and values," created a culture that facilitated violence in the home.[22]

By 1977, the national movement gained momentum, with Texas spearheading many developments, largely due to the national IWY conference to address gender inequality.[23] Before the National Women's Conference, states throughout the country held meetings to discuss women's issues and elect delegates to represent their state at the national event. From June 24 to 26, 1977, three thousand Texans met in Austin for their state-level conference. In the session "Violence Against Women," participants identified the origins of abuse and determined "socialization may be key to understanding the phenomenon."[24] Their report further argued, "Women's victimization has been excused and condoned by society, sanctioned by law, reinforced by institutions, and generally tolerated."[25] As a result, the Texas State Plan of Action called for shelters, legal change, and public education. Laws and resources would help survivors of abuse, but public education was essential to create the needed culture shift for eradicating abuse. Their ideas and delegates went on to influence the larger National Women's Conference in November of that year.

Instrumental to "widen[ing] the cracks in the wall of ignorance surrounding domestic violence" was the National Women's Conference held in Houston from November 18 to 21, 1977.[26] The National Women's Conference thrust Texas onto the national scene in part because Houston's Women's Advocate, Nikki Van Hightower, successfully persuaded the National Commission to choose Houston as the site for the conference. Twenty thousand people gathered from all US states and territories to develop a National Plan of Action. A panel discussed "social acceptance" of intimate partner violence throughout the United States and its territories, and participants called for change through public education, shelters, legal changes, and shifts in the media's portrayal of violence against women.[27] Ultimately, many of these recommendations were included in the final National Plan of Action resolution on battered women. ·

Many Texans attended the 1977 National Women's Conference, including members from six shelters across the state.[28] They sought to network and learn methods for combating abuse, and their fruitful exchanges, including with national leaders in NOW's Domestic Violence Taskforce, led to the formation of the Texas Council on Family Violence (TCFV). The TCFV sought representation from throughout the state to coordinate a unified effort to combat family violence; they focused on obtaining funding for shelters, engaging in policy advocacy, and working with experts to create law enforcement training programs. Within the first year alone, the TCFV successfully petitioned the legislature for $200,000 to be used in part for shelters in the state.[29] It also successfully lobbied for critical changes in the Texas Family Code. The revision enabled victims of abuse to secure a civil protective order, placing Texas ahead of many other states that did not make such changes for another few years.[30]

About the time of TCFV formation, the Houston Area Women's Center (HAWC) opened. Efforts to realize the HAWC had begun a few years previously when the Houston YWCA received one hundred to two hundred calls a month asking for help to escape abuse.[31] Houston women began organizing to acquire data and start identifying funding sources. The findings painted a dire picture in the area. The Houston Police Department reported that no less than 40 percent of calls received involved "domestic disturbances."[32] In December 1976, the YWCA engaged author Del Martin to speak in Houston and raise money for a shelter. Martin called shelters a needed refuge for those escaping abuse, but she also pointed to a culture that enables abuse, asserting, "Our culture sets women up to be victims and then blames them if they are." Martin continued with how to create a cultural shift: "We should start in family life classes in elementary school to educate children in attitudes and values that will prevent wife beating" as well as "exert social pressure on men who are beating women, or even joking about it."[33] Shelters were necessary but ultimately would not eliminate the cause of intimate partner violence.

The HAWC eventually received enough aid to open a small shelter on June 1, 1978, and, speaking to the enormity of the problem, served more than four hundred women and children within the first year.[34] The demographics of women assisted at HAWC aligned with findings from the first survey on spousal abuse in Texas by the Criminal Justice Center at Sam Houston State University in 1979. Collecting data from 138 counties throughout the state, the report found high rates of intimate partner violence in all counties with a greater number of victims in population-dense/urban areas. On average, eighty-seven thousand Texans were abused on a weekly basis, and 11.3 percent of women in the statewide survey reported abuse between 1978 and 1979. The survey also discovered the racial/ethnic background of abuse victims was proportionate to population ratios within the state and that 80 percent of the abuse went unreported. The report emphasized, however, that the estimates were in the low range given the limits of the study being a survey of only several hundred Texans who self-reported the information.[35] With the pressing data, HAWC and other Texas shelters continued to expand to meet the state's needs and increased their services to eliminate a culture of violence, including educating the public through workshops and the media.

During the 1970s, the movement across the country consisted largely of grassroots activism and support from the local and state governments. The federal government provided little directive during the decade aside from some funding. The Law Enforcement Assistance Administration (LEAA) provided millions of dollars during the late 1970s through the Victim Witness Assistance Program and other family violence projects. Some of those funds helped compile data from the National Crime Survey to gain preliminary statistics about abuse across the nation.[36] Twenty-one states began using Title XX of the Social Security Block Grant (SSBG) funds for shelters, citing abused women as ideal recipients for money allocated to "protective services."[37] By 1978, the Department of Labor began encouraging local governments to use Comprehensive Employment Training Act (CETA) funds to help staff shelters.[38] However, the federal government did not allocate any appropriations targeted specifically for intimate partner violence during the 1970s.

While no federal legislation came to fruition during the 1970s, some politicians at least began considering the issue, but the economic crises of the decade and the shifts in the political party system stymied much development. Conservative opponents to federal programming that combated intimate partner violence cited fiscal conservatism and the need to reduce the national budget. In addition, although the Republican Party in the late 1970s drew increasing support from the Christian right and espoused a pro-family platform, some opponents to federal domestic family programming argued such legislation would undermine the family structure by facilitating the victim to leave the violent relationship. Blocking anti–intimate partner violence measures would supposedly keep the family intact and, as lobbyist Karl Moor argued, "counter the federal government's intrusion into the domestic realm." Despite the economic crises and the growing social conservatism in politics, President Jimmy Carter (D) established the Office of Domestic Violence (ODV) in 1979 to develop policy and gather information on family violence. Unfortunately, because of budget cuts and conservative backlash, the ODV was closed in 1981.[39] Legislators proposed acts in the federal Congress but without success. In June 1977, Senator Wendell R. Anderson (D-MN) introduced Senate Bill 1728, which sought to establish grants for projects that "develop methods for the identification, prevention, and treatment of domestic violence . . . and for emergency shelter and protection."[40] The bill failed. In 1977, two pieces of legislation regarding intimate partner violence were proposed but did not pass. Again, in 1978, the Committee on Education and Labor in the House of Representatives held hearings for the Domestic Violence Prevention and Treatment Act of 1977. Despite more than four hundred pages of expert testimony supporting federal assistance, including prepared documents by the HAWC board of directors, the bill failed in part due to differences on where funds should be spent and who would maintain control.[41]

Despite limited gains on the federal level, intimate partner violence "had become a household word" and a "top crime" in Texas as well as the nation by the 1980s.[42] Consequently, the movement began to shift from the mainly reactionary approach of the 1970s movement to a more holistic and preventative approach. The movement began to focus on addressing culture, medicine, and the legal system. A first step to stopping a culture of violence required increased awareness and data on the problem. The 1980s saw improved recordkeeping in regard to intimate partner violence due to governmental agencies requiring statistics on abuse. Most studies and law enforcement agencies, however, focused exclusively on violence within legally married couples rather than all forms of intimate partners, which skews the rates considerably. But even with a focus on spousal abuse alone, studies in the 1980s estimated between 23 and 66 percent of spouses experienced violence during their lifetime, with an average of 16 percent each year. All studies agreed on the continuation of underreporting of intimate partner violence.[43]

Contributing to awareness across the country, the National Coalition Against Domestic Violence (NCADV), a newly formed organization established with the help of Texan Toby Myers, declared October 17, 1981, a Day of Unity. The day of recognition grew into a week-long program and eventually became Domestic Violence Awareness Month (DVAM) by 1987.[44] Congress officially declared October DVAM in 1989, stating that "domestic violence is the single largest cause of injury to women in the United States."[45] President George H. W. Bush signed the first proclamation for DVAM, and since then, every president has issued a proclamation reconfirming October as DVAM to help bring national attention to the problem.

On the local level, news outlets increasingly covered stories on violence in the home, raising public awareness and educating Texans to change social attitudes on violence. *Texas Monthly*'s "Sins of the Fathers" started with the pointed question, "By ignoring violence in the family, are we breeding violence in the streets?"[46] The article traced the most lethal form of family violence and the lack of prosecution, arguing, "It seems perfectly in tune with our belief that what goes on inside the four walls of a home—even murder—is no one's business, let alone the state's." The author concluded that instead of Americans fearing street violence, they should look to the source of much violent behavior— family violence. Similar to the March 1981 article in *Texas Monthly*, the *Times Record News* in Wichita Falls, Texas, published an article in 1988 titled "Denouncing the Myth," in which the writer asserts that "keeping a 'wife in line' with 'behind the door' tactics is no longer tolerable."[47]

Likewise, KHOU-TV aired "Family Violence Exposed," documenting the problem of intimate partner violence. The TCFV and Bay Area Chapter of NOW expressed appreciation for the film's being "one of the most sensitive and factual accounts of domestic violence that has been presented to the public."[48] Numerous other articles began being published in Texas newspapers, and collectively, the media served as a form of public education to shift the culture that enabled intimate partner violence during the 1980s.

Spotlighting the movement in Texas, CBS's *60 Minutes* episode "A Place to Go" aired in 1981 investigating spousal abuse and featuring the Austin Center for Battered Women. Journalist Dan Rather interviewed several survivors from different racial, ethnic, and socioeconomic backgrounds during the first part of the segment. Graphic images of their injuries flashed across the screen as the women described in detail the harrowing abuse they had endured. One woman spoke about her partner having been jealous and having beaten her in the face to ruin her looks. She said the worst incident had occurred in a car: he fractured her nose, knocked out her front teeth, and bruised her eyes to the point she could not see because of the swelling. Rather then spoke on the limits of seeking legal redress through the police and the courts, concluding, "There's no doubt the law thinks twice before reaching behind closed doors and calls a wife beater to account. In America, a man's home is still very much his castle."[49] In the next segment, Rather highlighted the main source of aid for victims—shelters—by touring the ACBW with Director Tucker. As they moved around the building, the camera showed the dilapidated conditions, including a leak in the laundry room and the one small bathroom shared by six families. Luckily, John McPhaul solicited donations from the community and worked with members from the Austin Association of Builders to construct a brand new facility for the ACBW.[50] But, Rather concluded that society needed to do more to address intimate partner violence. With new levels of awareness, organizers began pushing the national government for funding targeted specifically for combating abuse and succeeded with the passage of the Family Violence Prevention and Service Act (FVPSA) of 1984.

Shelters remained central in combating domestic violence, but national activists and experts in the 1980s looked beyond the stopgap measure of emergency shelters to systemic changes in culture, medicine, and the law. Organizers began pursuing methods to stop the violence. In Austin, approximately half of women who stayed at the ACBW returned to their abusers. Tucker spoke to the problem: "I don't have a success story to tell about those women who go back home. . . . We don't know if the situation really changes or not."[51] Experts began creating batterer programs to counsel abusers. The Duluth model provided the framework for counseling male batterers, focusing on unequal power dynamics between men and women and helping male abusers to establish egalitarian relationships and make positive choices.[52] Programs in Texas embraced this interventionist and preventative approach within a few years.[53] In Austin, abusers could enter a plea of no contest/guilty and attend six-month counseling sessions run by the ACBW instead of paying the fine, then have the assault charges expunged from their record.[54] Houston began a similar counseling service called PIVOT for Men, and a statewide program began when the TCFV successfully lobbied the Texas legislature to establish the Battering Intervention and Prevention Project (BIPP) in 1989 as an effort to rehabilitate batterers through counseling, behavioral retraining, and education. The approach to reduce recidivism by treating batterers marked a change in the movement's efforts to combat the culture of violence that enables intimate partner violence.

The shift in the national modern movement against intimate partner violence also included changing the justice system during the 1980s. In particular, issues with law enforcement took precedent. In a 1982 Texas legislative debate, speakers voiced concern over views among leaders in police departments who saw intimate partner violence as a lower-priority crime, which contributed, in one study, to the 89 percent of abuse victims who use shelters to avoid turning to the police.[55] Essentially, the public viewed law enforcement as ambivalent. Two court cases settled in 1979 paved the way for national changes in police tactics with domestic calls. *Scott v. Hart*, a class action lawsuit against the Oakland Police Department in California, resulted in massive changes to the police department's approach toward abuse victims, including requiring officers to provide resources for victims and to be trained in more responsive approaches to domestic disturbances.[56] *Bruno v. Codd* similarly impacted police policies in handling reports of abuse. The case mandated that New York City police send officers to investigate calls of intimate partner violence, assist in finding medical help for the injured party, and arrest batterers who either committed a felony assault or violated a protection order.[57]

In addition to these two court cases, the Minnesota Domestic Violence Experiment (MDVE) studied police response and found arresting the batterer lowered the risk of the abuser reoffending. The MDVE's scientific findings and the precedent-setting cases influenced states to change their legal response to combat intimate partner violence more effectively.[58] By the early 1980s, most states, including Texas in 1981, had changed their laws to statutes to allow for warrantless arrests in the case of abuse.[59] State legislatures also began mandating special training and improved reporting on intimate partner violence. Some states even passed laws to waive filing fees for protective orders and created criminal sanctions for violations of protective orders to make them more effective. Texas successfully passed bills on all of these issues during their legislative session in 1983.[60] Organizations such as the Texas Young Lawyers Association published pamphlets for abuse victims detailing their new choices. The information included gathering important birth certificates, taking photographs of injuries, pursuing criminal and civil options, and acquiring help even if the abuser or victim is not a citizen.[61]

Another key legal shift that occurred in the 1980s involved treatment in the courts of those who kill their abusers. Leonore Walker published *The Battered Woman* in 1979, which defined the cycle of violence and "learned helplessness." Walker's cycle of violence theory identifies a repetitive pattern of abuse from tension building to the battering phase to the honeymoon phase that contributes to the inability for a victim to escape the abuse.[62] In 1984, she built on her groundbreaking work with *The Battered Woman Syndrome,* which explores how abuse creates a psychological disorder that is a subcategory of posttraumatic stress disorder (PTSD). In an interview with Walker by HAWC's Toby Myers and Burnet Oliveros, Walker described why battered woman syndrome (BWS) leads to lethal forms of self-defense: "When the women strike back, they strike back with a tremendous amount of force. . . . The first thing that goes in their minds after the first blow is 'oh, I better get him good because if he gets up, he's gonna kill me.'"[63] Even before Walker's book, however, Texas juries generally refrained from convicting abuse victims for murdering their batterer in what one assistant district attorney referred to as a "Texas Divorce."[64] Although controversial in recent decades, Texas courts largely embraced the BWS defense and use of expert testimony during the late 1970s and 1980s. Consequently, the state was hailed at the time as a progressive leader in the movement against intimate partner violence.[65]

Along with substantial changes in the legal system, the medical field increasingly engaged in the movement to end abuse. Medical experts often come into contact with victims seeking help and have the potential to affect change. In a 1985 report, Surgeon General C. Everett Koop declared intimate partner violence a public health problem, altering approaches in viewing and treating abuse victims. Calling for a multidisciplinary approach, Koop recommended the entire health field work together on how to respond to victims of violence, educate the public, and research the problem.[66] The Centers for Disease Control and Prevention and the National Institute of Mental Health called for focus on problems in the field and helped fund studies.[67] Experts researched a wide array of factors related to intimate partner abuse, such as emergency department staff responses to dealing with battered women, the impact of abuse on mental health, and the impact of assault during pregnancy.[68] In a Texas Woman's University study, researchers found 42 percent of abuse victims reported being assaulted during pregnancy, with abuse ranging from slaps to kicks to choking to broken ribs.[69] The medical field's new foothold, along with numerous changes in the legal system, helped gain momentum for the movement against intimate partner violence through the 1980s.

During the 1990s, the movement continued to make significant gains and expanded its understanding of intimate partner violence, and it continued to raise awareness through new methods. The Clothesline Project began in Massachusetts in 1990 to bring attention to the problem of intimate partner violence. Survivors and loved ones touched by gender-based violence decorate t-shirts that are color coded to represent different types of abuse. Currently, the project is often part of Take Back the Night events to provide a visual protest of the impact of abuse. To raise awareness to the issue of intimate partner homicide, the NCADV partnered with *Ms.* magazine to start the Remember My Name Project in 1994. The project collects names of individuals murdered by an intimate partner and memorializes them on its website and a poster. Since 2008, the TCFV has a similar project called Honoring Texas Victims.[70] All of these projects seek to generate awareness about the problem.

National organizing increased at an even faster pace during the 1990s with Texans helping found many of the organizations. In 1993, the Battered Women's Justice Project was formed to serve as "the national resource center on civil and criminal justice responses to domestic violence" from funding from the FVPSA's reauthorization. The National Resource Center on Domestic Violence (NRCDV) formed the same year with funding from the US Department of Health and Human Services. The NRCDV seeks to help programs combating abuse, aid research on the issue, and lobby for better public policies. In addition, medical experts organized to establish the National Health Resource Center on Domestic Violence to change social attitudes, collaborate with experts in various fields, and educate medical professionals on abuse. Texans cofounded and helped to establish national organizations during the decade. In 1990, Tucker, who was the first executive director of the TCFV, cofounded the National Network to End Domestic Violence (NNEDV). The NNEDV formed as a coalition of organizations to end intimate partner violence and sexual assault and to influence public policy and public education.[71] In 1996, when funding ran out, Texan Christina Walsh, who later became a member and webmaster of the NCDSV, helped secure funding for the National Domestic Violence Hotline to open as a project of the TCFV and based it in Texas. The hotline received a thousand calls on the first day alone.[72] In 1998, Tucker cofounded the NCDSV to assist with conferences and provide training to stop abuse across the nation.

These new organizations helped successfully push for changes in the legal system, continuing a predominately legal approach to the movement, as in the prior decade. As experts came to better understand intimate partner violence, however, stalking and dating violence entered into public discussion and became areas in need of addressing.[73]

Texans' roles in national organizations helped them keep abreast of current information and approaches to combating intimate partner violence. In this case, Tucker's role with the NCDSV influenced her work with the TCFV, which pushed successfully for the anti-stalking law that was added to the Texas criminal code in 1993. Congress did not enact a federal anti-stalking law until 1997.[74]

Arguably the largest achievement of the movement came in 1994 with the passage of the Violence Against Women Act (VAWA). Spearheaded by the NNEDV, VAWA created the Office on Violence Against Women within the Department of Justice and sought to change public attitudes, raise awareness, fund services, and improve legal responses.[75] In Texas, reports identified three key areas to use funds: victim services, law enforcement training, and prosecution of abusers.[76] VAWA also encouraged mandatory arrests and no-drop policies. A majority of district attorneys did adopt no-drop policies by 2000.[77] Overall, VAWA had a substantial impact on the anti–intimate partner violence movement. The act committed the federal government to the fight against intimate partner violence—from ending a culture of violence to providing funds for services for victims. Studies show VAWA quickly led to a 21 percent decrease in the rate of intimate partner violence from 1993 to 1998.[78]

During the 2000s and 2010s, the movement to end intimate partner violence shifted again to address new challenges as well as aspects previously neglected. Male victims and abuse in same-sex relationships had previously been neglected in studies and excluded from services. Since the 2000s, language and legal protections, especially with the 2013 VAWA Reauthorization, have become more inclusive in recognizing men are also victims and violence occurs in any type of intimate relationship. Dating violence gained increased awareness during the 2000s with love is respect project. Love is respect and similar programs provide information and services for youths in abusive relationships. Abuse within military families also emerged as an area needing attention. At a 2004 senate committee hearing, Tucker of the NCDSV served as an expert witness and testified about the problem of intimate partner violence. She pointed to a culture that enables violence against women, stating, "Number one is that attitudes about women underlie violence against women. . . . And the culture shift that is so critical within the

Department of Defense was the number one recommendation coming out of the Defense Task Force."[79]

Activists also increasingly recognized the need for culturally sensitive approaches for immigrants, refugees, and victims of color. Some gains were made in the 1990s with shelter outreach programs, but people of color established independent organizations to combat intimate partner violence by the 2000s. In Texas, for example, Asians Against Domestic Violence was formed in Houston to "promote equal and healthy family relationships in the Asian community" and offer "culturally and linguistically appropriate care" for Asian Americans seeking help.[80] Understanding the role of faith in combating intimate partner violence, Toby Myers, often called the mother of the battered women's movement, cofounded Aid to Victims of Domestic Abuse to meet spiritual and physical needs of Jewish survivors as well as to run Shalom Bayit, a teen dating violence program.[81]

Despite VAWA's impact on reducing the number of incidents by 53 percent from 1993 to 2008, intimate partner violence remains a pressing problem experienced by approximately a third of all Americans.[82] The movement has met with new struggles since 2000, with the most evident challenges occurring primarily in the legal system. Efforts to decriminalize intimate partner violence gained ground. Views on decriminalization varied in the exact meaning. To some, decriminalization meant "a more balanced policy approach" through deemphasizing criminal solutions and instead treating abuse as "an economic, public health, community, and human rights problem."[83] Others viewed decriminalization as stopping prosecution on misdemeanor domestic violence charges as a cost-saving method.[84] Collectively, these arguments led to critiques of legal solutions and practices. Critics of decriminalization agree that intimate partner violence is a multifaceted issue requiring a comprehensive approach but fear reducing the criminal focus will send the social message that abuse is not taken seriously. Moreover, the low conviction rate nationally (22 percent) of misdemeanor abuse charges means that, even without decriminalization, a large number of abusers face little to no legal consequence.[85] As courts both influence and are influenced by social opinion, the conviction rate speaks to a larger sociolegal issue in which intimate partner violence is deemed as less serious. This, some argue, perpetuates a culture in which intimate partner violence thrives.

A second important challenge in the legal system came with reauthorization of VAWA. VAWA, despite being viewed as a bipartisan issue, became increasingly politicized in 2012. VAWA lapsed for five hundred days as politicians debated whether protections should be extended to immigrants, Native Americans living on reservations, and LGBTQ individuals.[86] Texas US Senators Ted Cruz (R) and John Cornyn (R) were among those who voted against the 2012 version, citing issues with tribal rights and the issue as belonging to the states.[87] Cornyn even sponsored a stripped-down version of VAWA that did not include protections to victims in same-sex relationships, Native Americans on reservations, or immigrants, which reflected a growing social conservatism opposed to legal protections for LGBTQIA+ individuals and other marginalized populations. Eventually, Congress passed the more comprehensive version, but the heated debate demonstrated cracks in the movement. In 2019, VAWA became the center of debate again. Additions such as the "boyfriend loophole," which would prohibit abusive dating partners and stalkers from owning a gun, generated difficulties in reauthorization of the bill. Although a 2016 Supreme Court ruling allowed for convicted abusers to be prohibited from owning a firearm, the boyfriend loophole controversy created divisions in Congress, and Second Amendment debates replaced the focus on domestic violence.[88]

During the 2010s, intimate partner homicides have risen across the United States.[89] Nationally, intimate partner homicides had declined from 1981 to 1998 by 47 percent and continued to decrease by 27 percent from 1999 to 2009.[90] From 2010 to 2014, the FBI's Supplementary Homicide Reports of the Uniform Crime Reporting Program noted the annual intimate partner homicides remained at similar levels to the prior decade--neither increasing or decreasing.[91] However, recent years marked a notable rise by 19 percent from 2014 to 2017, and preliminary data from the "Shadow Pandemic" (the growth of intimate partner violence during the COVID-19 pandemic) indicates a continued increase during 2020.[92] In 2020, 228 Texans were murdered by a current or former partner, marking the highest number of intimate partner homicides in the state in a decade.[93] As with mass murderers, those who murder their current or former partner often have a prior history of abuse. A study of Fort Worth, Texas, found that 55 percent of batterers who committed intimate partner homicide had a prior documented history of abuse.[94] A link between mass shooters and domestic violence and misogyny also exists. The 2017 mass murder at First Baptist Church in Sutherland Springs, Texas, was perpetrated by an individual whose known violent behavior began with beating and choking his first wife and ended with killing men, women, and children who attended the same church as his estranged second wife. Unquestionably, domestic abuse remains a pressing issue that leads to increased numbers serious physical, emotional, and mental injuries, fatalities, and economic and social costs for victims. Texas and the nation as a whole must continue to uproot a culture of violence that perpetuates intimate partner violence.

Notes

1. "Narrative on Funding Proposal," Austin Center for Battered Women, 1979, A 362.8292 CE, Austin History Center.

2. Council on Criminal Justice, "New Analysis Shows 8% Increase in U.S. Domestic Violence Incidents Following Pandemic Stay-At-Home Orders," accessed August 8, 2022, https://counciloncj.org/new-analysis-shows-8-increase-in-u-s-domestic-violence-incidents-following-pandemic-stay-at-home-orders/#:~:text=WASHINGTON%2C%20D.C.%20%E2%80%93%20A%20report%20released, orders%20during%20the%202020%20pandemic.

3. National Coalition Against Domestic Violence, "Statistics," accessed February 23, 2020, https://ncadv.org/statistics.

4. Laura M. Holson, "Murders by Intimate Partners Are on the Rise, Study Finds," *New York Times,* April 12, 2019, https://www.nytimes.com/2019/04/12/us/domestic-violence-victims.html.

5. Judy Klemesrud, "International Women's Year World Conference Opening in Mexico," *New York Times,* June 19, 1975, https://www.nytimes.com/1975/06/19/archives/international-womens-year-world-conference-opening-in-mexico.html.

6. United Nations, *Report of the World Conference of the International Women's Year: Mexico City, 19 June–2 July 1975* (New York: United Nations, 1976), 78. For more information on the IWY Mexico City conference, see Jocelyn Olcott, *International Women's Year: The Greatest Consciousness-Raising Event in History* (New York: Oxford University Press, 2017).

7. This chapter uses the phrase "women's movement" to refer to activism in the 1960s and 1970s instead of the more common phrase "second-wave feminism" because of inadequacies of the wave theory. See Nancy Hewitt, ed., *No Permanent*

Waves: Recasting Histories of U.S. Feminism (Piscataway, NJ: Rutgers University Press, 2010).

8. Karen Dill Bowerman, *Family Violence: Children Within the Cycle* (Austin: Texas Commission on the Status of Women, 1978).

9. *Ms.,* summer special edition (August 1976).

10. Although some TBTN events focus exclusively on sexual assault, the TBTN foundation includes intimate partner violence.

11. Kathleen J. Tierney, "The Battered Women Movement and the Creation of the Wife Beating Problem," *Social Problems* 29, no. 3 (February 1982): 207–20.

12. Barbara Cooper, *Wife Beating: Counselor Training Manual #2* (Ann Arbor, MI: NOW Domestic Violence and Spouse Assault Fund, 1976).

13. James S. Stachura and Raymond H. C. Teske Jr., *Special Report on Spouse Abuse in Texas* (Huntsville, TX: Survey Research Program Criminal Justice Center, Sam Houston State University, 1979), 18.

14. National Organization for Women, *Broadside* 7, no. 11 (November 1976), University of Houston Libraries Special Collections, Carey C. Shuart Women's Research Collection, Houston and Texas Feminist and Lesbian Newsletters, https://id.lib.uh.edu/ark:/84475/d068945s738.

15. The DVIA did expand its services and offered a shelter called The Family Place, which opened in 1978.

16. Austin Center for Battered Women, 1979, A 362.8292 CE, Austin History Center.

17. Hogg Foundation, "Family Violence: The Well-Kept Secret," 1979, box 8, folder 2, Toby M. Myers, Deborah D. Tucker, and Maria Jose Angelelli, Texas Council on Family Violence Records, 1998-005, University of Houston Libraries Special Collections.

18. Funding for the shelter came from the Hogg Foundation for Mental Health, Travis County, and the City of Austin. The Austin Center for Battered Women merged with the Austin Rape Crisis Center to become what is presently called SafePlace.

19. United Way, "The Center for Battered Women, Austin, Texas," 1979, box 8, folder 20, Toby M. Myers, Deborah D. Tucker, and Maria Jose Angelelli, Texas Council on Family Violence Records, 1998-005, University of Houston Libraries Special Collections. Other publications cite different numbers. Given many shelters emerged during the same time and many out of women's homes, the exact number of shelters is difficult to give with absolute certainty. See Tierney, "Battered Women Movement," 208. For information on a nineteenth-century precursor to the shelter, see Jayme A. Sokolow and Mary Ann Lamanna, "Women and Utopia: The Woman's Commonwealth of Belton, Texas," *Southwestern Historical Quarterly* 87, no. 4 (Apr., 1984): 371–92.

20. Toby Myers, "A Plea for Help: One Community's Response," *Victimology* 2, no. 3–4 (1977–78): 652.

21. Austin Center for Battered Women.

22. Hogg Foundation, "Family Violence."

23. The movement against intimate partner violence was labeled the "Battered Women's Movement" in the 1970s, but this chapter examines a longer time frame and argues the modern movement against intimate partner violence did not end in the 1970s. As such, the phrase "modern movement against intimate partner violence" will be used even during the 1970s.

24. Texas Coordinating Committee, *Texas Women's Meeting: Summary of the Final Report to the National Commission on the Observance of International Women's Year by the Texas Coordinating Committee,* September 1977, box 2, folder 11, Marjorie Randal National Women's Conference Collection, 1996–007, University of Houston Libraries Special Collections, https://id.lib.uh.edu/ark:/84475/d09078gh508.

25. Texas Coordinating Committee, *Texas Women's Meeting.*

26. "Houston Area Women's Center," Houston Area Women's Center Records, 1996-005-a, Facts and History, 1977-1992, 1997, Box: 1, Folder: 4. Houston Area Women's Center Records, 1996-005-a. University of Houston Libraries Special Collections. For more on the conference, see Marjorie J. Spruill, *Divided We Stand: The Battle Ove Women's Rights and Family Values That Polarized American Politics* (New York: Bloomsbury Publishing, 2018).

27. Battered Women, Rape, and Abused Children, selections from the Marjorie Randal National Women's Conference Collection, box 1, folder 25, University of Houston Libraries Special Collections, https://id.lib.uh.edu/ark:/84475/d09351hm143.

28. Maria Swall-Yarrington, "Texas Council on Family Violence," *Handbook of Texas Online,* published October 1, 1995, updated August 13, 2020, http://www.tshaonline.org/handbook/online/articles/pwtfg.

29. Texas Council on Family Violence, *The Essential Guide: An Introduction to Advocating for Survivors of Family Violence* (Austin: Texas Council on Family Violence), 5; K. J. Wilson, *When Violence Begins at Home* (Alameda, CA: Hunter House, 2006): 249.

30. Steve Russell, "The Futility of Eloquence: Selected Texas Family Violence Legislation 1979–1991," *South Texas Law Review* 33 (1992): 356; Texas Council on Family Violence, *Legislative Development of Domestic Violence Issues in Texas Report,* Toby M. Myers, Deborah D. Tucker, and Maria Jose Angelelli, Texas Council on Family Violence Records, 1998-005, University of Houston Libraries Special Collections.

31. Pokey Anderson, "Sex and Violence," *Pointblank Times* 3, no. 1 (January 1977): 9, Carey C. Shuart Women's Research Collection, University of Houston Libraries Special Collections, https://id.lib.uh.edu/ark:/84475/d03071nh65f.

32. National Organization for Women, *Broadside* 9, no. 6 (June 1978), Carey C. Shuart Women's Research Collection, Houston and Texas Feminist and Lesbian Newsletters, University of Houston Libraries Special Collections, https://id.lib.uh.edu/ark:/84475/d03515bd71v.

33. Ann Harris, "'Battered Wives' Author Talks on Crisis Housing," *Houston Breakthrough* 2, no. 2 (February 1977): 14, Carey C. Shuart Women's Research Collection, Houston and Texas Feminist and Lesbian Newsletters, University of Houston Libraries Special Collections, https://id.lib.uh.edu/ark:/84475/d084644t34j.

34. Susan A. Eggert, *HAWC Volunteer Training Manual,* Action Grant, undated, box 9, folder 2, Houston Area Women's Center Records, 1996-005-a, University of Houston Libraries Special Collections.

35. Stachura and Teske, *Special Report on Spouse Abuse,* 18.

36. D. A. Gaquin, "Spouse Abuse; Data from the National Crime Survey," *Victimology* 2, no. 3–4, (1977–78): 632–43.

37. Tierney, "Battered Women Movement," 209; Merle H. Weiner, "From Dollars to Sense: A Critique of Government Funding for the Battered Women's Movement," *Law & Equality* 9, no. 2 (1991): 208.

38. Tierney, 209.

39. Commission on Civil Rights, *The Federal Response to Domestic Violence: A Report of the United States Commission on Civil Rights* (Washington, DC: The Commission, 1982), 65.

40. Domestic Violence and Treatment Act, S. 1728, 95th Cong. (1977).

41. *Domestic Violence: Hearings before the Subcommittee on Select Education on the Committee on Education and Labor House of Representatives on H.R. 7927 and H.R. 8948 to Authorize the Secretary of Health, Education, and Welfare to Establish a Grant Program to Develop Methods of Prevention and Treatment Relating to Domestic Violence, and for Other Purposes,* 95th Cong., 2nd Sess., March 16 and 17 (1978) (statement of Carl D. Perkins).

42. Sandy Long, Houston Breakthrough, February 1980, Carey C. Shuart Women's Research Collection, Houston and Texas Feminist and Lesbian Newsletters, University of Houston Libraries Special Collections, https://id.lib.uh.edu/ark:/84475/d00921gj47n; Bob Tutt, "Battering of Women Is Termed Top Crime Problem in State, US," *Houston Chronicle*, July 15, 1982, University of Houston Libraries Special Collections, accessed August 10, 2022, https://digitalcollections.lib.uh.edu/concern/texts/2n49t298z.

43. Murray A. Straus, "Prevention of Family Violence," *The Prevention of Mental-Emotional Disabilities,* resource papers to the report of the National Mental Health Association, Commission on the Prevention of Mental-Emotional Disabilities (Washington, DC: National Mental Health Association, 1986). Other important studies included M. Roy, *The Abusive Partner* (New York: Van Nostrand Rheinhold, 1982); M. A. Gelles and R. J. Gelles, "Societal Change and Change in Family Violence from 1975 to 1985 as Revealed by Two National Surveys," *Journal of Marriage and the Family* 48, No. 3 (Aug. 1986): 465–79.

44. For more on the work of Toby Myers, see "Myers Honored for Work Against Domestic Abuse," *Houston Chronicle,* June 28, 2010, https://www.chron.com/

neighborhood/heights-news/article/Myers-honored-for-work-against-domestic-abuse-1712085.php.

45. S.J. Res. 113, Pub. L. No. 101-112, 101st Cong. (Oct. 6, 1989): A joint resolution designating October 1989 as "National Domestic Violence Awareness Month."

46. Jim Atkinson, "Sins of the Fathers," *Texas Monthly* (March 1981): 144.

47. Alden Brown, "Denouncing the Myth," *Times Record* (Wichita Falls, TX), July 26, 1988, Toby M. Myers, Deborah D. Tucker, and Maria Jose Angelelli, Texas Council on Family Violence Records, 1998-005, University of Houston Libraries Special Collection.

48. NOW News Bay Area Chapter, 11, no. 10 (October 1983), pg. 7, Houston and Texas Feminist and Lesbian Newsletters, University of Houston Libraries Special Collections, accessed December 28, 2019, https://digitalcollections.lib.uh.edu/concern/texts/s1784n49r?locale=en.

49. Dan Rather, "A Place to Go," *60 Minutes,* Dan Rather: American Journalist, Briscoe Center for American History, University of Texas at Austin, accessed December 29, 2019, https://danratherjournalist.org/investigative-journalist/60-minutes/60-minutes-additional-videos/video-place-go.

50. Steve Vinson, "Battered Women's Center Opens Shelter," *Daily Texan,* Toby M. Myers, Deborah D. Tucker, and Maria Jose Angelelli, Texas Council on Family Violence Records, 1998-005, University of Houston Libraries Special Collections.

51. Mary Dudley, "Battered Women Seek Refuge: Center Marks First Year," *Austin American-Statesman,* 1978, Toby M. Myers, Deborah D. Tucker, and Maria Jose Angelelli, Texas Council on Family Violence Records, 1998-005, University of Houston Libraries Special Collections.

52. Edward W. Gondolf, *Gender-Based Perspectives on Battering Programs: Program Leaders on History, Approach, Research, and Development* (Lanham, MB: Lexington Books, 2015).

53. Senate Concurrent Resolution 87, 1983, Texas Council on Family Violence, Legislative Development of Domestic Violence Issues in Texas Report, Toby M. Myers, Deborah D. Tucker, and Maria Jose Angelelli, Texas Council on Family Violence Records, 1998-005, University of Houston Libraries Special Collections; Toby Myers and Sandra Gilbert, *Victimology* 9, no. 1–2 (1983): 238–48; Melissa J. Eddy and Toby Myers, *Helping Men Who Batter: A Profile of Programs in the U.S.,* report prepared for the Texas Department of Human Resources, August 1984, Toby M. Myers, Deborah D. Tucker, and Maria Jose Angelelli, Texas Council on Family Violence Records, 1998-005, University of Houston Libraries Special Collections.

54. Irene Virag, "Plan Offers Option to Batterers," *Austin American-Statesman,* July 3, 1981, Toby M. Myers, Deborah D. Tucker, and Maria Jose Angelelli, Texas Council on Family Violence Records, 1998-005, University of Houston Libraries Special Collections.

55. One speaker used a statistic of a Dallas shelter, where only 11 percent of women who stayed there called the police. Committee on Human Resources,

work session on Domestic Violence Senate Committee on Human Resources 9-8-82, Texas Law Center, tape 4, sides 7 & 8, H.R. 125, September 8, 1982, 67th 3rd C.S., 670702a, Texas State Library and Archives Commission.

56. P. W. Gee, "Ensuring Police Protection for Battered Women: The *Scott v. Hart* Suit," *Signs* 8, no. 3 (Spring 1983): 554–61.

57. Susan Schechter, *Women and Male Violence* (Boston: South End Press, 1982), 160.

58. The MDVE encouraged mandatory arrest laws, and while some police departments adopted such policies and some states passed legislation to the effect, mandatory arrest remained debated in the 1980s. Texas did not pass any legislation on mandatory arrest laws. David Hirschel, *Domestic Violence Cases: What Research Shows about Arrest and Dual Arrest Rates* (Washington, DC: National Institute of Justice, 2008).

59. House Bill 1743, TCFV Legislative Development on Domestic Violence Issues in Texas, 1995, Toby M. Myers, Deborah D. Tucker, and Maria Jose Angelelli, Texas Council on Family Violence Records, 1998-005, University of Houston Libraries Special Collections.

60. SB878, SB997, and SCR88, TCFV Legislative Development on Domestic Violence Issues in Texas, 1995, Toby M. Myers, Deborah D. Tucker, and Maria Jose Angelelli, Texas Council on Family Violence Records, 1998-005, University of Houston Libraries Special Collections.

61. Committee on Legal Rights of Battered Women, *Family Violence: Legal Choices for Battered Women* (Austin: Texas Young Lawyers Association, 1985).

62. Leonore A. Walker, *The Battered Woman* (New York: Harper and Row, 1979).

63. Interview with Leonore Walker, 1980, Toby Myers Papers, 2010-018, University of Houston Libraries Special Collections.

64. Morris Edelson, "Till Death Do Us Part," Toby Myers Papers, 2010-018, University of Houston Libraries Special Collections.

65. Barbara J. Hart, "State Codes on Domestic Violence: Analysis, Commentary, and Recommendations," *Juvenile and Family Court Journal* 43, no. 4 (1992): 75; Mark Hansen, "Battered Child's Defense," *ABA Journal* 78 (May 1992): 28.

66. US Department of Health and Human Services and US Department of Justice, *Surgeon General's Workshop on Violence and Public Health Report* (Washington, DC: Health Resources and Services Administration, 1986).

67. Anne Flitcraft, "Physicians and Domestic Violence: Challenges for Prevention," *Health Affairs* 12, no. 4 (Winter 1993): 154–61.

68. Demie Kurz, "Emergency Department Responses to Battered Women: Resistance to Medicalization," *Social Problems* 34, no. 1 (February 1987): 69–81.

69. Anne Stewart Helton, "Battering during Pregnancy: A Prevalence Study in a Metropolitan Area," Texas Woman's University College of Nursing, August 1985, Barbara Karkabi Papers, 2012-003, University of Houston Libraries Special Collections.

70. You can find the report, which is updated annually, here under the subheading, "Texas Intimate Partner Fatality Report," accessed August 1, 2022, https://tcfv .org/publications/.

71. The organization was known as the Domestic Violence Coalition on Public Policy for four years before its name was changed to NNEDV.

72. National Domestic Hotline, *Making a Real Difference: National Domestic Hotline Five Year Report, 1996–2001,* Toby M. Myers, Deborah D. Tucker, and Maria Jose Angelelli, Texas Council on Family Violence Records, 1998-005, University of Houston Libraries Special Collections.

73. Jan E. Stets and Maureen A. Pirog-Good, "Violence in Dating Relationships," *Social Psychology Quarterly* 50, no. 3 (Sept. 1987), 237–46.

74. Texas Council on Family Violence, *Legislative Development of Domestic Violence Issues in Texas Report,* Toby M. Myers, Deborah D. Tucker, and Maria Jose Angelelli, Texas Council on Family Violence Records, 1998-005, University of Houston Libraries Special Collections.

75. Lisa N. Sacco, *The Violence Against Women's Act: Overview, Legislation, and Federal Funding* (R42499), Congressional Research Service, May 26, 2015.

76. Planning Council for S.T.O.P. Violence Against Women, *S.T.O.P. Violence Against Women in Texas Statewide Strategy,* Office of the Governor, Austin, Texas, October 1995, Toby M. Myers, Deborah D. Tucker, and Maria Jose Angelelli, Texas Council on Family Violence Records, 1998-005, University of Houston Libraries Special Collections.

77. Robert C. Davis, Barbara E Smith, and Heather J Davies, "Effects of No-Drop Prosecution of Domestic Violence on Conviction Rates," *Justice Research Policy* 3, no. 2 (Fall 2001): 1–13.

78. Bonnie S. Fisher, ed., *Violence Against Women and Family Violence: Developments in Research, Practice, and Policy,* NCJ 199701 (2004), National Criminal Justice Resource Center, https://www.ncjrs.gov/pdffiles1/nij/199701.pdf.

79. United States, *Policies and Programs for Preventing and Responding to Incidents of Assault in the Armed Services, Hearing Before the Subcommittee on Personnel of the Committee on Armed Services, United States Senate, One Hundred Eighth Congress Second Session, February 24, 2004* (Washington, DC: US Government Printing Office, 2005): 208.

80. "Asians Against Domestic Abuse Non-Residential Policy and Procedure," Asians Against Domestic Abuse Records, 2010-005, box 1, folder 5 University of Houston Libraries Special Collections; Asians Against Domestic Abuse, "AADA's History," accessed December 29, 2019, https://www.aadainc.org/history.

81. Toby Myers, "Jewish Perspectives in Domestic Violence," in *Domestic Violence: Cross Cultural Perspective,* ed. M. Basheer Ahmed (North Texas: MCC for Human Services, 2009), 45–55.

82. Monica N. Modi, Sheallah Palmer, and Alicia Armstrong, "The Role of Violence Against Women Act in Addressing Intimate Partner Violence: A Public Health

Issue," *Journal of Women's Health* 23, no. 3 (March 2014): 253–59; Sharon G. Smith et al., *National Intimate Partner and Sexual Violence Survey: 2015 Data Brief—Updated Release* (Atlanta, GA: National Center for Injury Prevention and Control, Centers for Disease Control and Prevention, November 2018).

83. Leigh Goodman, *Decriminalizing Domestic Violence: A Balanced Policy Approach to Intimate Partner Violence* (Oakland: University of California Press, 2018).

84. Shelley M. Santry, "Penny Wise but Pound Foolish in the Heartland: A Case Study of Decriminalizing Domestic Violence in Topeka, Kansas," *Journal of Law & Family Studies* 14 (2012): 223–44.

85. Erica L. Smith, Matthew R. Durose, and Patrick A. Langan, *State Court Processing of Domestic Violence Cases,* NCJ 214993 (February 2008): 1. While some of the accused are proven innocent, many plea bargain or evade prosecution for various reasons, including the victim dropping charges. Whether a charge is a felony or misdemeanor makes a difference in conviction rate: felonies are more successfully prosecuted.

86. Jane K. Stoever, *The Politicization of Safety Critical Perspectives on Domestic Violence Responses* (New York New York University Press, 2019).

87. Ted Cruz, "Statement on Sen. Ted Cruz's Vote Regarding VAWA," February 12, 2013, https://www.cruz.senate.gov/?p=press_release&id=201.

88. *Voisine v. United States,* 579 US (2016).

89. Emma E. Fridel and James Alan Fox, "Gender Differences in Patterns and Trends in US Homicides, 1976–2017," *Violence and Gender* 6, no. 1 (March 2019).

90. Leonard J. Paulozzi et al., "Surveillance for Homicide Among Intimate Partners—United States, 1981–1998," Morbidity and Mortality Weekly Report, CDC Surveillance Summaries 50 no. 3 (October 21, 2001): 1–16; Federal Bureau of Investigation Crime Data Reporter, Expanded Homicide Offense Characteristics in the United States, accessed August 4, 2022, https://crime-data-explorer.app.cloud.gov/pages/explorer/crime/shr.

91. Federal Bureau of Investigation Crime Data Reporter, Expanded Homicide Offense Characteristics in the United States, accessed August 4, 2022, https://crime-data-explorer.app.cloud.gov/pages/explorer/crime/shr.

92. Emma F. Fridel and James Alan Fox, "Gender Differences in Patterns and Trends of US Homicide, 1976–2017," Violence and Gender6, No. 1 (March 2019): 27–36; UN Women, "The Shadow Pandemic: Violence against women during COVID-19," accessed August 4, 2022, https://www.unwomen.org/en/news/in-focus/in-focus-gender-equality-in-covid-19-response/violence-against-women-during-covid-19.

93. Texas Council on Family Violence, " Honoring Texas Victims: Family Violence Fatalities in 2020 accessed August 1, 2022, https://tcfv.org/publications/. This report is updated annually on the website of the Texas Council on Family Violence.

94. Katie Zezima et al., "How Domestic Violence Leads to Murder," *Washington Post,* December 9, 2018.

3

FIGHTING THE KILLING TRAIL

LGBTQ Activism and the Hate
Crime Epidemic in Texas

Christopher P. Haight

In February 1995, *Vanity Fair* published a lengthy article titled "The Killing Trail," which highlighted the murders of eight gay Texas men in the early 1990s.[1] The writer followed "the killing trail" from urban centers such as Houston into the rural areas of East and West Texas, weaving a story of gay bloodshed at the hands of homophobic attackers. Although the article placed the murders in the context of a national hate crime epidemic and admitted that Texas may not be entirely unique, the subtext was that the Lone Star State was a particularly violent place for gay men. To help make sense of the brutality visited upon gay men in the state, the article quoted the openly gay Reverend Mel White: "We molest, we recruit, we eat shit, we're not fit to be in the military. All this rhetoric goes on and they wonder why kids are beating the shit out of us." The writer pointed the finger at antigay rhetoric spewed from Texas pulpits, in particular, and added: "When you take the [homophobic] rhetoric and combine it with the macho culture of a state where the cowboy and six-shooter still hold powerful sway, it makes the trail of death seem not aberrational but inevitable."[2]

By 1995, gay activists and the mainstream and gay media had painted a picture of a Lone Star State reeling from an antigay violence wave. At the beginning of the year, the statewide gay publication *This Week in Texas* (*TWT*) published an article on the spate of gay murders in 1993 and 1994; the writer ominously warned that recent events "should make everyone in the community think both about their own safety and about such crimes as a continuing societal problem."[3] This rhetoric did not simply serve as a warning to the gay community; other media outlets (such as *Vanity Fair*) picked up on the high-profile murder stories and painted the crisis, to some degree, as a Texas problem created by an oppressively homophobic culture, government, and legal system.

The Lesbian/Gay Rights Lobby of Texas (LGRL), the state's leading gay rights organization, seized on the local, state, and national media coverage of antigay hate crime in Texas and organized a Stop the Violence rally in Austin. Held in April 1995, the march drew at least five thousand people. Democratic State Representative Glen Maxey of Austin, the first and only openly gay legislator in Texas at the time, spoke to the marchers and invoked the state's torrid racial history, drawing a line from the lynching tradition to gay bashing: "Some 70 years ago, the Ku Klux Klan roamed the Piney Woods and North Texas Plains beating, robbing, and murdering Texans simply because of the color of their skin. In the nineties, it is gay men and lesbians who are the victims of the new Saturday-night pastime: fag bashing."[4] Following the tactics of early twentieth-century lynching activists, the march revolved around the murders of specific gay Texans, and hate crime activists saw themselves in a civil rights framework. For many in the crowd, it was also a deeply personal march as they carried photographs of murdered loved ones. While gay advocacy organizations and the media often spoke in abstract terms about a hate crime "epidemic," individual marchers and activists were moved by personal experiences in their own families and localities. The movement against antigay violence in Texas, embodied by the 1995 march, took on a distinctly Texan character as it focused on local and state solutions to this perceived local and state problem.

By the 1990s, gay activists were convinced—based on a series of murders that targeted gay men—that a deep culture of violence existed in Texas that specifically targeted gay people.[5] They believed not only that Texas was uniquely violent but also that state and local institutions (from the legislature to the courts to law enforcement) neglected to pursue justice for gay Texans who were victims of violence. These activists, led by the LGRL, formed a movement in support of a hate crime law that included specific protections for people victimized because of their sexual orientation. Previously, activists raised alarm that gay people were being targeted and brutalized by police, but by the 1990s, these activists turned toward law enforcement and the criminal justice system to protect them from the scourge of antigay violence. In many ways, the gay rights movement that existed in Texas in the 1990s was centered on the push for a hate crime bill. The legislation activists sought was modeled after language championed by the Anti-Defamation League (ADL) and National Gay and Lesbian Task Force (NGLTF) and called for penalty enhancements for bias-motivated crimes.[6] The proposed bill in Texas, which built on a vague 1993 hate crime law providing for sentence enhancements but not protected categories, sought to add the explicit categories of race, color, disability, religion, national origin, and sexual orientation. This movement culminated with the passage of the gay-inclusive James Byrd Jr. Hate Crimes Act, which Republican Governor Rick Perry signed into law in 2001, following an intense legislative push in the aftermath of the infamous 1998 murder of James Byrd Jr. The inclusion of sexual orientation in the final bill, which seems out of step with the socially conservative Texas political environment, was possible only because of sustained gay and lesbian activism on the issue throughout the 1990s.[7]

This chapter argues that the culture of violence that Texas gay and lesbian activists perceived was real, at least in part. This does not mean that Texas has led the nation in antigay violence. Although hate crime reporting is spotty at best, FBI statistics from 1996 (the earliest year such statistics were available) to 2001 show that Texas has never led the nation in the number of reported hate crimes. Furthermore, crimes committed against gay Texans were always far outnumbered by crimes committed against racial minorities.[8] However, statistics aside, the Lone Star State has been the center of some of the most notorious and symbolically important antigay hate crime cases in the country. Prior to the infamous 1998 murder of Matthew Shepard in Wyoming, *the* "national" antigay hate crime was the 1991 murder of Paul Broussard in Houston. Texas was also (justifiably) seen as a center for state-sanctioned homophobia. Before Broussard's murder, the hate crime case that shook the national gay community took place in Dallas and resulted in the 1988 decision by Judge Jack Hampton to hand down a purposely lenient sentence to the perpetrator. The perceived culture of violence in Texas was real, but it was more cultural than statistical.

Violence targeting LGBTQ Texans did not begin in the 1990s when gay activists began to organize in support of a comprehensive hate crime law, nor did it end in 2001 when the law was finally passed. This chapter, which seeks to provide a narrative of anti-LGBTQ violence in Texas history, is nevertheless centered on the 1980s and 1990s, when such violence was given a legal name ("hate crime") and the gay and lesbian community in Texas focused its attention on combating that violence. I utilize a broad definition of violence that encompasses state violence (police brutality and harassment) as well as bias-motivated acts of violence by anti-LGBTQ attackers (hate crime). The chapter begins in the 1970s, when politically organized gay communities first began to take shape in Texas—and when police exercised a kind of state-sanctioned violence against gay Texans. I then examine the gay movement's transition from a focus on state violence to an emphasis on combating hate crime by *using* law enforcement for protection. The gay struggle for a hate crime law in Texas, which was a central civil rights goal for gay Texans in the 1990s, forms the bulk of the chapter. Finally, the chapter considers anti-LGBTQ violence in the twenty-first century as well as the limitations of the James Byrd Jr. Hate Crimes Act.

By the late 1970s, Texas was home to vibrant gay communities and institutions, particularly in urban centers such as Dallas and Houston. The Dallas gay community, centered in the Oak Lawn neighborhood, also consisted of political organizations such as the Dallas Gay Political Caucus and (later) the Dallas Gay and Lesbian Alliance.[9] Houston's gay community, centered in the Montrose neighborhood, featured the Gay Political Caucus (GPC) and the Houston Human Rights League (HHRL). After leading antigay advocate Anita Bryant's 1977 visit to the Texas State Bar Association meeting in Houston, gay organizing ignited like never before. Soon, Houston's gay community became a major political and cultural force within the city. Gay Houstonians (and other gay Texans) also had alternative newspapers, such as *This Week in Texas*.[10] Relations between gay Texans and the police were not as widely covered by the mainstream media as was racial tension in the 1970s, but gay activists and organizations did fight against police brutality, making the issue a centerpiece of their gay rights agenda. This antiviolence activism, like the struggle against racist police abuse, was centered in the Dallas and Houston urban areas.[11] In Texas, gay sex was a special target of the "sodomy" ban found in Section 21.06 of the Texas Penal Code, adding an extra layer of criminality to the struggle for gay rights and likely fueling tensions between the gay community and the police.[12] By the mid-1970s, in the context of the national gay liberation movement, activists in the large, well-developed, and politically organized gay communities of Houston and Dallas began to assert their right to exist free of police harassment and violence.[13]

In 1976, for example, police raided nearby Galveston's Kon Tiki bathhouse. The raid resulted in the arrest of thirty-nine gay Galvestonians and Houstonians and the eventual trial of thirty on indecent exposure charges. Gay activists claimed that this was just another in a series of police harassment episodes targeting gay establishments. Houston gay leader Ray Hill called for the gay communities of Houston, Galveston, and Dallas (also a perceived hotbed of antigay police harassment) to finally stand up against this wave of police brutality: "The vast majority of us have been silent, and some gays have even voiced support of these clear abuses of police power. . . . But my concern is not with police homophobia. I always knew it was there. What bothers me is gay apathy."[14]

Houston and Dallas gay newspaper headlines related to police harassment and brutality were voluminous throughout the 1970s and early 1980s. Police raids of gay establishments were perhaps the most documented alleged police violence cases. In addition to the Galveston raid, which directly affected gay Houstonians, the end of 1976 saw a raid by Houston Police Department (HPD) vice officers on an after-hours party at Levi's, a popular Houston gay bar. The raid resulted in forty arrests for consuming liquor "after hours." While seeming to admit that liquor laws were indeed violated, *TWT* wondered "if the raid can be considered completely coincidental."[15] The Houston GPC, the city's leading gay organization, published a call for police brutality victims during the Galveston raid to come forward with information.[16] On February 25, 1977, HPD vice officers raided six adult bookstores and arrested ten employees as a part of an antipornography campaign.[17] While the raids targeted pornography in general, Hill placed the action in the context of antigay harassment by the HPD and "red neck lunatic homophobes."[18] A GPC progress report in 1976, while optimistic about its efforts to improve relations with the HPD, urged individuals who felt "hassled" by the police to contact the organization to provide "more raw information" on the problem.[19] Despite the GPC's optimism, Hill and a coalition of gay businessowners concerned about HPD harassment founded the HHRL in 1977 "to combat official abuses of power aimed at gay people and gay businesses," citing bookstore raids and a recent beating of a gay bookstore customer by HPD officers.[20] In Dallas, a similar coalition of gay businessowners and managers formed the Dallas Alliance for Individual Rights (DAIR) in 1976, citing "continuous and unprovoked police harassment of gays in the Dallas area."[21]

In the late 1970s, gay activism against police brutality intensified. This was especially true in Houston, where the US Department of Justice (DOJ) Civil Rights Commission had opened an investigation in 1979 in response to civil rights abuse allegations by racial minorities. The GPC announced in February 1979 that it was going to become involved in the DOJ hearings by testifying about antigay police harassment allegations. The organization launched Operation: Documentation in order to gather information about specific police harassment and brutality incidents in Houston's gay community.[22] In April, gay leaders organized a rally in front of Houston City Hall to protest "numerous incidents of harassment and abuse" carried out by the HPD.[23] The rally drew more than one thousand people from various Houston minority communities concerned about police violence as well as representatives from the Hispanic Coalition and Democratic US Representative Mickey Leland's office.[24] In June, news that GPC president Steve Shiflett had been subpoenaed to testify before a DOJ hearing dovetailed with the findings of Operation: Documentation, which uncovered more than one hundred cases of reported verbal and physical brutality, murder cover-ups, and prejudiced testimony by the HPD.[25] Shortly after the police abuse rally in Houston, Operation: Documentation moved to Dallas through the efforts of DAIR, with the purpose of sending a report on Dallas Police Department (DPD) harassment to the DOJ Civil Rights Commission and Congress.[26]

In 1980, relations between police and the gay community reached a nadir, centering on a series of violent incidents in Houston. On June 20, immediately before the city's Gay Pride Week celebrations, the HPD carried out a major raid on Mary's, a popular gay bar. HPD officers arrested sixty-one people in the raid, with reports that "the vice [officers] were shoving people against the wall" and "select[ing] at random all those people who looked different, those without shirts or in leather." Highlighting gay impatience with HPD harassment, one of those arrested said, "Next time, it'll be a Stonewall."[27] While there was no "Stonewall" moment following a police raid in Houston, the Mary's raid provided an ominous backdrop for the Houston gay community's Pride celebration. It also foreshadowed the complete collapse of trust between the gay community and the police.

Only six days after the Mary's raid, another expression of state violence rocked the Houston gay community: the police shooting death of Fred Paez, who was the GPC secretary and a self-taught expert on gay-related police procedures. According to the official HPD press release, Paez approached off-duty officer K. M. McCoy and another officer, suggested they follow him to the side of the building, and then touched McCoy between his legs. When McCoy attempted to arrest him for public lewdness, Paez reportedly grabbed McCoy's .45 automatic gun, which discharged after a short struggle and fatally struck Paez in the back of the head.[28] The HPD's version of events stretched credulity in the eyes of the gay community, considering Paez's familiarity with police procedure and especially after a firearm expert's testimony that the gun could not have discharged accidentally.[29] A grand jury indicted McCoy, but he was acquitted at trial. The gay community, however, used the opportunity to protest against police harassment and brutality, culminating in a march of approximately one thousand people from City Hall to the HPD headquarters.[30] After the Paez shooting, an emphasis on police brutality became evident in literature produced by the HHRL, which Paez cofounded. The HHRL lambasted the "open attack by the Houston Police Department and other violent homophobic extremists" on gay community institutions.[31]

Police harassment and brutality continued to dominate the agenda of Houston and Dallas gay activists in the early 1980s.[32] During the 1980s, in response to gay and racial minority pressure, both Houston and Dallas underwent a series of police reforms seeking to make the HPD and DPD more accountable and responsive to the needs and issues of minority communities. HPD implemented a community policing model, and DPD was placed under the supervision of a civilian review board, both of which saw some level of success in reducing tensions between police and minorities (although substantial distrust between minority communities and the police would continue to exist).[33] As these reforms unfolded, attention placed on police violence—which did not completely subside as a result of the reforms—morphed into a focus on general violence levels, which activists believed were reaching "epidemic" proportions. By the end of the decade, the focus on state violence began to shift to hate crimes perpetrated by antigay assailants. Indeed, the community came to *rely* on the police both to protect gay neighborhoods such as Houston's Montrose and Dallas's Oak Lawn and to adequately classify bias-motivated assaults. This shift was likely also influenced by moments that seemed to confirm activists' suspicions that law enforcement and the judicial system were rigged against gay victims of crime and needed reform.

One high-profile example was a 1988 case involving Richard Bednarski, who was accused of shooting two gay men in Dallas's Reverchon Park, a well-known gay meeting place. Republican Judge Jack Hampton heard the case, and when a jury convicted Bednarski, Hampton sentenced him to thirty years in prison rather than the life sentence sought by prosecutors. He explained his reasoning to the *Dallas Times Herald:* "I don't much care for queers cruising the streets picking up teenage boys." He added, "I put prostitutes and gays at about the same level. And I'd be hard put to give somebody life for killing a prostitute."[34] The comments sparked gay protesting that rippled throughout the state and even across the country in addition to a failed attempt to oust Hampton.[35] Activists continued to use Hampton's words and antigay caricature throughout the 1990s as proof of the need for sentence enhancements.

The gay community's emphasis on curbing and prosecuting antigay hate crimes flourished in the 1990s, in Texas and elsewhere. In Dallas, the Dallas Gay Alliance started an Anti-Violence Project, which organized volunteer antiviolence patrols in Oak Lawn to reduce the number of assaults against gay residents. Off-duty Dallas police officers aided and supplemented these patrols.[36] Gay Houstonians launched similar efforts, which by the 1990s took the form of the Houston chapter of Queer Nation, a national organization that existed to directly and flamboyantly challenge homophobia.[37] Across the Lone Star State, local gay and lesbian communities implemented efforts to address, contain, and prosecute antigay violence. What fueled these efforts were individual murders profiled by the media that exposed the shortcomings of the Texas criminal justice system where it concerned gay crime victims.

While hostility between gay people and the police still ran rampant at the end of the 1980s, police reforms in Houston and Dallas helped ease tensions between police and community leaders. Having made tangible progress on police relations, the gay community began to depend on the police as a tenuous partner by the end of the decade to control crime in their neighborhoods. Gays in Houston's Montrose launched the successful Keep Our Police Station (KOPS) project in 1988 to raise money and retain the Montrose substation amid budget cuts—a clear departure from the antipolice anger of the early 1980s.[38] In short, gay activists shifted from fighting "the system" to *using* the system to combat oppressive acts of violence. This change in tone and strategy did not occur because police violence came to an end but rather because gay people in Texas and nationwide faced what they believed were epidemic levels of hate crime in the late 1980s and 1990s. Protection of their communities from vigilantes suddenly took priority over police reform.

Beginning in the late 1980s, antiviolence activism in the Texas gay community took aim at hate crime, a legal category originating in the early 1980s. The parameters of this legal construct varied from state to state, but activists in Texas defined it as a crime committed on the basis of real or perceived race, color, religion, national origin, or sexual orientation. In particular, activists targeted light sentencing of perpetrators, which they saw as a kind of state sanctioning of hate crime.[39] In Texas, activists focused on a few highly publicized hate crime cases that the gay community used to paint the criminal justice system as corrupt and neglectful at best—and complicit in antigay violence at worst.

Most notably, the Houston gay community experienced a murder in the early 1990s that shaped local and statewide activism for years to come. On July 4, 1991, a gang of ten youths from the master-planned exurb The Woodlands, located approximately thirty miles north of Houston—later dubbed "The Woodlands Ten"—savagely beat Paul Broussard, a gay banker, and left him to die on a Montrose street. On the night of the attack, Broussard and two of his friends were visiting nightclubs in Montrose. They had just left a nightclub when two vehicles containing the youths pulled up to the group of friends. One of the youths asked Broussard and his friends for the directions to Heaven, a popular gay club. When the men indicated they knew the way to the club, the youths emerged from the vehicles, and a foot chase ensued. Broussard's two friends escaped unscathed; Broussard was not so fortunate. The youths reportedly beat him with nail-studded boards and left him for dead. Suffering multiple stab wounds, he died shortly after arriving at the hospital.[40]

The Broussard murder was a transformational event for the Houston gay community—many individuals became activists as a direct result of the murder. One such activist, Adrian Ozuna, was a student at the University of Houston at the time of Broussard's killing. Although Ozuna was already active as the president of the university's gay-straight alliance, Broussard's death filled him with an anger that drove him to join Queer Nation. When he first joined Queer Nation, meetings averaged at about a dozen members each. But according to Ozuna, as the Broussard incident received more attention, the organization swelled to forty or fifty members. In the wake of the murder, Queer Nation used its newfound manpower to organize Q-Patrol, in which Ozuna took part. Q-Patrol was a volunteer patrol that walked the streets of Montrose and reported crime to authorities.[41] In addition, the gay community joined forces with the Houston police, some of whom posed as gay couples in an antiviolence sting operation. One such police officer reportedly suffered an antigay beating during the operation.[42] This was a notable shift in police relations from the early 1980s and before, when police brutality dominated the minds of activists.

The gay community also took its anger into the streets, led most prominently by Queer Nation. On July 13, Queer Nation activists led the Take Back the Streets rally in Montrose. The organizers of the rally demanded the prosecution of the Broussard murder as a hate crime and sought to bring wider attention to the issue of antigay violence. Gay leaders expected eight hundred to nine hundred people to participate, but the rally drew more than two thousand people. After the demonstration, representatives of Queer Nation read a list of demands, all of which indicated the gay community's desire to work with and reform the criminal justice system in combating violence. The demands included the proper classification and prosecution by the HPD of hate crimes, gay-inclusive sensitivity training for HPD officers, the hiring of gay and lesbian police officers, and a promise to treat hate crime victims with confidentiality.[43] The stated purpose of this rally was to end the underreporting of hate crimes by victims who feared publicity and discrimination at the hands of the HPD.[44]

By mid-August, a grand jury indicted all of The Woodlands Ten.[45] In the end, the youths received sentences ranging from fifteen to forty-five years. However, gay activists considered the sentences too light.[46] Aside from the sentencing, a great deal came out of the incident for the gay community. Houston's city council unanimously passed a resolution calling on the Texas Legislature to pass gay-inclusive hate crime legislation. In addition, state representatives Paul Colbert and Debra Danburg, both of Houston, introduced HB 52, a gay-inclusive hate crime law, in the legislature's July special session.[47] Important changes also came about within the HPD. On September 10, 1991, the commissioner of the HPD issued an order mandating that hate crimes be viewed as "major, possible organized criminal acts [that] will be given the highest investigative priority." Significantly, the order added sexual orientation to the list of biases motivating a hate crime.[48]

Later in his life, gay activist Ray Hill—who played a significant role in demanding the incarceration of The Woodlands Ten—had doubts that the incident was even an antigay hate crime. As a prisoner (in addition to gay) rights advocate who forged a relationship with Jon Buice, the assailant who remained in prison the longest, Hill believed Buice and the other assailants were misunderstood as homophobes in the early 1990s. He advocated for Buice's parole, and he dropped his support for hate crime legislation because of what he viewed as draconian sentencing.[49] However, Broussard's mother and other activists continued to actively fight Buice's parole, and he remained in prison until 2015 despite coming up for review a total of eight times throughout his imprisonment.[50] He was finally released on parole in December 2015.[51] Whether The Woodlands Ten were actually homophobes or simply misunderstood troublemakers, the gay community saw the Broussard murder as an antigay hate crime in the 1990s, and the crime played an instrumental role in uniting the community behind hate crime legislation.

In the following months and years, the LGRL used the Broussard murder to bring attention to the need for comprehensive hate crime legislation in Texas.[52] The role of the LGRL expanded when hate crimes occurred in relatively small cities with nascent gay communities that lacked institutional infrastructure (which was not the case in Houston following the Broussard murder). Two particular acts of violence perpetrated against gay men in smaller Texas cities were especially important in shaping the movement for hate crime legislation: the murders of Tommy Musick in Midland and Nicholas Ray West in Tyler. In addition to organizing rallies in these communities and attempting to build local movements where none had existed before, the LGRL folded these murders into a broader discussion of hate crime statewide and built the case that antigay murders were spiraling out of control in Texas.

On April 14, 1993, teenagers Michael Scott Thomas and Ramsey Blake Harrell called forty-eight-year-old gay Midland hairdresser Tommy Musick, asking for a ride home from a campground. Thomas knew Musick because he had occasionally used his swimming pool. How exactly the murder unfolded remains murky, but there are some known facts. During the drive from the campground, Harrell, who was sitting in the back seat, shot Musick in the back of the head four times with a .22-caliber gun. The boys drove Musick's body to an isolated area and dumped it. They then left his car near the city airport and immediately went to Musick's house, where they told his partner of twenty years that Musick had never arrived at the campground. It did not take much investigation on the part of the local police department before authorities arrested Thomas and Harrell for Musick's killing. They later stood trial on charges of capital murder.[53]

Convicting the teenagers was no easy task for the prosecution. Harrell and Thomas made a "gay panic" defense, claiming Musick aggressively made a pass at Thomas, immediately after which Harrell became temporarily irrational and shot Musick in the back of the head. Even though Thomas confessed on tape that Musick did not sexually assault him, that evidence was ruled inadmissible. The attention of the court shifted to Musick's personal life. The defense presented him as a promiscuous gay man, and his HIV-positive status entered the court transcript. The defense even went so far as to enter Musick's thong bathing suit into evidence, apparently in an attempt to show he was not normal.[54] The strategy worked; in February 1994, the jury convicted Harrell of murder instead of capital murder, meaning he would serve up to twelve years in prison with the possibility of parole in three years.[55]

After the judge handed down the sentence in the trial, members of the small Midland gay community expressed frustration and outrage over what they perceived as another in a line of "judicial gay-bashings." The LGRL used the opportunity to call for a Midland rally. Linking the Musick case to the Broussard killings and others, LGRL executive director Dianne Hardy-Garcia noted that the cases "illustrate that not only are lesbians and gays victims of violence in Texas, but lesbians and gays are also not being treated fairly by the judicial system."[56] On April 9, 1994, at least five hundred people gathered in Midland for the region's first-ever gay event to protest the verdict.

The same year as Musick's murder, a similar killing occurred across the state in Tyler. On the evening of November 7, 1993, Nicholas Ray West, an openly gay twenty-three-year-old Hispanic man, left to run an errand and never returned. Teenagers found his body two days later facedown in a sandpit. He had been shot nine times with a shotgun and two .357-caliber Magnum pistols in addition to being struck with both a fist and a gun. His pants, wallet, and truck had been stolen. Chief sheriff's deputy Johnny Beddingfield called the murder a "sick, sadistic crime," adding that he would "prosecute someone who treated a dog like this, much less a human being."[57]

Linking the case to a previous antigay assault, police officers arrested three adults and two juveniles in connection with West's murder. Three of the men—Donald Aldrich, David McMillan, and Henry Dunn—confessed on video to murdering West. Not only did they admit to the killing, but they also boasted that, under Aldrich's leadership, they had targeted members of the gay community to assault and rob for months. Police connected the gang with a string of Tyler robberies and arsons in previous months.[58] Unlike in other Texas cities—and interestingly, given East Texas's reputation—gay activists never had a major complaint about law enforcement's handling of the case or the trial. The three men faced capital murder charges, and Aldrich was sentenced to death in 1994.

West's murder spurred a movement against antigay violence in rural East Texas that was impressive considering the gay community was not organized in the area. In conjunction with the LGRL, Tyler and Dallas area gays and lesbians came together to plan a Stop the Hate rally in Tyler a little over a month after West's death. Wesley Beard, a twenty-one-year-old who became something of a gay leader in East Texas after the killing and played a role in organizing the rally, estimated that two hundred people would attend the event.[59] In the end, at least one thousand people showed up in Tyler to rally against violence. Rally participants gathered in Bergfield Park and persisted as cars reportedly circled the park and passengers shouted, "Faggots!" and "Kill 'em! Kill 'em all!" Antigay counterprotesters also made their presence known, many of them holding signs with Bible verses against homosexuality.[60]

In 1994, another high-profile incident of violence struck the Houston area gay community that reverberated across the state. On July 30, a car was found, abandoned and burned, in Harris County north of Houston. Nearby, car owner and gay Houstonian Michael Burzinski's body was discovered, shot once execution-style in the back of the head and possibly beaten. While the Harris County Sheriff's Department did not know the motive for the killing, the fact that twenty-nine-year-old Burzinski had last been seen alive earlier that morning in Montrose gay bars led detectives to investigate the incident as a possible hate crime. To many in Houston, the crime was eerily similar to the brutal death of Paul Broussard in Montrose only three years prior to Burzinski's murder. The similarities increased when, following a CrimeStoppers tip, police arrested four teenagers from Aldine, north of Houston. Hardy-Garcia later claimed, "I started to see very clearly there is a pattern. The teenage-boy syndrome."[61] Activists began to paint a picture of gay neighborhoods under siege by homophobic suburban youths with too much time on their hands. Although the Burzinski murder did not inspire protests on the level of the Broussard killing, the LGRL took note of the Burzinski case, and his name continued to be used throughout the 1990s alongside Broussard's, West's, and Musick's in the push for stronger hate crime protections.

In April 1995, building on the activist momentum after this spate of murders, the LGRL planned a massive march on Austin in response to the wave of violence targeting gay Texans. Dubbed the Stop the Violence rally, the march on the State Capitol had a specific goal in mind: the passage of a strong, gay-inclusive hate crime bill, which had become one of the LGRL's top priorities by 1995. The march was to be followed by a Lobby Day in which ordinary gay and lesbian Texans could take the opportunity to discuss the hate crime bill with their legislators' offices. In all, at least five thousand people participated in the march, according to the Texas Department of Public Safety; the LGRL reported that more than seven thousand people attended.

While gay and lesbian Texans marched for hate crime protections, transgender Texans argued that the movement was not inclusive of their concerns. One San Antonio transgender writer excoriated the LGRL in 1995 for using the headline "Lesbians and Gays March on Austin." She rhetorically asked, "Excuse me, LGRL, but don't you want transgender people to join with you in the march? . . . The great LGRL gaffe drives a wedge of exclusion and isolationism of the lesbian/gay equal rights movement from all others." The hate crime bill itself, as transgender activists reminded the LGRL, did not include gender identity as a protected category, which Hardy-Garcia denied, asserting (falsely) that most transgender people would be covered in the bill as written because transgender people are often confused for gay or lesbian.[62] Despite transgender objections to their exclusion from the bill and broader hate crime movement, the gay and lesbian movement marched on under the leadership of the LGRL in support of a gay-inclusive, transgender-exclusive hate crime bill. However, the 1995 march did not result in the passage of the bill. Although the bill passed out of the Senate, it died in the House.[63]

The LGRL's hate crime activism did not end after its disappointing legislative defeat in 1995. However, the continuation of the hate crime struggle hinged on further media coverage of bias-motivated murders that seemed to prove the LGRL's point that a strong legislative response was needed. One particularly important hate crime that fueled both local activists and statewide lobbying efforts was the 1996 killing of forty-six-year-old Fred Mangione by neo-Nazis in Katy, a small suburban city located on the western side of metropolitan Houston. The Mangione murder ignited a protest movement the likes of which had not been seen since the 1991 killing of Paul Broussard.

Mangione and his partner of sixteen years, Kenneth Stern, celebrated the New Year in 1996 at Dolly's Place, a bar in Katy. In the *Houston Voice* article on the murder, the writer remarked that the couple had been "basking in the hope and promises of an idyllic, American Dream–world lifestyle" in suburban Katy. Whatever feelings Mangione and Stern had regarding their "American Dream" were certainly shattered on New Year's Day. Half-brothers Daniel Christopher Bean and Ronald Henry Gauthier, ages nineteen and twenty-one, respectively, lived in Montana but were in Katy visiting their mother at the time of the incident. Mangione and Stern crossed their paths in Dolly's Place, and the night ended in a brutal attack outside the bar. Stern was severely beaten, but the worst was reserved for Mangione, whom the half-brothers stabbed at least thirty-five times. Stern survived the assault, but Mangione died at the scene.[64]

The case, from the outset, seemed as open and shut as a hate crime case could be, with Harris County Sheriff Tommy Thomas stating confidently, "This was definitely a hate crime."[65] Bean and Gauthier were not simply random assailants; they were self-professed members of the German Peace Corps, a California-based neo-Nazi hate group. Numerous witnesses in the bar recalled hearing the pair boast of their

plans to "get a fag" that night. The half-brothers were quickly identified, arrested, charged in the slaying, and held without bond.[66] From
the beginning, activists had no substantive complaint about the police
handling of the case, and it was understood to be a hate crime by all
relevant authorities. Bean was easily convicted of murder and sentenced to the maximum of life in prison.[67] However, nearly a year later,
Gauthier was convicted and sentenced only to ten years of probation
because jurors felt the prosecution did not prove his active role in the
murder.[68] This relatively light sentence did not, however, seem unjust
enough to spark protests in 1997.

Despite the swift response of police and prosecutors, the brutal
nature of the murder and the obvious role that antigay hate played in
the crime mobilized the gay community in the Houston area. Houston's
Queer Nation chapter, which had recently rebooted after disbanding,
immediately took to the streets in a way reminiscent of its role in the
Broussard case. Queer Nation's activism following the murder was
the first major direct action of the restarted organization. The group
organized a march in Montrose that it called (again reminiscent of the
street protests after the Broussard murder) Take Back the Streets Four:
A Candlelight March in Memory of Fred Mangione on January 20.
Queer Nation planned for the march to begin on the corner of West
Drew Street and Montrose Boulevard, the site at which Broussard was
stabbed. The group clearly saw the Mangione murder as just the latest
in a series of gay bashings that plagued Houston.[69]

In addition to local activism, the Mangione murder fueled statewide
lobbying efforts by providing yet another stark example of Texas hate
for the LGRL to seize upon in convincing Texans and legislators to take
action. All of this local and statewide mobilization on the issue of hate
crime led to the LGRL's next rally in Austin, scheduled for March 1997
and dubbed the March in March. The event drew approximately five
thousand people, mirroring the conservative Stop the Violence rally
estimate. The event included people from San Antonio, Dallas, Denton,
Waco, and Southwest Texas. The following day, approximately three
hundred people took part in the Lobby Day to personally urge their
legislators to support the hate crime bill.[70] Despite the intense push
from gay activists, no hate crime bill would move forward in 1997.

In 1998, however, the political landscape fundamentally changed for the hate crime movement. The gay-led hate crime movement had been trying to build legislative momentum by highlighting the murders of gay men in Texas. But the event that would finally catapult a comprehensive hate crime bill to the governor's desk was the brutal slaying of an African American man reminiscent of the Lone Star State's lynching past. On June 7, 1998, white supremacists in Jasper, Texas, brutally chained and dragged James Byrd Jr. behind their truck. Byrd was conscious throughout most of the ordeal, attempting to keep his head above the pavement until his body hit the edge of a culvert, decapitating him and severing his right arm. The East Texas hate crime, dubbed a modern-day lynching, captured the attention of the United States and world.[71] Newspapers such as the *New York Times* reported on an East Texas drenched in white supremacy and racist violence, in turn pressuring the Texas Legislature to act.[72]

With the high-profile Byrd murder, what had once been a gay-led movement transformed into a broadly based coalition of organizations supporting hate crime law reform, including the LGRL, NAACP, American Civil Liberties Union (ACLU), Texas Civil Rights Project, and American Jewish Congress. The construction of this coalition, in addition to sympathetic media coverage, eventually led to the final passage of the James Byrd Jr. Hate Crimes Act in 2001. While the Byrd murder was the primary catalyst for the renewed push for a hate crime law, the final bill included sexual orientation at the insistence of both the Byrd family and a coalition of progressive white, African American, Mexican American, and gay Texas legislators who refused to allow protections for gay people to be stripped from the bill. Governor Rick Perry signed the bill into law on May 10, 2001—but not before lamenting that it would "create new classes of citizens," referring to the explicit categories protected under the law.[73]Although it was the murder of an African American man that put hate crime legislation back on the table for the Texas Legislature, the failure of socially conservative lawmakers to strip sexual orientation from the bill speaks volumes about the groundwork laid by the Texas gay movement. Without the decade-long gay movement that built the case for hate crime protections, it is unlikely that such a feat—arguably the most significant gay rights victory in the state's history up to that point—would have been possible in the increasingly conservative Texas political environment.[74]

Despite the passage of the James Byrd Jr. Hate Crimes Act in 2001, its shortcomings have become clear, especially concerning the exclusion of transgender Texans from the law's protections. Recent events have resulted in a contemporary debate over the law's efficacy and purpose. In January 2015, Ty Underwood—a twenty-four-year-old African American transgender woman—was found fatally shot in her car in North Tyler, Texas. The local media reported on her murder using male pronouns, and when police identified twenty-one-year-old African American Carlton Ray Champion Jr. of Longview as a suspect, newspaper reporting focused on a homosexual relationship gone wrong.[75] Champion was charged, and a jury convicted him of the murder, after which he shouted, "I'll be back on the streets!" and had to be restrained by officers in the courtroom.[76] He was later sentenced to life in prison.[77] Immediately after the killing, Underwood's friends demanded that the case be treated as a hate crime carried out because of bias against her gender identity, and the Twitter hashtag #JusticeForNunne (one of Underwood's nicknames) called for justice not only in the Underwood murder but also for the transgender community at large, which had reportedly seen an "epidemic" of hate crime.[78] In the end, Underwood was likely a victim of domestic, rather than hate, violence, but her murder opened a public discussion in the Lone Star State about the limits of existing hate crime legislation.[79] This discussion became even more important by 2019, when Texas led the nation in the number of murdered transgender women.[80]

The Underwood case is just one high-profile example of the holes in the Byrd Act. Some have even called the legislation's overall effectiveness into question. A 2012 *Austin American-Statesman* article, "Texas Hate Crime Law Has Little Effect," makes the argument that the law is largely unused, leaving little reason for its existence aside from sending a symbolic message to would-be hate crime perpetrators.[81] In the years after the passage of the Byrd Act, hate crime reports steadily declined in Texas along with other violent crime, with the number of reported hate incidents hovering close to two hundred per year.[82] However, in the first ten years of the Byrd Act, only ten convictions were secured under the law. Possible reasons range from subjective standards to blatant holes in the law's coverage to reluctance on the part of prosecutors (who often use hate crime charges as leverage to secure a plea bargain). Former Travis County District Attorney Rosemary Lehmberg blames local law enforcement, which sometimes fails to treat incidents as hate crimes from the beginning, and Equality Texas (the LGRL's successor group) maintains that Texas is unique in its lax enforcement of its hate crime law.[83] Whether the reason is the difficulty of proving bias motivations, the failure of authorities to use the law appropriately, or some combination of the two, it is clear that the Lone Star State's hate crime law has been relatively ineffective in the years after its passage. A logical question follows: Was the Byrd Act worth the effort that activists and legislators poured into it? Scholars are beginning to debate the merits of hate crime legislation in general, with some arguing that it is not effective and others claiming it is harmful to society and helpful only to the expanding "prison industrial complex."[84]

Answering such a question—if an answer is even possible—is beyond the scope of this chapter. Regardless of the Byrd Act's ultimate effectiveness, gay and lesbian activists saw hate crime legislation as the best possible means to combat the culture of violence they believed existed in Texas and threatened the gay community. After police violence subsided as a major issue for gay and lesbian Texans, activists viewed law enforcement as the answer to the perceived hate crime epidemic—and because they believed the criminal justice system was historically rigged against them, only adequate legislation could compel the police and courts to take the issue seriously. Advocates saw the James Byrd Jr. Hate Crimes Act as an imperfect civil rights measure that would move state law toward adequate prosecution of hate crime at a time when many lacked faith in the Lone Star State's ability and willingness to protect its LGBTQ citizens.

Notes

1. The material in this chapter includes work that the author has already published on the Texas gay movement against violence. See Christopher Haight, "The Silence Is Killing Us: Hate Crime, Criminal Justice, and the Gay Rights Movement in Texas, 1990–1995," *Southwestern Historical Quarterly* 120, no. 1 (July 2016).

2. Buzz Bissinger, "The Killing Trail," *Vanity Fair,* February 1995.

3. "Hate Crimes Pose Continuing Threat to Gay and Lesbian Texans," *This Week in Texas,* December 30, 1994–January 5, 1995, 77.

4. Stefanie Scott, "5,000 Gays, Lesbians Urge Putting an End to 'Bashing,'" *San Antonio Express-News,* April 3, 1995.

5. Although violence against lesbians certainly existed, prominent murders of gay men drove the headlines and the activist response against antigay violence.

6. See Phyllis B. Gerstenfeld, *Hate Crimes: Causes, Controls, and Controversies* (Thousand Oaks, CA: Sage, 2004) for more general information on hate crime legislation.

7. See Jennifer Petersen, *Murder, the Media, and the Politics of Public Feelings: Remembering Matthew Shepard and James Byrd Jr.* (Bloomington: Indiana University Press, 2011) for more information on the Byrd murder and the legislative wrangling over the James Byrd Jr. Hate Crimes Act in Texas.

8. Uniform Crime Reports 1996–2001, Criminal Justice Information Services, Federal Bureau of Investigation, https://www.fbi.gov/about-us/cjis/ucr/hate-crime/. Reported hate crimes based on race numbered 233 in 1996, 209 in 1997, 184 in 1998, 166 in 1999, 159 in 2000, and 197 in 2001; reported hate crimes based on sexual orientation numbered 62 in 1996, 54 in 1997, 60 in 1998, 57 in 1999, 50 in 2000, and 55 in 2001.

9. See "The Resource Center LGBT Collection: Dallas Gay Political Caucus," University of North Texas Libraries Exhibits, https://exhibits.library.unt.edu/resource-center-exhibit/dallas-gay-political-caucus, and "The Resource Center LGBT Collection: Dallas Gay and Lesbian Alliance," University of North Texas Libraries Exhibits, https://exhibits.library.unt.edu/resource-center-exhibit/dallas-gay-lesbian-alliance.

10. See Bruce Remington, "Twelve Fighting Years: Homosexuals in Houston, 1969–1981" (master's thesis, University of Houston, 1983) for more on the history of the Houston gay community.

11. See Dwight Watson, *Race and the Houston Police Department, 1930–1990: A Change Did Come* (College Station: Texas A&M University Press, 2005) for more on tensions between racial minorities and the police in Texas.

12. See Dale Carpenter, *Flagrant Conduct: The Story of* Lawrence v. Texas (New York: W. W. Norton & Company, 2013) for more on Section 21.06 and the long legal fight for its repeal.

13. See David Carter, *Stonewall: The Riots That Sparked the Gay Revolution* (New York: St. Martin's Press, 2004), and David Eisenbach, *Gay Power: An American Revolution* (New York: Carroll & Graf Publishers, 2006) for more national context on the gay liberation movement.

14. "Kon Tiki Bath Raid," *This Week in Texas,* July 17–23, 1976, 9–10; "Ray Hill Speaks Out," *This Week in Texas,* August 7–13, 1976, 36.

15. "Police Raid After Hours Party," *This Week in Texas,* December 25–31, 1976, 9.

16. "GPC's Policy Statement in Response to Raid on Levi's," *This Week in Texas,* December 25–31, 1976, 41–42.

17. "The Book Store Hassle," *This Week in Texas,* March 5–11, 1976, 7.

18. Ray Hill, editorial, *This Week in Texas,* March 19–25, 1977, 47.

19. Mort Schwab, editorial, *This Week in Texas,* August 28–September 3, 1976, 25, 38.

20. "Human Rights League Formed," *This Week in Texas,* May 28–June 3, 1977, 7.

21. "DAIR to Be Seen & Heard!," *This Week in Texas,* November 13–19, 1976, 6.

22. "Gay Political Caucus Operation: Documentation," *This Week in Texas,* February 17–23, 1979, 7, 54.

23. "A Spring Rally," *This Week in Texas,* April 6–12, 1979, 7.

24. "This Week," *This Week in Texas,* April 13–19, 1979, 7.

25. "Shiflett Subpoenaed," *This Week in Texas,* June 8–14, 1979, 7; "Operation Documentation," *This Week in Texas,* June 15–21, 1979, 7.

26. "Operation Documentation Comes to Dallas," *This Week in Texas,* May 18–24, 1979, 7.

27. "61 Arrested at Mary's," *This Week in Texas,* June 27–July 3, 1980, 9.

28. "GPC Secretary Fred Paez Shot and Killed," *This Week in Texas,* July 4–10, 1980, 11–13.

29. Barbara Canetti, "Gun That Killed Paez Couldn't Have Discharged Accidentally, Expert Says," *Houston Post,* July 2, 1980.

30. Barbara Canetti, "1,000 Protest: March Notes Injustice to Homosexuals, Memorializes Member Slain by Police," *Houston Post,* July 23, 1980.

31. Memorandum by Ray Hill, Houston Human Rights League papers, Charles V. Botts Library and Resurrection Archives, Houston, TX.

32. "Crime, Violence, and Harassment," *This Week in Texas,* December 28, 1979–January 6, 1980, 11–12; "Harassment and Violence," *This Week in Texas,* December 26, 1980–January 1, 1981, 9–11.

33. See Dwight Watson, *Race and the Houston Police Department, 1930–1990: A Change Did Come* (College Station: Texas A&M University Press, 2005) for more on 1980s police reform.

34. Lori Montgomery and Jeff Collins, "Prejudice and Presumption: Views of Victims' Lifestyle Blur Truth in Gay-Bashing Case," *Dallas Times Herald,* January 8, 1989.

35. David Jackson, "Groups Protest Judge's Comments About Gays," *Dallas Morning News,* December 17, 1988.

36. Tammye Nash, "Anti-Violence Patrols Out in Full Force This Weekend," *Dallas Voice,* April 13, 1990.

37. Clifford Pugh, "Proud and Loud," *Houston Post,* April 12, 1994, D-2.

38. "Police Station Remains Open," *This Week in Texas,* April 8–14, 1988, 25–26.

39. From 1981 to 1993 (the year Texas passed its first hate crime law), thirty other

states had passed some form of hate crime legislation. Ten of those states passed laws in the first half of the 1980s, with fourteen following suit in the latter half. See Valerie Jenness and Ryken Grattet, *Making Hate a Crime: From Social Movement to Law Enforcement* (New York: Russell Sage Foundation, 2001), 74.

40. Sheri Cohen Darbonne, "Murder Sparks Calls for Action from Activists, Officials," *The New Voice,* July 12–18, 1991.

41. Adrian Ozuna to Christopher Haight, October 20, 2012, interview (tape in possession of the author).

42. Stephen Johnson and R. A. Dyer, "Police Officer Posing as Gay Is Beaten," *Houston Chronicle,* August 7, 1991.

43. Sheri Cohen Darbonne, "Unexpectedly Large Crowd Turns Out for 'Take Back the Streets' Rally," *The New Voice,* July 19–25, 1991.

44. "Queer Nation to Hold Anti-Violence March in Montrose," *The New Voice,* July 12–18, 1991.

45. "Grand Jury Indicts Ten Suspects in Broussard Killing," *This Week in Texas,* August 9–15, 1991, 19.

46. "Lesbian and Gay Activists Protest Sentences in Paul Broussard Murder Case," *The New Voice,* January 22–28, 1993.

47. Sheri Cohen Darbonne, "City, State Officials, Others Want Tough Hate Crimes Laws," *The New Voice,* July 26–August 1, 1991.

48. Earnest L. Perry, "HPD Puts Hate Crimes High on Priority List," *Houston Chronicle,* September 11, 1991.

49. Ray Hill to Christopher Haight, October 31, 2011, interview (tape in possession of the author).

50. "Jon Buice Denied Parole in Gay Houston Man's 1991 Murder," *Dallas Voice,* October 17, 2013.

51. Allan Turner, "Man Convicted in Montrose Gay Murder Freed on Parole," *Houston Chronicle,* December 31, 2015.

52. "Gays Murdered in Texas," date unknown, Lesbian/Gay Rights Lobby of Texas, Charles V. Botts Library and Resurrection Archives. https://findingaids.lib.uh.edu/repositories/2/resources/276. This is a flyer produced by the LGRL that lists the names of murdered gay men in Texas. At the time of research, the box was not processed, so no box number is currently available.

53. Garry Boulard, "The Anti-Twinkie Defense," *The Advocate,* June 14, 1994, 33.

54. Boulard, "The Anti-Twinkie Defense."

55. Kay Longcope, "Verdict Questioned in Trial of Gay's Killer," *Texas Triangle,* February 23, 1994.

56. "Lobby Demands Justice in Texas Gay Murders," *San Antonio Marquise,* March 10–23, 1994, 8.

57. Kay Longcope, "Death of a Texan," *The Advocate,* February 22, 1994, 46.

58. "Gay-Hating Gang Linked to Slaying and Assaults," Associated Press, January 7, 1994.

59. Frank Trejo, "Many Set to Attend Rally in Gay's Death," *Dallas Morning News,* January 8, 1994.

60. Phil Johnson, "On the Edge of the Tyler Rally," *This Week in Texas,* January 14–20, 1994, 27–29.

61. Bissinger, "The Killing Trail."

62. Tere Frederickson, "The Great LGRL Gaffe," *San Antonio Marquise,* March 1995, 14.

63. "One-Word Change Made to State's Old Hate Crime Law," *This Week in Texas,* June 2–8, 1995, 68.

64. Sheri Cohen Darbonne, "Fatal Intolerance," *Houston Voice,* January 12, 1996.

65. "Gay Man Slain in Hate Killing Near Houston," *This Week in Texas,* January 12–18, 1996, 53.

66. Cohen Darbonne, "Fatal Intolerance."

67. "Neo-Nazi Guilty of Murder in Death of Houston-Area Gay Man," *This Week in Texas,* September 6–12, 1996, 60.

68. "Second Defendant Convicted in Murder of Gay Man Near Houston," *This Week in Texas,* July 4–10, 1996, 70.

69. "March, Meetings Set in Response to Hate Crime," *Houston Voice,* January 12, 1996.

70. "Thousands March on Capitol in Push for Hate Crime Law," *This Week in Texas,* March 28-April 3, 1997, 68.

71. For more on the Byrd murder, see Joyce King, *Hate Crime: The Story of a Dragging in Jasper, Texas* (New York: Pantheon Books, 2002), and Dina Temple-Raston, *A Death in Texas: A Story of Race, Murder, and a Small Town's Struggle for Redemption* (New York: Henry Holt & Company, 2002).

72. Carol Marie Cropper, "Black Man Fatally Dragged in a Possibly Racial Killing," *New York Times,* June 10, 1998.

73. Petersen, *Murder, the Media, and the Politics of Public Feelings,* 127; "Governor of Texas Signs a Hate Crimes Bill," *New York Times,* May 12, 2001.

74. For more on the legislative wrangling that ultimately resulted in the passage of the James Byrd Jr. Hate Crimes Act, see Petersen, *Murder, the Media, and the Politics of Public Feelings.*

75. Adam Russell, "Relationship Had Sexual Connotations, Police Say," *Tyler Morning Telegraph,* February 9, 2015.

76. Risa Morris, "Champion Found Guilty in January Murder of Ty Underwood," *Tyler Morning Telegraph,* December 17, 2015.

77. Elizabeth Daley, "College Football Player Sentenced to Life for Killing Texas Trans Woman," *The Advocate,* December 18, 2015.

78. Samantha Michaels, "More Transgender People Have Been Killed in 2015 Than Any Other Year on Record," *Mother Jones,* November 20, 2015.

79. Hannah Smothers, "In Texas, There's No Such Thing as a Transgender Hate Crime," *Texas Monthly,* February 3, 2015.

80. Lauren McGaughy, "Texas Leads the Nation in Transgender Murders: After the Latest Attack, the Dallas Trans Community Asks Why," *Dallas Morning News,* September 30, 2019.

81. Eric Dexheimer, "Texas Hate Crime Law Has Little Effect," *Austin American-Statesman,* January 24, 2012.

82. Uniform Crime Reports 2001–2010, Criminal Justice Information Services, Federal Bureau of Investigation, https://www.fbi.gov/about-us/cjis/ucr/hate-crime/. Reported hate crimes based on race numbered 197 in 2001, 181 in 2002, 154 in 2003, 157 in 2004, 122 in 2005, 124 in 2006, 130 in 2007, 131 in 2008, 84 in 2009, and 85 in 2010. Reported hate crimes based on sexual orientation numbered 55 in 2001, 52 in 2002, 54 in 2003, 61 in 2004, 63 in 2005, 47 in 2006, 46 in 2007, 55 in 2008, 36 in 2009, and 39 in 2010.

83. Dexheimer, "Texas Hate Crime Law Has Little Effect."

84. See James B. Jacobs and Kimberly Potter, *Hate Crimes: Criminal Law and Identity Politics* (Oxford, UK: Oxford University Press, 1998), Valerie Jenness, *Making Hate a Crime: From Social Movement to Law Enforcement* (Thousand Oaks, CA: Sage, 2004), and Christina B. Hanhardt, *Safe Space: Gay Neighborhood History and the Politics of Violence* (Durham, NC: Duke University Press, 2013) for more discussion on this topic.

4

"THOSE BOYS DIDN'T LEARN TO HATE HERE"

Racial Violence in Texas, 1965 to 2020

Betsy Friauf and Michael Phillips

Racial violence in Texas was fundamentally transformed in the cultural and political climate that prevailed after passage of the 1964 Civil Rights Act and the 1965 Voting Rights Act. After a bloodstained history that included slavery, the Ku Klux Klan, lynching, and race riots, most racial violence and intimidation in Texas during the late twentieth and early twenty-first centuries took place out of public view. The overwhelmingly black and brown targets of individualized terrorism died lonely deaths that generated little national press coverage.

This change happened in part because white supremacy became professionalized. Previously, enraged mobs and private groups such as the Klan mobilized to suffocate labor-organizing efforts and battles for justice by people of color. As the state rapidly urbanized, industrialized, diversified, and assumed a more prominent role on the world stage, the desire for social order, as well as an insistence that the state present a more sophisticated face to the world, transformed the nature of racial oppression in Texas. After 1965, the most visible and politically important instances of racially motivated violence stemmed not from rabbles carrying ropes and setting fire to crosses but from the poisoned interactions between white-dominated police departments and African Americans and Latino/a communities. Officers injuring and killing people of color, sometimes under highly questionable circumstances, benefited from the respect afforded those donning police uniforms and, typically, earned media approval. Even when the injury or death of African American and Latino/a victims of police violence inspired intense local outcry, these incidents usually failed to mobilize protest on the national stage.

Police departments in Texas played a key role in racial violence since 1965 in two ways. First, they themselves repeatedly precipitated racial violence. Second, law enforcement agencies in the state failed to take racially-motivated crimes committed by civilians seriously. They ignored evidence that crimes were racially motivated and did not participate in programs meant to track the hate crime phenomenon. In doing so, Texas police departments further strained an already bad relationship with black and brown Texans that undermined the police investigative work needed to reduce crimes stemming from bias.

Texas had changed since the first half of the twentieth century in ways that, on the surface, challenged its often-sinister racial past. The state's population became more diverse and more urbanized, while the economic focus of the state diversified and industrialized. These changes, and the desire to attract outside dollars, prompted Texas elites in the early 1960s to loosen the state's moorings to the Old South and its more bloodstained legacies. Increasingly, elites linked the state to the West, a region with a still violent racist past but (for whites) a more triumphant mythology than the Lost Cause. The most outsized Texas political leader of the decade, Lyndon Johnson, often wore cowboy hats and famously lived on a Western-style ranch in Central Texas.[1]

Newcomers to the state were not all necessarily antiracists, but by obscuring the face of racism, they slowly altered the forms of white supremacy. In the 1950s and 1960s, white Texans congratulated themselves on avoiding the "troubles" unfolding elsewhere in the former Confederacy: the church bombings, lobbed tear gas canisters, and televised scenes of civil rights protesters beset by snarling police dogs and blasted by fire hoses in places such as Birmingham, Alabama. Meanwhile, they fretted that their luck might run out. Fearing that the flow of international capital might dry up, the ruling class used a propaganda film and other forms of soft power to warn Dallas citizens to not engage in massive resistance when token integration began in Dallas schools in 1961. Particularly during the peak of the mid-twentieth-century civil rights movement in the 1960s, Texas elites walked a tightrope between maintaining racial and economic hegemony while avoiding white backlash and/or resistance from African Americans and the Latino/a community that might attract bad publicity.[2] Mass, disorganized racial assaults gave way to institutionalized, as well as punctuated and more narrowly directed, violence.

Nevertheless, the century before the peak of the civil rights movement in the mid-1960s left African Americans deeply aware of their vulnerability. Memories from an earlier, bloody era served as a form of psychological violence stalking people of color for the African American and Latino/a population coming of age in the mid-1960s. Dr. Henry Masters, who served as the senior pastor at St. Luke "Community" United Methodist Church in Dallas from 2012 to 2014, remembered confronting Texas' tragic racial past during a truck ride with his siblings and father in the 1950s in Rosebud, about thirty-five miles from Waco. "We were very young—six, seven, eight years old, I guess—and while riding in the back of my dad's truck," Masters said, "we actually whistled at a [white] girl. That was the angriest I've ever seen my dad. . . . And though my dad, because he didn't read the newspapers so he wouldn't have been aware of Emmett Till [a 14-year-old boy murdered in Mississippi in 1955 after supposedly whistling at a white woman] per se . . . he was aware enough that those kinds of things did happen, and were happening. . . . He wanted to make sure that I was aware of that also. . . . He just told me that that's not something you do. Don't do that ever again because, literally, your life depends on it."[3]

Racial danger continued to take more concrete forms. A bullet hole remains in the window of the home of Opal Johnson Smith, who worked for decades as a teacher and administrator in the Dallas Independent School District. She moved with her husband to a formerly all-white neighborhood in the Red Bird area of southern Dallas in the 1960s. Smith kept the bullet hole as a memento of the risks her family took to break racial barriers.[4] In the mid- and late 1960s, a bullet hole in a Dallas window, or the often lonely but deadly encounters between African Americans or Latino/a persons and white police officers across Texas, couldn't compete for national media attention with some of the more famous moments of the civil rights movement. In the eyes of the outside media, and later historians, the front lines of the civil rights struggle always seemed to be somewhere other than Texas.[5] With attention focused elsewhere, white violence against black and brown people in Texas unfolded outside of the spotlight, giving rise to a myth that race relations were better and white terrorism less virulent in the Lone Star State than elsewhere, particularly the rest of the South.

Despite the outward appearance of progress, serious racial problems remained. Houston, for example, became a murder capital in the 1960s. A study in 1961 indicated that 60 percent of the city's murders happened in African American neighborhoods. By 1967, the city had the fourth-highest per capita homicide rate in the country. The body count only accelerated as the decade progressed. In spite of the escalating body count, white Houston elites refused to extend social services to black neighborhoods or to make the economic investments that might alleviate poverty and its side effect, violence. "Perhaps callousness toward murder resulted because it affected largely a politically impotent minority and because the conservative temperament of the society insisted on low taxes and a frontiersman's reliance upon himself for survival," wrote Houston historian David G. McComb.[6]

The disdain for social services that benefitted the poor and the working class, and a desire to stanch the bloodshed, led the city leadership and much of the white public to give wide latitude to the Houston police to curb crime by any means necessary. The city met street crime with police violence. Locally, Houston police acquired a reputation for brutality to all civilians, particularly African Americans, subjecting suspects to ruthless interrogations. The crossover between the Houston police payroll and the Ku Klux Klan membership lists had been known for decades. In the 1960s, a hyper-conservative department stood on perpetual lookout for black revolutionaries and was determined to crush any black revolt in its infant stages. The hostile stance by the police department toward black and brown communities created a vicious cycle. "The police, on one hand, looked at all minorities as potential criminals, but on the other, they rarely tried to prevent crime in minority neighborhoods," said Dwight Watson, a historian of the racism within the Houston Police Department. "The HPD interpreted public fears caused by the rising crime rates as a willingness to accept more aggressive policing."[7]

During the late 1960s, black Texans often viewed the police as particularly hostile to their communities. One of the more famous instances of police confrontations with black residents occurred at Texas Southern University (TSU), an historically black institution in Houston, in May 1967. In response to the May 8th death of Victor George, an eleven-year-old African American child who drowned after falling into a pond at one of the many landfills placed near the city's black neighborhoods, students began protesting. On May 15, TSU student protesters, in an attempt to get the city to close down the landfill where George had died, sought to block the entrance of garbage trucks to the landfill. Rumors spread on May 16 that a white man had murdered a black child. Protesters held a sit-in at the dump, and when they returned to TSU, police surrounded the campus and blocked all entries. Students responded by hurling rocks and other projectiles at officers and barricading themselves in dorm rooms. A shot was fired from Lanier Dormitory. Houston police responded with massive firepower, pounding the dorm with at least three thousand rounds of ammunition, and arrested nearly five hundred students. One Houston police officer, rookie Louis Kuba (whose wife was pregnant) died in the melee, struck by a ricocheted bullet fired by a fellow officer. The Houston press reported that TSU students had been massively armed, not just with guns but also with Molotov cocktails, but in fact investigators uncovered only a single .22 caliber pistol in the dorm rooms.[8]

In response, the local press responded to police accounts of violent encounters with communities of color with utter credulity. The ruling class may have divided on lynching and the Klan in earlier decades, but it spoke with one voice regarding police power. Referencing Houston Mayor Louie Welch's response to the TSU uprising, one headline on the front page of the May 17, 1967, *Houston Chronicle* declared, "Welch: Minority Group to Blame." Other page-one headlines on that day and on May 18 echoed that tone: "Police 'Did the Right Thing,' Leader Says"; "Shocked TSU Officials Pledge to Rid Campus of Agitators"; "New Breed Negroes Grab Campus Revolts."[9]

Suffering no official repercussions after the overreaction at TSU, the Houston police responded "by using increasing levels of brutality," Watson said. In 1968, for instance, police battered and kicked Johnny Coward, a member of a group affiliated with the Black Panthers, the People's Party II. Coward lost sight in his left eye because of the beating. A trial jury acquitted officers of all charges.[10] The department believed it had received a green light to suppress black radicalism by any means necessary. On July 17, 1970, Houston police confronted a twenty-one-year-old African American man, Carl Hampton, selling copies of a Black Panther newspaper on Dowling Street. Hampton ran inside the nearby offices of the People's Party II and then emerged armed and accompanied by other men bearing weapons. Police units swarmed to the area, preparing for a siege. Hampton and his allies retreated into the party office, and a police officer entered as well, hoping to negotiate a surrender. Police ended up arresting no one that night but shot Hampton to death on July 26 under dubious pretexts.[11]

Just as the Houston media pinned the tragedy at TSU on the students, the local press blamed Hampton and the People's Party II for the loss of life in the Dowling Street incident. "The explosive hours of Sunday night came from a time fuse which had been burning slowly all week," a July 28, 1970, *Houston Post* editorial claimed. "The Houston Police Department had been exercising a deliberate restraint for eight days, hoping to avert armed confrontation." When a Harris County grand jury no-billed police involved in the Hampton shooting, the newspaper declared, "Reasonable men will accept the validity of the jury's conclusions."[12]

Police culpability was unmistakable, however, in the murder of a twelve-year-old Mexican American boy, Santos Rodriguez, on July 24, 1973, in Dallas. After a break-in at a gas station, Dallas police handcuffed Rodriguez and his thirteen-year-old brother and began interrogating them in the back of a squad car. Officer Darrell L. Cain later claimed he thought he had emptied his pistol of bullets when he tried to bully Santos into a confession by pressing the barrel of the .357 Magnum against the boy's temple and squeezing the trigger, firing a fatal bullet into Santos Rodriguez's head. A fingerprint check later proved neither of the Rodriguez brothers had anything to do with the break-in. Cain was arrested and released on five thousand dollars' bail. Rodriguez's age, the fact that the child was unarmed and securely in custody, and that he died while an officer tried to terrify him, provoked an explosive response: a July 28 uprising involving one thousand black, brown, and white protesters. Demonstrators set two police motorcycles ablaze, raided downtown department stores, and shattered windows at Dallas City Hall. Later found guilty of murder, Cain served only half of his five-year sentence before being released.[13]

A similar outcome unfolded after Houston police beat and drowned an intoxicated and unarmed Vietnam War veteran, José Campos Torres, the night of May 5, 1977. Officers arrested and repeatedly struck Torres after he had scuffled with a bar manager at the end of a twelve-hour drinking binge. When police delivered him to the jail, the duty sergeant refused to book Torres until he had been examined by doctors. Patrolman Stephen Orlando instead drove him to the edge of Buffalo Bayou and, accompanied by other officers, whipped him for five minutes. Officers told Torres they would release him if he could swim his "wetbacked ass across the bayou." When he didn't jump into the water, they pushed him off a twenty-foot cliff and drove away, leaving Torres to drown. Only two of the six officers, Orlando and Terry W. Denson, were indicted for murder. Orlando and Denson were convicted of negligent homicide, a misdemeanor, given a one-dollar fine, and sentenced to a year on probation. The US Justice Department later charged those two and Joseph Janish with violating Torres's civil rights. The three served nine months in prison. As in the Santos Rodriguez case, the Latino/a community responded with rage to the murder and the light punishments given the responsible officers. On the first anniversary of Torres's death, during Cinco de Mayo observances, chaos ensued when police tried to break up a crowd that had gathered at Moody Park. The crowd hurled rocks and bottles at police and overturned squad cars while they shouted, "Justice for Joe Torres!"[14]

Police shootings of black and brown suspects in Dallas and Fort Worth continued in the late 1970s and 1980s. This bloodshed, and the public indifference to it, came in the context of a moral panic over narcotics instigated by the Nixon presidency. Richard Nixon declared that the White House was launching a "war on drugs" in 1971. Drugs had long been associated in the white mind with African Americans and immigrants. The popular culture in the 1970s and 1980s depicted African Americans as drug dealers and undocumented workers as narcotics smugglers. Elites exploited this association in order to roll back the gains of the civil rights movement in the 1950s and 1960s.[15] In 1994, disgraced former Nixon Chief of Staff H. R. "Bob" Haldeman admitted in an interview with author Dan Baum the cynical and deliberately racially inflammatory reasons for the now decades-long antidrug crusade. "You want to know what this was really all about?" Haldeman asked Baum. "The Nixon campaign in 1968, and the Nixon White House after that, had two enemies: the antiwar left and black people. We knew we couldn't make it illegal to be either against the war or black, but by getting the public to associate the hippies with marijuana and blacks with heroin, and then criminalizing both heavily, we could disrupt both communities. We could arrest their leaders, raid their homes, break up their meetings, and vilify them night after night on the evening news."[16] Over five decades, the drug war may not have effectively curbed drug use and addiction, but it did increase racial profiling by police, racial disparities in arrests, the militarization of law enforcement agencies, and lethal police brutality.[17]

Texas Governor William Clements, who served two nonconsecutive terms (1979–83 and 1987–91), announced his own war on drugs on May 10, 1980. "It's time that we in Texas get serious about this drug problem, and it's time to get dope off of the streets and put the pushers in our jails, and I'm ready to lock them up," Clements declared.[18] Clements tapped the hyperkinetic Dallas billionaire Ross Perot, founder of Electronic Data Systems, to be the "commander in chief" of the Texas War on Drugs. Perot brought a showman's zest to his role as the chair of the state's War on Drugs Committee, tirelessly touring the state in a campaign that brought numerous celebrities, including First Lady Nancy Reagan in 1982, to warn of the ominous dangers of drugs. The chairman told parents that even casual marijuana use represented a "gateway" to heroin addiction and violent criminal behavior. He urged parents to listen in on their children's phone conversations in order to nip drug sales in the bud. Perot was accused of racializing the drug problem and proposing aggressive police policies that endangered the civil liberties of African Americans and Latinos/as. *Dallas Times Herald* columnist Laura Miller (who later became that city's controversial mayor) quoted Perot as saying that black and brown neighborhoods should be "cordoned off" to allow heavily armed police SWAT teams to conduct house-to-house searches for cocaine, crack, and other illegal substances. Perot did not challenge the comments at the time but later suggested Miller had engaged in "flights of fancy." Nevertheless, Miller's account was essentially verified by another journalist, James Ragland of the *Dallas Morning News*, who reported that Perot said during a meeting with police officers that police "ought to just go in there [neighborhoods with high crime rates], cordon off the whole area, going block-by-block, looking for guns and drugs." Years later, during an October 25, 1989, appearance on the *Today Show*, Perot used the violent language of literal combat to describe what he thought would be necessary to eliminate drug abuse. "You can simply declare civil war, and the drug dealer is the enemy," he said. "At this point, there ain't no bail. You go to POW camp. You can deal with this problem in straight military terms. . . . We don't have to have military troops do all this, but we can apply the rules of war."[19]

Perot's war proved costly and, in terms of battling violent crime, extremely counterproductive. Texas' spending on antidrug law enforcement and incarceration dwarfed funds allocated for education and drug and alcohol addiction treatment. Draconian laws followed in 1981 with Texas raising the sentencing minimum for many drug offenses from five to ten years, a fifteen-year minimum for drug dealing, and for those caught with fifty pounds of marijuana or more: life imprisonment. Fines for financing drug operations increased to $1 million. As a result of the new drug laws, the state's prison population increased by 44 percent between 1982 and 1992. Mass incarceration became a new form of racial violence. From the dawn of the Texas drug war in 1980 to 2002, the number of Texans in prisons and jails for drug offenses increased by a factor of 13, and those convicted were disproportionately black and brown. The number of African Americans sent to prison after drug convictions was seven times higher than white offenders from 1986 to

1999, and African Americans accounted for 81 percent of the increase in prison admissions in that period. Nineteen percent of prisoners were Latino/a. Here, Texas followed national trends. As historian Heather Ann Thompson notes, between 1970 and 2010, the United States led the world in the incarceration of its citizens. This trend was fueled not only by the war on drugs but also by what Thompson calls the "criminalization of urban space" in which authorities disproportionately confined people of color in jails and prisons for sleeping in public spaces, begging for food, and eating on public transportation. Increasingly, schools relied on police to enforce discipline on campus, with African American and Latino/a children increasingly getting arrested for fighting in school or truancy. Mass arrests reduced wage earners in black and brown communities, increasing the poverty that is often a predicate for property crime, while at the same time increasing the chances of police-civilian interactions resulting in bloodshed.[20]

Once in overcrowded Texas prisons, black and brown inmates, along with their white peers, faced a relentless nightmare of brutality—rape, beatings, and murders—at the hands of other inmates and guards, with much of it racially motivated. An inmate, David Ruiz, filed a lawsuit challenging the constitutionality of Texas' incarceration policies in 1972, a case that lasted for more than two decades. In 1980, federal district court Judge William Wayne Justice ruled in *Ruiz v. Estelle* that the state's prison system violated the Eighth Amendment of the United States Constitution's ban on "cruel and unusual punishment." The case resulted in orders that the state cap prison populations at 95 percent of capacity, separate the most violent prisoners from the rest of the population, and increase the number of guards tasked with reducing violence within the prison walls. The Texas Department of Corrections, to a large degree, failed to comply. Texas sought to escape federal supervision of its penitentiary system, reopening the *Ruiz* case. As author Robert Perkinson argued, Texas prisons remained, as the war on drugs dragged on, "crowded, poorly supervised cell blocks and dormitories" where "prison gangs preyed on the weak, reducing some to sexual enslavement, while officers themselves continued to engage in 'sadistic and malicious violence' unchecked by supervisors." A mass construction program of new prisons followed, which reduced overcrowding, and in 2002, a federal judge released the Texas Department of Criminal Justice from federal oversight.[21]

Outside the prison walls, for not the first time in its history, Texas militarized its border with Mexico as part of the war on drugs. The Texas National Guard supplemented the customs service on the border in hopes of drug interdiction even as military reconnaissance planes patrolled the southern Texas skies.[22] With black and brown people already widely depicted as murderous dope peddlers bent on destroying the state's youth, such escalation in firepower reinforced for some Anglos the need to engage in mortal combat against a lawless, dark-skinned horde. Perhaps because of the sense of menace created by national drug war propaganda, surveys indicated that a large majority of the white community in the United States was willing to give police the benefit of a doubt after incidents involving violence against suspects, and so were a surprising number of African Americans. The number of Americans accepting police violence against suspects rose significantly during the first two decades of the drug war in the 1970s and 1980s. According to the General Social Surveys conducted by the National Opinion Research Center between 1973 and 2016, the percentage of African Americans saying it was permissible for a police officer to strike an adult male during a stop went up from 42.4 percent in the early 1970s to 57.6 percent in the late 1980s.[23] The numbers were more stable but significantly higher for whites, rising from 76.9 percent in the early 1970s to 79.10 percent in the late 1980s, with Southern whites more likely to approve of the use of violent force by police than whites in other regions. Nationally, although there is some support for "tough on crime" law enforcement in the black and brown communities, more whites consistently support "punitive" anticrime measures than do African Americans and the Latino/a community.[24] Furthermore, a substantial portion of the public has consistently regarded "reasonable" racial discrimination on the part of law enforcement to simply be part of good police work.[25]

Drug war propaganda combined with a general inclination of more influential, affluent and middle-class Texans to assume guiltlessness on the part of police officers after violent encounters with the public created an atmosphere in which police violence has continued through the early 2020s. Community activists in Houston fought a lonely battle when they protested a 1979 incident where police shot to death an African American man officers claimed had pointed a gun at them. Witnesses said, to the contrary, that the victim had begged for his life. In a November 1981 incident, a dozen off-duty white Houston police officers drank at a barbecue and subsequently beat black residents of a nearby apartment complex. Just a few days later, an African American man with a history of mental health problems "staged a bizarre martial arts display in front of police headquarters," in the words of the *New York Times,* as approximately thirty police officers watched. When the man lunged with a knife, he was instantly shot and killed. The department later said it had no nets or other equipment other than handguns available to subdue the man.[26]

Meanwhile, police violence against people of color accelerated in Dallas during the 1980s. Dallas officers killed or wounded an average of twenty-one people a year during the 1980s, with the number of African American and Latino/a victims out of proportion to either group's numbers in the city's total population. Dallas police had violent confrontations with thirty people of color in 1983, setting a dubious record, and another twenty-nine in 1986. Age provided no protection from police shootings. In the most infamous incident, officers shot to death seventy-year-old Etta Collins, who had called police to her South Dallas home after hearing burglars in her neighborhood. Soon thereafter, Dallas police gunned down another innocent, elderly African American resident of South Dallas, David Horton.[27] Incidents like these led the Dallas City Council to create a Citizens Police Review Board in 1987, but a backlash ensued the following year when three Dallas police officers violently died in the line of duty. The Dallas Police Association asked for the review board to be abolished. Ross Perot, father of the Texas drug war, intervened on behalf of the police, spent one hundred thousand dollars to pay for a survey to measure public support for the board, and privately lobbied then-City Manager Richard Knight to gut the board's power. Subsequently, the board lost the power to subpoena witnesses to police shootings or to conduct independent investigations into such matters, which left it to a large degree dependent on police accounts of officer-involved shootings.[28]

Outrage at police violence in Texas was mostly confined to African American and Latino/a activists, but it spilled into the suburbs in the July 11, 1975, fatal shooting of a white teenager, Billy Keith Joyvies, and the February 8, 1978, slaying of another white youth, Randy Webster, in Houston. What tied the two incidents together was that in order to justify later claims of self-defense, officers in both cases planted guns near the bodies of the unarmed youths after they died. So-called throw-down guns and the Houston police practice of shooting at fleeing suspects when their backs were turned came under increased scrutiny from white critics.[29]

"By the 1980s, the Houston Police Department had earned its reputation as mean, racist, and brutal because of its long history of episodic violence against citizens of Houston," Watson wrote. A halting effort to rein in out-of-control police abuse of civil liberties marked that decade, in part because of the Department of Justice's demands for civic reforms that ended the city's racist, exclusively at-large system for electing members of the city council, providing more diverse representation. The ascension of Kathy Whitmire as mayor in 1982 marked an era of change in the city's law enforcement and the appointment of the first African American police chief, Lee P. Brown. The Houston Police Officers Association claimed that the non-Houstonian had been picked to head the department solely because of his race and persistently objected to his efforts to improve the department's relationship with the community through methods such as neighborhood policing. Officers objected that such methods placed them in "hostile territory." Brown's efforts to increase the number of African American sergeants on the force and to implement civil service reforms also met a cold response from many veteran white officers. By 1990, Brown was gone. The department in many ways had become more professional, but a profound distrust between the Houston police and black and brown citizens remained, and police encounters with those communities still often ended in injury and/or death well into the second decade of the twenty-first century. Between 2007 and 2012, the city recorded 550 incidents in which Houston officers discharged their weapons, killing or injuring residents or animals. Victims were sometimes unarmed, as was wheelchair-bound Brian Claunch, a mentally ill man lacking one arm and one leg who was shot to death after pointing a ballpoint pen at an officer. While 706 excessive force complaints were filed in that five-year period, only fifteen officers were disciplined.[30]

An exceptionally gruesome, racially motivated murder at the end of the twentieth century gave law enforcement a new responsibility in battling racial violence, one they often neglected. On June 7, 1998, Shawn Berry, embittered by his bleak economic prospects, and Lawrence Brewer and John King, two devoted white supremacists and convicted criminals, killed James Byrd Jr. in Jasper, Texas. On the night of the murder, Berry, Brewer, and King offered James Byrd a ride and eventually yanked him out of the car, threw him to the ground, kicked his head, sprayed black paint on his face, secured a thirty-foot logging chain to his ankles, and dragged the still-conscious Byrd to his death.[31] Even though the courts convicted the killers, sentencing King and Brewer to death and Berry to life in prison, Byrd's murder produced far-reaching consequences and became the impetus for hate crime bills at the state and national levels.[32] After two years of political debates, the Texas Legislature passed, and the governor signed, the James Byrd Jr. Hate Crime Act on May 12, 2001. This act enhanced penalties for those guilty of criminal acts motivated by bias against victims due to race, color, religion, sex, sexual orientation, disability, age, or national origin.[33]

Eight years passed before enactment of a similar federal law. In 2009, Congress passed, and President Barack Obama signed, the Matthew Shepard and James Byrd Jr. Hate Crimes Prevention Act (also named in honor of a University of Wyoming student murdered by gay-bashers in Laramie, Wyoming). The legislation built on a 1969 federal hate crimes law and expanded the ability of the Federal Bureau of Investigation (FBI) to probe such incidents. In addition to race, the statute covered crimes motivated by bias based on the gender, gender identity, sexual orientation, or disability of the victim.[34]

Passage of the Texas and federal laws was delayed because many white politicians and law enforcement officials refused to recognize racial violence as a phenomenon distinct not only in motive but in impact. Racial crimes not only harm targeted individuals but have negative consequences for all within their communities. Throughout history, racial attacks often exceeded other crimes in levels of cruelty, with torture a frequent element. Texas law enforcement proved reluctant to acknowledge that racism remained a powerful force in the state's life, politics, and culture. This denial undermined the ability of police to gain the trust of African Americans, the Latino/a community, and other marginalized groups and hindered efforts to prevent future attacks. The hesitance to confront deep-rooted Texas racism made itself evident from the earliest days of the Byrd murder investigation. Jasper County Sheriff Billy Rowles drew sneers from some African Americans attending a press conference on June 9, 1998, shortly after suspects in the killing were arrested. "Those boys didn't learn to hate here," Rowles said, drawing "hoots of derision" from African Americans listening in, including one who shouted, "Yeah, right."[35]

Passage of the hate crime law did little to change the attitude of law enforcement toward racial violence that prevailed from the 1990s to the early twenty-first century. While police and law enforcement officials remained a threat to black and brown Texans, those same communities depended on often-antagonistic or indifferent law enforcement agencies to solve hate crimes and, beginning in the 1990s, to track and analyze them. Texas law enforcement agencies across the state did not seem to take this duty with uniform seriousness. Police departments such as Houston's that accepted a high degree of violence by officers against people of color worked in a culture that encouraged blind indifference to racially motivated crimes by the public. The rate of racially motivated hate crime and trends in racial violence across the state were difficult to calculate until passage of the federal Hate Crimes Statistics Act of 1990. Even when data began to be compiled, the numbers proved unreliable and thus not conducive to meaningful analysis. The 1990 law required the FBI to count crimes in which there was "manifest evidence of prejudice" against the victim based on race, ethnicity, religion, or sexual orientation; to document where the crimes were committed; and to describe the traits of victims and perpetrators. The FBI relies on local law enforcement agencies to collect the data, but thousands of agencies do not.[36] As a 2018 report in *Buzzfeed News* observed, according to the FBI's 2017 statistics, Texas reported only 0.68 hate crimes per 100,000 residents compared to 2.77 in California, 2.8 in New York, and

2.34 across the entire United States. The low participation rates in the FBI data collection program in Texas clearly suggest that racially based hate crimes in the state have been consistently undercounted.[37]

As the Southern Poverty Law Center notes, nearly half of hate crime victims never report such incidents to the police, and "many of the country's . . . law enforcement agencies do a poor job collecting or categorizing hate crime data . . . nearly nine out of 10 [agencies] reported zero hate crimes." In 2020, police recruits in Texas were not required to learn about hate crimes during their training at law enforcement academies. A December 7, 2017, *ProPublica* investigation suggests that police often ignore evidence indicating a crime was motivated by racism, Islamophobia, and other biases. In 2016 in the Dallas suburb of Mesquite, police did not report as hate crimes the beating of a Mexican American by white suspects who called him a "wetback" nor an incident in which an African American had a gun pulled on him by white assailants who called him "nigger." Roy Austin, a one-time US Justice Department deputy assistant attorney general in the Civil Rights Division, was blunt in his assessment of the value of the FBI numbers. "The current statistics are a complete and utter joke," he said. In any case, Texas police and courts also seem not to take hate crimes seriously. Between 2010 and 2015, police investigated 981 potential hate crimes. According to *ProPublica,* these investigations resulted in only five convictions.[38] Police resistance to completely and accurately recording the number of hate crimes contributed to the relative unawareness of the extent of racial violence in Texas in the post-1965 era. It also hampered efforts to understand the hate crime phenomenon and design social and law enforcement strategies to prevent racial violence in the future.

Substantial caveats aside, the fragmentary and unreliable information on hate crimes collated by the Texas Department of Public Safety (DPS) since 1999 indicates that hate crimes in Texas (murder, rape, robbery, aggravated assault, arson, and other violent crimes as well as intimidation and vandalism motivated by bias) stem mostly from racism or xenophobia. From 1999 to 2017, the DPS was not consistent in how it reported hate crimes per category of bias (hate crimes motivated by antiblack bias or anti-Hispanic bias, for instance.). The DPS's yearly reports provided raw numbers of incidents per bias until 2012. From 2013 on, the DPS provided only the percentage each category of bias represented out of the total number of hate crimes. However, some patterns remain clear. Between 1999 and 2012, hate crimes motivated by the race and ethnicity of the victim (as opposed to, for example, sexual orientation or religion), represented 70.3 percent of the total number of hate crimes. From 2013 on, hate crimes based on race and ethnicity represented between a low of 55.9 percent in 2015 and a high of 73.6 percent in 2016, the year Donald Trump ran what some critics called a racially divisive first campaign for president. In Texas, hate crimes, by a wide margin, are overwhelmingly committed by white people, and the victims are most often African Americans. Even as non-Hispanic whites declined from 45 percent to 41 percent of the total Texas population from 2010 to 2020, they still made up 2,219 of 4,561 hate crime offenders, 49 percent of the total number of perpetrators. It is unknowable how distorted that number is due to the numerous lapses in hate crime reporting in the state and because the race of the perpetrator was unknown in roughly 32 percent of the hate crime incidents in that nineteen-year period. Whites greatly outnumber the next highest number of racially identified perpetrators, African Americans. African Americans, who made up less than 12 percent of the Texas population, were slightly overrepresented (681 of all perpetrators in the selected time period, or 14.9 percent of the total), just as whites are underrepresented, but the giant gaps in the data make this count highly unreliable. Latino/a hate crime offenders are invisible in the statistics because the DPS's yearly reports define "Hispanics" as an ethnic rather than a racial group, and offenders are classified only by race. Racial categories are socially constructed and vaguely defined in any case, so in the DPS's yearly hate crime reports, Latino/a offenders might have been defined as white, black, or multiracial based in part on the varying judgments of the arresting officers. Hate crime victims, by a wide margin, are people of color. The percentage of the Texas population represented by African Americans held steady between 11 and 13 percent from 1990 to 2020. They were a much higher percentage of hate crime victims, however. According to the DPS, antiblack bias was involved in about 40 percent of the hate crimes from 1999 to 2012 and between 24.1 percent and 49 percent of such incidents between 2013 and 2017, when raw numbers were not provided by the agency.[39]

To the extent that the numbers can be relied on, Texas hate crime is largely an urban phenomenon, although those numbers may be primarily a function of the diligence of local law enforcement agencies in reporting such offenses. According to the DPS, between 1999 and 2016, the five most urban counties—Dallas, Harris, Tarrant, Bexar, and Travis—accounted for 59.2 percent of the state's hate crimes in those seventeen years. These counties also experienced the most rapid population and economic growth in the early twenty-first century, a period when older community ties and sense of shared identity were strained. Such conditions have served as predicates for racial violence in Texas throughout its history.[40]

One of the most identifiable spikes came in the wake of the September 11, 2001, attacks on the World Trade Center and the Pentagon by Al Qaeda. Hate crimes in Texas jumped from 305 in 2000 to 464 in 2001. Texans of Arab descent, who represented only 1.3 percent of hate crime victims in 2000, accounted for 13.8 percent of the victims in 2001, a bigger percentage than the much larger Latino/a community (10.8 percent of all victims that year). Victims identified by the DPS as Muslims went from 1 percent of the victims in 2000 to 6.3 percent in 2001.[41] Muslims suffer harassment not just because some blame them as a group for the September 11 attacks but also because of anti-immigrant prejudice (58 percent of American Muslims are immigrants). Muslims also suffer from the perception that they are a disloyal population that seeks to subvert American legal traditions with oppressive Shariah law (based on Islamic religious codes). Finally, six in ten American Muslims are classified as nonwhite and thus have inherited the consequences of the state's almost 180-year white supremacist history. Twenty percent are African Americans, 28 percent are Asian Americans, and 8 percent are Latino/a. (A similar notable spike in hate crimes against Jewish Texans took place between 2000 and 2001. As with Arabs, the whiteness of Jewish people has long been questioned. Some anti-Semitic conspiracy theories held that Jewish people plotted the terrorism of September 11, 2011.)[42]

Racial anxieties provoked one of the worst series of anti-Muslim hate crimes in the state's history. The September 11 terrorist attacks enraged Mark Anthony Stroman, a Dallas resident who had joined the white supremacist Aryan Brotherhood gang while imprisoned for murder. Stroman shot to death two men he believed were Muslims (one of the slain was a Hindu immigrant from India) and wounded a third on September 15, September 21, and October 4, 2001. The murders happened at a politically sensitive time as President George W. Bush was seeking assistance from Muslim nations in his newly declared war on terror. While some Texas elites embraced Islamophobia, others were also aware of the economic importance of the rapidly growing Muslim population in the state. The state of Texas executed Stroman, never charged with a hate crime, for capital murder on July 20, 2011, despite pleas from his lone surviving victim, Rais Bhuiyan, a Bengali immigrant and former Air Force pilot blinded after being shot by the gunman and who said that his Muslim religion taught him to forgive the attack.[43]

Attacks on the Muslim community, committed predominantly by white men, reflect fears of lost Western cultural and religious hegemony in the state. The state became more religiously diverse between 2000 and 2010. Muslims represented only 1.68 percent of the state population in 2010. They nevertheless stood as the fifth-largest body of believers in Texas by 2010, and the state had the largest Muslim population in the nation. This increase occurred even as the number of Texans belonging to any religious faith declined. These facts combined to inflame unfounded fears of some that Texas was about to fall under the tyrannical control of Muslim religious law and that the state would somehow become "foreign."[44] For example, in 2015, Beth Van Duyne, then the mayor of Irving, a Dallas–Fort Worth suburb, spread a panic about a local mosque operating a "sharia law court" as part of a plot to impose Muslim religious law in the United States.[45] A season of psychological violence against Muslims in the North Central Texas area ensued.

On November 22, 2015, a militia calling itself the Bureau on American-Islamic Relations (BAIR) held a rally outside the Islamic Center of Irving. Taking advantage of the state's open-carry laws, BAIR brandished twelve-gauge shotguns and other weapons. They marched in camouflage and masks, bullying men, women, and children as they

entered the mosque for prayers. BAIR supported Van Duyne and protested against allowing refugees from the Syrian Civil War to enter
the United States. On December 12, heavily armed BAIR protesters
moved their intimidation campaign to a mosque in Richardson, fifteen
miles north of Dallas. The group claimed that the Richardson mosque
supported Hamas, a politically powerful fundamentalist Palestinian
political and military resistance force dominant in the Gaza Strip and
officially labeled by the United States, Israel, and the European Union
as a terrorist organization. Counterprotesters outnumbered BAIR, and
the militia was forced to wave its firearms across the street from the
mosque. BAIR had already hit its high mark. BAIR threatened to carry
its anti-Muslim campaign to a Nation of Islam mosque in South Dallas,
a heavily African American part of the city. On April 2, 2016, the day
the BAIR rally was scheduled, several hundred mostly black counterprotesters, showed up, chanting, "Whose streets? Our streets." BAIR
members withdrew from the scene. "This is what they fear—the black
man," local activist Olinka Green said of BAIR. "This is what America
fears."[46]

That July, at a meeting of the City Council of Farmersville, a town of
four thousand north of Dallas, some attendees bullied Muslims who
hoped to open a cemetery, threatening to pour pig" blood on graves
and scatter pigs' heads on the burial ground, should it ever open.[47]
Islamophobia, however, proved to be not only a white phenomenon,
and in at least one highly visible case, a member of a community targeted by racism joined in the anti-Muslim crusade. On January 28, 2017,
Marq Vincent Perez burned down the Victoria Islamic Center, the only
mosque in that city 127 miles southwest of Houston. Perez reportedly
called Muslims "towelheads" and "was jumping up and down like a
little kid" as the mosque went up in flames. A federal jury later handed
him a twenty-four-year-plus sentence for the crime.[48]

Violence against Muslims seemed inspired by the notion that they
are "outsiders" and not truly part of the American family. In this way,
the fate of Muslims and the Latino/a in Texas unexpectedly entwined.
Often, the Latino/a individuals who are attacked are assumed by the
assailants to be undocumented. For instance, when a group of anti–
death penalty Hispanic protesters demonstrated outside the Walls Unit

in Huntsville, where authorities held the execution of Karla Faye Tucker for murder on February 3, 1998, a mob began screaming at them, "This is our state, go back where you came from," "Mexicans just come in to trash our country," and "They should all be killed."[49]

Muslims were not the only group to be targeted by escalating assaults after September 11. By a wide margin, Latino/a suffered racially motivated violence rather than committing it. Recorded hate crimes motived by anti-Hispanic bias doubled in 2001 from the previous year, from twenty-five incidents to fifty, and stayed at a comparable level in 2002 when forty-five such crimes were recorded.[50] In 2010, Representative Louie Gohmert, a Republican from Tyler in East Texas, conflated the threat of Muslim terrorists to the United States and the supposed need to tighten security along the Mexican border. He claimed that pregnant terrorist sympathizers were crossing the border in order to give birth to so-called anchor babies in the United States. Gohmert claimed he received his information from a "retired F. B. I. agent." In a speech in the House of Representatives, he warned that "it appeared they would have young women who became pregnant [and] would get them into the United States to have a baby. They wouldn't even have to pay anything for the baby. And then they would return back where they could be raised and coddled as future terrorists. And then one day, 20, 30 years down the road, they can be sent in to help destroy our way of life."[51]

As the Latino/a community rapidly increased in size in Texas, growing from 6.7 million in 2000 to 10.7 million fifteen years later, hate crimes against the entire Latino/a community climbed. The FBI calculated that 11 percent of hate crime victims nationwide were Latino/a. California and Texas led the union in anti-Latino/a hate crimes from 2003 to 2007. But again, there was no clear picture of how bad the problem was because, as Mark Potok, a onetime spokesperson for the Southern Poverty Law Center, said in a 2017 interview, "Latinos, and in particular undocumented immigrants, are among the least likely to report hate crimes because they fear deportation."[52]

The attacks on Latino/a victims in recent years often have included the sadism seen in the lynchings of an earlier era and are intended to police rigid racial sexual boundaries. For instance, on April 22, 2006, in the Houston area, neo-Nazi "skinheads" broke sixteen-year-old David

Ritcheson's jaw, attempted to carve a swastika into his chest, and sodomized him with a patio umbrella pole after they saw him kiss a white girl, an underage sister of one of the assailants. Ritcheson knew some of his attackers, who had been drinking and consuming drugs with him before the assault. Racial animus clearly provided at least one motive for the attack. During the torture, the skinheads screamed, "White Power!" and called their victim a "beaner," "a spic," and a "wetback." Ritcheson survived the attack but in the coming months endured thirty surgeries and had to wear a colostomy bag. Juries convicted his assailants, swastika-tattooed David Henry Tuck and Keith Richard Turner, of aggravated sexual assault. Ritcheson testified before Congress and declared, "I'm glad to tell you today that my best days still lay ahead of me." The event haunted him, however, leaving him deeply depressed. A little more than two months after this testimony in Washington, DC, on July 1, 2007, he jumped off the upper deck of a cruise ship, killing himself.[53]

Hate crimes motivated by anti-Hispanic bias almost doubled in 2016. This is the same year that Donald Trump opened his presidential campaign declaring that "when Mexico sends its people, they're not sending their best. . . . They're sending people that have lots of problems, and they're bringing those problems with us. They're bringing drugs. They're bringing crime. They're rapists." Anti-Hispanic hate crimes almost doubled in Texas from 2015 to 2016, from 7.7 percent of hate crimes to 14.6 percent.[54]

The legacy of white racial violence in Texas—lynchings, beatings, the destruction of not only black and brown lives but black and brown property, and the exterminationist language heard by the death penalty protesters—bore bitter fruit in Dallas on the night of July 7, 2016. That evening, during a peaceful downtown protest of police brutality, Micah Johnson opened sniper fire on Dallas police officers. Johnson, an African American former private in the US Army Reserve, shot to death five and wounded nine other officers and two civilians before a tactical squad killed him in a parking garage at a nearby college with a remotely controlled explosive carried by a bomb-disposal robot. The downtown protest and Johnson's sniper attacks represented dramatically different responses to the police shooting earlier that week of

Philando Castile near St. Paul, Minnesota, a killing captured by his girlfriend's cellphone video, and the Baton Rouge police officers' killing of Alton Sterling. Before his death, Johnson told negotiators "he was upset about the recent police shootings. The suspect said he was upset at white people. The suspect stated he wanted to kill white people, especially white officers," according to then-Dallas Police Chief David O. Brown.[55]

An African American himself, Brown argued, unlike many of his white peers, that the Black Lives Matter movement (which arose in 2013 in response to police killings of African Americans) "brought awareness." Before the sniper attacks, Brown won praise in some quarters for emphasizing de-escalation of violence in police training, increasing the number of squad car cameras and body cameras to document events in the cases of police shootings, and making information on officer-involved shootings more available to the public. As a result of the de-escalation program, police and civilian encounters resulted in fewer injuries in Dallas, from 478 officer and 789 civilian injuries in 2013 (1,267 injuries in police encounters in total) to 234 police and 629 civilian injuries in 2016 (863 in all.) The Dallas police reported a decline in officer-involved shootings from ten in 2014 to five the following year. Excessive force complaints dropped from 147 in 2009 to 21 in 2016. However, the reforms led to angry objections from the Dallas Police Association, which has consistently opposed civilian review. Deputy Chief Malik Aziz, the chair of the Black Police Association, complained that second-guessing of officers undermined the effectiveness of officers who hesitated to get involved in any interaction with suspects that might provoke an investigation. Brown retired as the Dallas police chief in 2016. John Fullinwider, the cofounder of Dallas-based Mothers Against Police Brutality, said that Brown had "a reputation as a reformer. But this police department has not been reformed." Fullinwider said in a 2019 interview that he first got involved in the police brutality issue after meeting Santos Rodriguez's mother, Stephanie, as the family prepared a civil rights case against Officer Cain. Noting that American police departments have their origin in antebellum slave patrols, Fullinwider said that police officers are a product of a violent American gun culture. The Dallas police have not kept complete records on the number of civilians killed by officers, so he admits his best estimate of civilian deaths is in the hundreds since 1973. The rate of police shootings, he said, is inextricably linked to racism. "I think race is paramount," he said. "There is no way to look at any of the shootings and not see racism as a major factor. The racial element is central in all of these cases, even when it's not fatal. There are proportionately more deadly encounters with police when it involves people of color." Dallas-area police reformers called for financial compensation for victims of police violence, for the local US Attorney to appoint a special prosecutor to investigate fatal police shootings, for routine drug testing and psychological evaluations of officers, and for the Dallas police to implement deadly force training approved by the US Justice Department. Fullinwider has asked for more. He pointed out in 2019 that most fatal encounters between police and the public occur when officers are alone. He called for officers to be trained to retreat to safety and call for backup before they use lethal force and for the creation of a single national standard for police use of lethal force. He said that legal accountability for instances of officers violating those standards is key to preventing future civilian deaths at the hands of police.[56]

Perot had characterized police as engaged in civil war against drug-saturated communities, and that martial mentality has not disappeared. In spite of reforms in large cities, Texas police as a whole remain anomalously and strikingly lethal in their use of firearms compared to law enforcement officers in the rest of the world.[57] At the funeral service for the five slain Dallas officers, President Obama acknowledged the gulf dividing many white police officers and their supporters from people of color, who often felt aggrieved by police killings in their communities. In his speech, Obama tried to split the difference, expressing empathy for the risks faced by police while acknowledging the frequency of racially motivated police brutality.[58]

Obama and many others expressed a hope that the July 7, 2016, murders might in some vague way inspire reflection on the scourge of racism and stop the bloodshed in a way the butchering of James Byrd did not. They were to be disappointed. On September 6, 2018, a five-year veteran of the Dallas Police Department, Amber Guyger, shot to death Botham Jean, a PricewaterhouseCoopers accountant, as he sat on a couch in his apartment eating ice cream and watching a football game. Jean sang in his church choir, but just as an earlier generation of police posthumously criminalized lynching victims, Dallas police smeared Jean. They leaked the search warrants for Jean's apartment, revealing the presence of marijuana at his residence. Meanwhile, Guyger, who is white, had a history of sharing racist texts with other officers and had posted comments on social media celebrating police violence. On Pinterest, she once posted, "I wear all black to remind you not to mess with me, because I'm already dressed for your funeral." After killing Jean, she said she had been exhausted after a long shift. She thought that Jean's unlocked apartment, located on the floor above hers, was her own and that she mistook him for a burglar. Fullinwider said he believes the Jean case illustrates how not holding police involved in unprovoked violence accountable can lead to a degeneration of standards leading to lethal consequences. He noted that Guyger's boyfriend and former patrol partner Martin Rivera had shot to death Brandon Washington while he allegedly ate a stolen candy bar in Dallas's Pleasant Grove neighborhood on March 22, 2007. (Guyger was texting Rivera in the moments leading up to her shooting Jean.) "Rivera had killed an unarmed black guy," Fullinwider pointed out. "He was Guyger's mentor. Maybe if he had been held accountable [for the Washington shooting], maybe Guyger would have had a different mentor. And maybe she would have hesitated [to shoot] in a life-and-death situation." On October 10, 2019, Guyger was sentenced to ten years in prison.[59]

Michael W. Waters, the founding pastor of the Abundant Life African Methodist Episcopal Church in South Dallas, said the sentence was too lenient compared to those for most convicted murderers in Texas and sent a message that black lives still did not matter in the state. "In the state of Texas, Amber Guyger is in the 1.9% of all persons who are sentenced for murdering someone in our state," Waters said in a National Public Radio interview. "So she's in very small company. And we're very clear that the well over 80% of incarcerates serving for murder who are serving 20 years or more tend to be of black and brown hue. And so there's a great deal of concern in terms of how justice is meted out in this case. In reality, over the last almost 50 years, of all the officer-related fatalities, only two officers have been convicted, and they will both have totally served or been sentenced to a time of 15 years. And we think that's a disgrace."[60]

Meanwhile, just two days after Guyger was sentenced for murdering Botham Jean, Fort Worth police officer Aaron Dean fatally shot twenty-eight-year-old Atatiana Jefferson through a window in her home where she was playing video games with her eight-year-old nephew. Police had been called to the Jefferson home by a neighbor who was concerned about the family's safety because the front door had been left open.[61]

Texas today remains poised at the intersection of serious racial and economic inequality, elements providing the soil from which racial brutality has grown. As of 2018, Texas ranked as the state with the eighth highest rate of income inequality. Poverty rates declined from a high of 18.5 percent in 2011 to a still significant 14.7 percent by late 2018, while incomes for most Texans remained flat for much of that period. As a result of the policies of the ruling class, malnutrition, a lack of health care, and exposure to environmental racism wounded black and brown bodies and shortened lives as surely as bullets and became a subtler form of racial violence. Meanwhile, "last place aversion"—the desire to not be perceived as occupying the bottom social rung—sometimes provoked marginalized whites such as James Byrd's killers to lash out at people of color.[62]

In the 1920s, when the Ku Klux Klan gained control of Texas, suspicion of immigrants fueled the rise of that hate group. In a 2015 poll, 22 percent of Texans rated "illegal immigration" as the greatest threat facing the nation, the top-rated anxiety, followed by 18 percent who mentioned foreign terrorist groups.[63] The combination of dislocation, alienation, and xenophobia that characterized racial violence in an earlier era again came together on August 13, 2019, when twenty-one-year-old Patrick Crusius, a resident of the Dallas suburb of Allen, used an AK-47-style rifle to slaughter twenty-three and injure twenty-three mostly Mexican and Mexican American victims at a Walmart in El Paso. Crusius had driven ten hours across the state to specifically target Mexicans he feared would displace real "Americans" such as himself. Crusius wrote, "This attack is a response to the Hispanic invasion of Texas. They are the instigators, not me. I am simply defending my country from cultural and ethnic replacement brought on by an invasion."[64]

Locked into a combat footing against communities of color and predisposed by a police culture to not perceive racial hatred as a major factor shaping Texas culture, state law enforcement ignores hate crimes as a serious threat. The exception is when the degree and the extent of violence, such as in James Byrd's murder and the El Paso massacre, draw the world's attention. At the same time, black and brown civilians see police as an occupying and often dangerous force, a fraught relationship that undermines public safety.

The ghosts of racial violence past, and specifically the specter of James Byrd, still stalk the Lone Star State. From 2013 to 2015, at least sixteen African Americans vanished near Jasper where Byrd was killed, with the US Department of Justice and the Texas DPS showing little interest in solving the mystery. Byrd has not been left in peace, even in death. An iron fence surrounds his grave, which was vandalized twice. Anglo Texans still do not perceive the persistence and commonality of white racial violence toward African Americans, wrote Bruce Glasrud, a historian of black Texas history, much less that of other people of color. "It is important to recognize that *all* race relations—in Texas, in the South, and in the United States—are colored not only by the fact and the history of white-on-black violence, but also by the differential awareness of it," Glasrud argues. "That whites repress that memory and seek to minimize the ongoing threat is all the more necessary to acknowledge in light of the fact that blacks are very aware of the past and often wary of the present."[65]

Notes

1. See Kent B. Germany, "Historians and the Many Lyndon Johnsons: A Review Essay," *Journal of Southern History* 75, No. 4 (November 2009), 1017–18; David G. McComb, *Houston: A History* (Austin: University of Texas Press, 1981), 114, 143; Michael Phillips, *White Metropolis: Race, Ethnicity, and Religion in Dallas, 1841–2001* (Austin: University of Texas Press, 2006), 14–15.

2. Robert F. Greenwald, *Race Relations and the Intergroup Climate in Dallas, Texas: Analysis and Comment on the Nature of Intergroup Problems and the Potential for Resolution* (Dallas: North Texas Chapter of the Association of Intergroup Relations Officials, April 1967), 1; W. Marvin Dulaney, "Whatever Happened to the Civil Rights Movement in Dallas, Texas?" in *Essays on the American Civil Rights Movement,* ed. W. Marvin Dulaney and Kathleen Underwood (College Station: Texas A&M

University Press, 1993), 81–82; William R. Carmack and Theodore Freedman, *Dallas, Texas: Factors Affecting School Desegregation* (New York: Anti-Defamation League of B'nai B'rith, 1962), 15–16, 20–21; Darwin Payne, *Big D: Triumphs and Troubles of an American Supercity in the 20th Century* (Dallas: Three Forks Press, 1994), 300–301; Jim Schutze, *The Accommodation: The Politics of Race in An American City* (Secaucus, NJ: Citadel Press, 1986), 128–33; *Dallas at the Crossroads with Walter Cronkite* (1961), documentary, Dallas Citizens Council and Sam Bloom, SMU Jones Film, September 26, 2019, video, 21:26, https://www.youtube.com/watch?v=GmjNx8dEC-8.

3. Henry Masters, interview by Michael Phillips and Betsy Friauf, October 9, 2013, Oral Memoirs of Henry Masters, audio, Baylor University Libraries, Digital Collections, https://digitalcollections-baylor.quartexcollections.com/Documents/Detail/oral-memoirs-of-henry-masters-audio/980870.

4. Opal Johnson Smith, interviewed by Michael Phillips and Betsy Friauf, audio recording, Dallas, Texas, April 26, transcript, Baylor Universities Libraries, Digital Collections. Smith discussed the bullet hole in her window after the recording for the interview ended. Smith had not finished her edits of the interview transcript by the time of her death on December 26, 2020, so the transcript had not been posted on the Baylor University Digital Collections website as of press time. It was in the process of being posted when this chapter was edited. By the time of publication, it should be accessible through this link: https://digitalcollections-baylor.quartex collections.com/documents?returning=true. Those searching should use the search terms "Phillips" and "Friauf." For more on Smith, see "PVAMU First-Class Alumna Opal Johnson Smith passes away (1934-202), https://www.pvamu.edu/blog/pvamu-first-class-alumna-opal-johnson-smith-passes-away/(accessed August 3, 2022.)

5. Taylor Branch, *Parting the Waters: America in the King Years, 1954–63* (New York: Simon & Schuster, 1988), 888–92; and *At Canaan's Edge: America in the King Years, 1965–1968* (New York: Simon & Schuster, 2006), 44–57, 284–85, 288–89, 293–99, 305–8.

6. McComb, *Houston,* 154–56.

7. Dwight Watson, *A Change Did Come: Race and the Houston Police Department, 1930–1990* (College Station: Texas A&M University Press, 2005), 19, 42, 64, 70, 131.

8. McComb, *Houston,* 170; Alex LaRotta, "The TSU Riot: 50 Years Later," *Houston Chronicle,* May 16, 2017, https://www.houstonchronicle.com/local/gray-matters/article/The-TSU-Riot-50-years-later-11149852.php; Ayodale Braimah, "Houston (TSU) Riot (1967)," *Black Past,* December 4, 2017, https://www.blackpast.org/african-american-history/houston-tsu-riot-1967; *Encyclopedia of American Race Riots, Volume 2,* ed. Walter C. Rucker and James N. Upton (Westport, Conn.: Greenwood Press, 2007), s.v. "Texas Southern University Riot of 1967"; Bernard Friedberg, "Houston and the TSU Riot," in *Anti-Black Violence in Twentieth Century Texas,* ed. Bruce Glasrud (College Station: Texas A&M University Press, 2015), 131–42.

9. J. R. Gonzales, "The Death of Carl Hampton," *Houston Chronicle,* July 26, 2010, https://blog.chron.com/bayoucityhistory/2010/07/the-death-of-carl-hampton.

10. Watson, *A Change Did Come,* 88–89.

11. J. R. Gonzales, "The Death of Carl Hampton."

12. Gonzales, "The Death of Carl Hampton."

13. "Latins, Blacks Hold Vigil for Rodriguez," *Dallas Morning News,* March 7, 1971; Terry Kliewer, "Rodriguez Rally: Protestors March in Shrine Parade," *Dallas Morning News,* March21, 1971; Stephen Power, "Fatal Flashback: Ex-Officer Looks Back with Regret 25 Years after Killing Boy in Interrogation," *Dallas Morning News,* July 24, 1998; Payne, *Big D,* 363–65; Stephen Power and Brenda Rodriguez, "'Flash Point in Dallas History Has Faded with Time," *Dallas Morning News,* July 24, 1998; Lauren Silverman, "How the Death of a 12-Year Changed the City of Dallas," *Code Switch,* July 24, 2013, https://www.npr.org/sections/codeswitch/2013/07/24/205121429/How-The-Death-Of-A-12-Year-Old-Changed-The-City-Of-Dallas; Tasha Tsiaperas, "Was 15-Year Sentence Enough for Ex-Cop Who Killed Jordan Edwards?" *Dallas Morning News,* August 30, 2018, https://www.dallasnews.com/news/courts/2018/08/30/15-year-sentence-enough-ex-cop-killed-jordan-edwards.

14. Watson, *A Change Did Come,* 110–25; Marialuisa Rincon, "40 Years Ago Police Killed Joe Campos Torres Sparking Massive Moody Park Riots," *Houston Chronicle,* May 10, 2017, https://www.chron.com/news/houston-texas/article/Joe-Campos-Torres-Moody-Park-riots-11135844.php.

15. Cigdim V. Sirin, "From Nixon's War on Drugs to Obama's Drug Policies Today: Presidential Progress in Addressing Racial Injustices and Disparities," *Race, Class, and Gender* 18, no. 3–4 (2011): 82.

16. Dan Baum, "Legalize It All: How to Win the War on Drugs," *Harper's Magazine* (February 4, 2016) https://harpers.org/archive/2016/04/legalize-it-all.

17. Hannah L. F. Cooper, "War on Drugs Policing and Police Brutality," *Substance Use and Misuse* 508, no. 8–9 (2015), 1188–94, https:doi.org/10.3109/10826084.2015.1007669; Peter B. Kraska and Victor E. Kappeler, "Militarizing American Police: The Rise and Normalization of Paramilitary Units," *Social Problems* 44, no. 1 (February 1997), 1–18.

18. James W. Marquart et al., "Ceremonial Justice, Loose Coupling, and the War on Drugs in Texas, 1980–1989," *Crime and Delinquency* 39, no. 4 (October 1993), 529.

19. Marquart et. al, "Ceremonial Justice," 531; Michael Isikoff, "Perot Championed Unorthodox War on Drugs," *Washington Post,* June 10, 1992, https://www.washington-post.com/archive/politics/1992/06/10/perot-championed-unorthodox-war-on-drugs/c8094304-bbf1-490e-9471-6c86dc9e8e2b/.

20. Marquat et al., "Ceremonial Justice," 530–31; Isikoff, "Perot Championed Unorthodox War; Justice Policy Institute, *Race and Imprisonment in Texas: The Disparate Incarceration of Latinos and African Americans in the Lone Star State* (Washington, DC: Justice Policy Institute, 2005), 5; Heather Ann Thompson, "Why Mass Incarceration Matters: Rethinking Crisis, Decline, and Transformation in Postwar American History," *Journal of American History* 97, no. 3 (December 2010), 703–34.

21. Robert Perkinson, *Texas Tough: This Rise of America's Prison Empire* (New York: Picador, 2010), 264, 326–27; *The Handbook of Texas,* s.v. "Prison System," updated September 24, 2020, https://tshaonline.org/handbook/online/articles/jjp03; Jorge

Antonio Renaud, *Behind the Walls: A Guide for Family and Friends of Texas Inmates* (Denton: University of North Texas Press, 2002), xii.

22. Marquat et al., "Ceremonial Justice," 530.

23. Support for police use of force was higher among African Americans who were wealthier and spent more years in school.

24. Christopher Everett Robertson, "Race, Class, and Attitudes Toward Uses of Force by Police" (master's thesis, University of Texas at Arlington, 2018), iii, 11, 25, 29; Nazgool Ghandnoosh, "Race and Punishment: Racial Perceptions of Crime and Support for Punitive Policies," The Sentencing Project, September 3, 2014, https://www.sentencingproject.org/publications/race-and-punishment-racial-perceptions-of-crime-and-support-for-punitive-policies/#B.%20The%20Racial%20Gap%20in%20Punitiveness.

25. Shaun L. Gabbidon and Helen Taylor Greene, *Race and Crime* (Thousand Oaks, CA: Sage, 2009), 116.

26. William E. Stevens, "Houston's Mayor and Police at Odds," *New York Times,* March 16, 1982, https://timesmachine.nytimes.com/timesmachine/1982/03/16/254604.html?pageNumber=18.

27. Robert Ingrassia, "Police Shooting Was Dallas Turning Point: Many Believe Furor over Black Woman's '86 Death Transformed Department," *Dallas Morning News,* October 27, 1996.

28. Jon Fortune, memorandum to members of the Public Safety and Criminal Justice Committee, *Citizens Police Review Board* (Dallas: Public Safety Criminal Justice Committee, February 11, 2019), 5, https://dallascityhall.com/government/Council%20Meeting%20Documents/pscj_2_citizen-police-review-board_combined_021119.pdf; Isikoff, "Perot Championed Unorthodox War on Drugs."

29. Watson, *A Change Did Come,* 105–7.

30. Watson, 130, 133, 139–45, 149; Joe DePrang, "The Horror Every Day: Police Brutality in Houston Goes Unpunished," *Texas Observer,* September 24, 2013, https://www.texasobserver.org/horror-every-day-police-brutality-houston-goes-unpunished.

31. Dina Temple-Raston, *A Death in Texas: A Story of Race, Murder, and a Small Town's Struggle for Redemption* (New York: Henry Holt & Company, 2002), 5.

32. Temple-Raston, *A Death in Texas,* 32–35, 199–200; Allan Turner, "Hate Crime Killer Executed," *Houston Chronicle,* September 22, 2011, https://www.chron.com/news/houston-texas/article/Hate-crime-killer-executed-2182684.php; Eliott C. McLaughlin and Steve Almasy, "John William King Had No Last Words before His Execution for the Heinous Dragging Death of James Byrd Jr.," CNN.com, April 25, 2019, https://www.cnn.com/2019/04/24/us/james-byrd-killer-execution-john-william-king/index.html.

33. J. Erik Jonsson Ethics Award: Rev. Zan Holmes, Jr., SMU Office of the Provost, accessed June 19, 2019, https://www.smu.edu/Provost/Ethics/Events/EthicsAward/Holmes; Jim Schutze, "Mystery of St. Luke," *Dallas Observer,* May 17, 2001, https://www.dallasobserver.com/news/mystery-of-st-luke-6392130; Zan Holmes interview

with Phillips and Friauf, Oral Memoirs of Zan Wesley Holmes, series 2, audio, Baylor University Libraries, Digital Collections, https://digitalcollections-baylor. quartexcollections.com/Documents/Detail/oral-memoirs-of-zan-wesley-holmes-jr.-series-2-audio/1602614; Associated Press, "Governor of Texas Signs a Hate Crimes Bill," *New York Times*, May 12, 2001.

34. US Department of Justice, "Hate Crime Laws," updated March 7, 2019, https:// www.justice.gov/crt/hate-crime-laws; Michelle Boorstein, "Matthew Shepard, Whose 1998 Murder Became a Symbol of the Gay Rights Movement, Will Be Interred at the Washington National Cathedral," *Washington Post,* October 11, 2018, https://www.washingtonpost.com/religion/2018/10/11/matthew-shepard-whose-murder-became-symbol-gay-rights-movement-will-be-interred-washington-national-cathedral/; David Crary, "Views Are Mixed on Hate Crime Law Named for Matthew Shepard," AP News, October 12, 2018, https://www.apnews.com/a6d811ece9254facbc68df40d20e931a.

35. Raston, *A Death in Texas,* 114.

36. For instance, Texas has 1,913 state and local law enforcement agencies. Between 1996 and 2017, the number of agencies participating in the FBI data collection program ranged from a low of only 65 in 2012 (about 3.4 percent) to a high of 1,097 in 2016 (about 57.3 percent). Ken Schwencke, "Documenting Hate: Why America Fails at Gathering Hate Crime Statistics," *ProPublica,* December 4, 2017, https://www.propublica.org/article/why-america-fails-at-gathering-hate-crime-statistics (accessed July 17, 2019); FBI/US Department of Justice, *Uniform Crime Reports: Hate Crime Statistics* (Washington, DC: US Government Printing Office, 1994), 1, https://www.ncjrs.gov/pdffiles1/Digitization/149507NCJRS.pdf.

37. Brian A. Reaves, *Census of State and Local Law Enforcement Agencies, 2008,* NCJ 233982 (Washington, DC: US Department of Justice Office, July 2011), 15, https:// www.bjs.gov/content/pub/pdf/csllea08.pdf; Edwin R. Byerly and Kevin Deardorff, *National and State Population Estimates: 1990 to 1994,* P25–1127 (Washington, DC: US Government Printing Office, 1995), v, https://www.census.gov/content/dam/Census/library/publications/1995/demo/p25-1127.pdf; Glen Kercher, Claire Nolasco, and Ling Wu, *Hate Crimes* (Huntsville, TX: Crime Victim's Institute, Criminal Justice Center, Sam Houston State University, 2008), 5; Peter Aldhous, "The Cities Where the Cops See No Hate," *BuzzFeed News,* December 13, 2018, https://www.buzzfeed news.com/article/peteraldhous/hate-crimes-miami-police-irving-syracuse. The FBI's Uniform Crime Reports between 1995 and 2017, which include data on the number of hate crimes per state and the number of reporting agencies each year, can be found at https://ucr.fbi.gov/hate-crime.

38. Swathi Shanmugasundaram, "Hate Crimes Explained," Southern Poverty Law Center, accessed July 17, 2019, https://www.splcenter.org/20180415/hate-crimes-explained; Schwenke, "Documenting Hate"; A. C. Thompson, Rohan Naik, and Ken Schwencke, "Hate Crime Training for Police Is Often Inadequate, Sometimes Nonexistent," *ProPublica,* November 29, 2017, https://www.propublica.org/article/

hate-crime-training-for-police-is-often-inadequate-sometimes-nonexistent; Aldhous, "Cities Where Cops See No Hate"; Ryan Katz, Hate Crime Law Results in Few Convictions and Lots of Disappointment," *ProPublica,* April 10, 2017, https://www.propublica.org/article/hate-crime-law-results-in-few-convictions-and-lots-of-disappointment.

39. Detailed, if incomplete and inadequate, statistics on Texas hate crimes can be found at Texas Department of Public Safety (DPS), Crime Records, accessed July 17, 2019, http://www.dps.texas.gov/administration/crime_records/pages/crimestatistics.htm; ; Nazrul Hoque, *Texas Population: Changes in Size, Composition, and Distribution, 2000–2010,* University of Houston Hobby Center for Public Policy, p. 9, accessed January 20, 2020, https://www.uh.edu/hobby/_docs/Texas%20Population%20Changes%20in%20Size%20Composition%20and%20Distribution%202000-2010.pdf; "Population of Texas: Census 2010 and 2000 Interactive Map, Demographics, Statistics, Quick Facts," CensusViewer, accessed July 17, 2019, http://censusviewer.com/state/TX; Texas Demographic Center, "Texas Demographic Trends and Projections and the 2020 Census," January 29, 2021, https://demographics.texas.gov/Resources/Presentations/OSD/2021/2021_01_29_MexicanAmericanLegislativeLeadershipFellowship.pdf; The Texas Demographic Center's website allows you to look up population numbers broken down by race/ethnicity and year using the "data" tab, see https://demographics.texas.gov/Data/TPEPP/.

40. Texas DPS, Crime Records; The Texas Demographic Center's website allows you to look up population numbers broken down by race/ethnicity and year using the "data" tab, see https://demographics.texas.gov/Data/TPEPP/.For examples of how dramatic economic growth and transformation has preceded racial violence in Texas history, see Brandon Jett, "Paris Is Burning: Lynching and Racial Violence in Lamar County, 1890–1920," in *Anti-Black Violence in Twentieth Century Texas,* ed. Bruce Glasrud (College Station: Texas A&M University Press, 2015), 17–24; and James A. Burran, "Violence in an 'Arsenal of Democracy': The Beaumont Race Riot, 1943," in Glasrud, ed., *Anti-Black Violence,* 116–30.

41. Texas DPS, Crime Records; Robert J. Samuelson, "Was the Great Recession Worse Than the Great Depression?," Washington Post, November 26, 2018, https://www.washingtonpost.com/opinions/was-the-great-recession-worse-than-the-great-depression/2018/11/26/8ba5ab7a-f1a9-11e8-bc79-68604ed88993_story.html; Terence Samuel, "The Racist Backlash Obama Has Faced During His Presidency," *Washington Post,* April 22, 2016, https://www.washingtonpost.com/graphics/national/obama-legacy/racial-backlash-against-the-president.html; Hanaa' Tameez, "Hate Crimes Fluctuated in North Texas Cities between 2016 and 2017, FBI Reports," *Fort Worth Star-Telegram,* November 20, 2018, https://www.star-telegram.com/latest-news/article221923915.html.

42. McCaig, Amy, "Islamophobia Represents a Form of Racism Mixed with Cultural Intolerance," *Rice News,* September 14, 2017, https://news2.rice.edu/2017/09/14/islamophobia-represents-a-form-of-racism-mixed-with-cultural-intolerance; Pew

Research Center, "Demographic Portrait of Muslim Americans," July 26, 2017, https://www.pewforum.org/2017/07/26/demographic-portrait-of-muslim-americans. For more on panic over Sharia law in Texas, see Christopher Hooks, "The Crank Factory: How the Right-Wing Media and a Small Band of Activists Turned Irving into a Hotbed of Hatred," *Texas Observer,* June 13, 2016, https://www.texas observer.org/irving-islamophobia-beth-van-duyne; David R. Brockman, "When Islamophobia Backfires," *Texas Observer,* June 1, 2018, https://www.texasobserver .org/when-islamophobia-backfires; Patrick Strickland, "US: Are Anti-Sharia Bills Legalizing Islamophobia?" Al Jazeera, October 1, 2017, https://www.aljazeera.com/ news/2017/09/anti-sharia-bills-legalising-islamophobia-170928150835240.html. See the Texas DPS Crime Reports for the years 2000 and 2001 for the numbers of anti-Jewish hate crimes. For more on Jews and whiteness in Texas, see Phillips, *White Metropolis,* 52, 75–76, 83–84, 86, 89, 102, 122, 140–41. For more on anti-Semitic conspiracy theories regarding September 11, see Linda Grant, "The Hate That Cannot Die," *The Guardian,* December 17, 2001, https://www.theguardian.com/world/2001/ dec/18/september11.israel.

43. Timothy Williams, "The Hated and the Hater, Both Touched by Crime," July 18, 2011," *New York Times,* July 18, 2011, https://www.nytimes.com/2011/07/19/ us/19questions.html ; Kari Huss, "A victim of 9/11 hate crime now fights for his attacker's life," NBC News, June 3, 2011, https://www.nbcnews.com/id/wbna43241014; "Bush Denounces Muslim Harassment," September 17, 2001, cnn.com, https:// www.cnn.com/2001/US/09/17/gen.hate.crimes/ ; "Timeline: US-Saudi Relations Since 9/11," May 16, 2008, reuters.com, https://www.reuters.com/article/us-saudi-relations-idUSL1686464320080516; Ahmed Afzal, *Lone Star Muslims: Transnational Lives and the South Asian Experience in Texas* (New York: New York University Press, 2015), 34.

44. Texas Almanac, "Religious Affiliation in Texas," accessed July 19, 2019, https:// texasalmanac.com/topics/religion/religious-affiliation-texas.

45. Talal Ansari, "This Controversial Texas Mayor Says She Is Joining the Trump Administration," *BuzzFeed News,* March 30, 2017, https://www.buzzfeed news.com/article/talalansari/this-controversial-texas-mayor-says-she-is-joining-the; Jeff Paul, "Irving City Council Passes Resolution Prohibiting Foreign Law," CBS News DFW, March 19, 2015, https://dfw.cbslocal.com/2015/03/19/irving-city-council-passes-resolution-prohibiting-foreign-law.

46. Hooks, "Crank Factory"; Gabriel Roxas, "Protestors Accuse Richardson Mosque of Supporting Terrorism," CBS News DFW, December 12, 2015, https://dfw.cbslo-cal.com/2015/12/12/protesters-accuse-richardson-mosque-of-supporting-terrorism; Sarah Mervosh, "Armed Clash Over Black Mosque Triggers Anger in South Dallas," *Dallas Morning News,* April 2, 2016, https://www.dallasnews.com/news/news/2016/ 04/02/tense-anti-mosque-protest-draws-armed-demonstrators-in-south-dallas.

47. David Milward, "Texans Threaten to Cover Land with Pig's Blood to Block Muslim Cemetery," *The Telegraph,* July 20, 2015, https://www.telegraph.co.uk/news/

worldnews/northamerica/usa/11750259/Texans-threaten-to-cover-land-with-pigs-blood-to-block-Muslim-cemetery.html. See also Michael Phillips and Betsy Friauf, "The World That Made the El Paso Shooter," *Jacobin,* August 12, 2019, https://www.jaco binmag.com/2019/08/patrick-crusius-texas-el-paso-massacre-shooting-gun-laws.

48. Christina Caron, "Texas Man Found Guilty of Hate Crime in Mosque Fire," *New York Times,* July 17, 2018, https://www.nytimes.com/2018/07/17/us/mosque-arson-guilty-verdict.html; "Update: Arsonist Marq Vincent Perez Gets 24-Year Federal Prison Sentence," *Victoria Advocate,* October 17, 2018, https://www.victori aadvocate.com/news/crime/update-arsonist-marq-vincent-perez-gets-24-year-federal-prison-sentence/article_39cfeb16-d21f-11e8-89c1-3f12fe348ad9.html.

49. William F. McDonald, *The Criminal Victimization of Immigrants* (Cham, Switzerland: Palgrave Macmillan, 2018), 57.

50. See the Texas DPS hate crime reports for the years 2000 and 2002.

51. Elise Hu, "HuTube: Texas Congressman Warns of Terrorist Babies," *Texas Tribune,* June 28, 2010, https://www.texastribune.org/2010/06/28/tx-rep-louie-gohm ert-warns-of-terrorist-babies; Daniel Schuman, "Rep. Louie Gohmert's 'Terror Baby' Meltdown," *Mother Jones,* August 13, 2010, https://www.motherjones.com/politics/2010/08/rep-louie-gohmerts-terror-baby-meltdown; Phillips and Friauf, "World That Made the El Paso Shooter."

52. Antonio Flores, "How the US Hispanic Population is Changing," Pew Research Center, September 18, 2017, https://www.pewresearch.org/fact-tank/2017/09/18/how-the-u-s-hispanic-population-is-changing; Texas DPS hate crime reports, 2015 and 2016; Mariana van Zeller, "Anti-Latino Hate Crimes Rise as Immigration Debates Intensifies," *Huffington Post,* October 18, 2011, updated December 6, 2017, https://www.huffpost.com/entry/anti-latino-hate-crimes-rise-immigration_n_1015668.

53. Brentin Mock, "Hate Crimes Against Latinos Rising Nationwide," *Intelligence Report,* November 28, 2007, https://www.splcenter.org/fighting-hate/intelli gence-report/2007/hate-crimes-against-latinos-rising-nationwide; "The Wages of a Hate Crime," *NewsWeek,* July 4, 2007, https://www.newsweek.com/wages-hate-crime-104219; "Police: Brutalized Teen Took Drugs Before Death," NBC News, August 17, 2007, http://www.nbcnews.com/id/20327022/ns/us_news-life/t/police-brutalized-teen-took-drugs-death/#.Xs63Vy-z0lI; Paige Hewitt, Eyder Peralta, and Peggy O'Hare, "Girl Says She Heard Ritcheson Talk about Jumping," July 4, 2007, *Houston Chronicle,* https://www.chron.com/news/houston-texas/article/Girl-says-she-heard-Ritcheson-talk-about-jumping-1531986.php.

54. "Full Text: Donald Trump Announces a Presidential Bid," *Washington Post,* June 16, 2015, https://www.washingtonpost.com/news/post-politics/wp/2015/06/16/full-text-donald-trump-announces-a-presidential-bid.

55. Manny Fernandez, Richard Pérez-Peña, and Jonah Engel Bromwich, "Five Dallas Police Officers Were Killed as Payback, Police Chief Says," *New York Times,* July 8, 2016, https://www.nytimes.com/2016/07/09/us/dallas-police-shooting.html.

56. Belinda Luscombe, "8 Questions with David Brown, Former Dallas Police Chief," *Time,* June 8, 2017, https://time.com/4810491/dallas-police-chief-david-brown-called-rise; Ted Robbins, "Dallas Has Been Called a Leader in Police Training, Transparency," npr.org, July 8, 2016, https://www.npr.org/2016/07/08/485274691/dallas-has-been-called-a-leader-in-police-training-transparency; Jon Buntin, "David Brown: Caught Between Reform and a Hard Place," *Governing,* November 2016, https://www.governing.com/topics/public-justice-safety/gov-dallas-police-chief-david-brown.html; US Commission on Civil Rights, *Police Use of Force: An Examination of Modern Policing Practices* (Washington, DC: US Commission on Civil Rights, 2018), 117–18; Cassandra Jaramillo and Tommy Magelssen, "Former Dallas Police Chief David Brown to Lead Chicago Police Department," *Dallas Morning News,* April 2, 2020, https://www.dallasnews.com/news/2020/04/02/former-dallas-police-chief-david-brown-to-lead-chicago-police-department; "David O. Brown Named Chicago Police Superintendent," *Security Magazine,* April 9, 2020, https://www.securitymagazine.com/articles/92094-david-o-brown-named-chicago-police-superintendent; John Fullinwider, phone interview with Michael Phillips and Betsy Friauf, October 30, 2019. For more on the roots of American police departments in slave patrols, see Otis S. Johnson, "Two Worlds: A Historical Perspective on the Dichotomous Relations between Police and Black and White Communities," *Human Rights* 42, no. 1 (2016): 7, https://www.jstor.org/stable/26423488.

57. During the first six months of 2016, Texas police shot to death fifty civilians, only five fewer than English and Welsh police combined had gunned down in the previous twenty-four years.

58. Rachel Moran, "In Police We Trust," *Villanova Law Review* 62, no. 953 (December 15, 2017), 985, https://digitalcommons.law.villanova.edu/vlr/vol62/iss5/4; Barack Obama, "Remarks by the President at Memorial Service for Fallen Dallas Police Officers," July 12, 2016, https://obamawhitehouse.archives.gov/the-press-office/2016/07/12/remarks-president-memorial-service-fallen-dallas-police-officers.

59. Erik Ortiz and Alex Johnson, "Amber Guyger Sentenced to 10 Years for Murdering Neighbor Botham Jean," NBC News, October 2, 2019, https://www.nbcnews.com/news/crime-courts/amber-guyger-sentencing-resumes-after-murder-conviction-death-botham-jean-n1061146; "Lawyers 'Disgusted' by Release of Search Warrant Showing Marijuana Found in Botham Jean's Apartment," Fox 4 News, September 13, 2018, https://www.fox4news.com/news/lawyers-disgusted-by-release-of-search-warrant-showing-marijuana-found-in-botham-jeans-apartment; Marjorie Owens and Jason Trahan, "State Reveals Racist and Violent Texts Social Media Comments during Amber Guyger Sentencing Phase," WFAA-TV, October 1, 2019, updated October 4, 2019, https://www.wfaa.com/article/news/special-reports/botham-jean/racist-and-violent-messages-social-media-posts-shown-during-sentencing-phase-of-amber-guyger-trial/287-c1afb7ab-255c-444f-ac25-e3ba14b2f337; Cassandra Jaramillo and David Tarrant, "Local Activists Call for Re-Investigating

Fatal Shooting Involving Amber Guyger's Former Police Partner," *Dallas Morning News,* September 25, 2019, https://www.dallasnews.com/news/2019/09/25/local-activists-call-for-re-investigating-fatal-shooting-involving-amber-guyger-s-former-police-partner; Erik Ortiz, "Texts between Amber Guyger , Dallas Police Partner Revealed at Murder Trial," NBC News, September 24, 2019, https://www.nbcnews.com/news/us-news/texts-between-amber-guyger-dallas-police-partner-revealed-murder-trial-n1058051; Fullinwider interview.

60. Michel Martin, "Barbershop: Botham Jean, Amber Guyger, and Forgiveness," npr.com, October 5, 2019, https://www.npr.org/2019/10/05/767572862/barbershop-botham-jean-amber-guyger-and-forgiveness.

61. "Woman Shot Dead by Texas Police through Bedroom Window," BBC News, October 13, 2019, https://www.bbc.com/news/world-us-canada-50032290.

62. Emmie Martin, "US States with the Highest Level of Income Inequality," June 8, 2015, CNBC, https://www.cnbc.com/2018/03/12/us-states-with-the-highest-levels-of-income-inequality.html; Alex Ura, "Poverty in Texas Continues to Drop, but Inequality Remains," September 13, 2018, KERA News, https://www.keranews.org/post/poverty-texas-continues-drop-inequality-remains. For more on the concept of last place aversion, see Felicia J. Wong et al., *The Hidden Rules of Race: Barriers to an Inclusive Economy* (Cambridge: Cambridge University Press, 2017).

63. Ross Ramsey, "UT/TT Poll: Texans Say Immigration, Terror Greatest Threats to US," *Texas Tribune,* November 17, 2015, https://www.texastribune.org/2015/11/17/utt-poll-immigration-terror-greatest-threats-us.

64. "El Paso Shooting Suspect Says AK-Style Gun Came from Romania," AP News, August 28, 2019, https://apnews.com/f519fb0254de409d93a751e4fa1f8e0b; Dana Branham, "El Paso Massacre Suspect Drove 10 Hours from Allen before Killing 22 in Crowded Walmart, Chief Says," *Dallas Morning News,* August 5, 2019, https://www.dallasnews.com/news/texas/2019/08/06/el-paso-massacre-suspect-drove-10-hours-from-allen-before-killing-22-in-crowded-walmart-chief-says; Nicholas Bogel-Burroughs, "'I'm The Shooter': Suspect Confessed to Targeting Mexicans, Police Say," *New York Times,* August 9, 2019, https://www.nytimes.com/2019/08/09/us/el-paso-suspect-confession.html; Kristen Gelineau and Jon Gambrell, "New Zealand Mosque Shooter Is a White Nationalist Who Hates Immigrants, Documents and Video Reveals," *Chicago Tribune,* March 15, 2019, https://www.chicagotribune.com/nation-world/ct-mosque-killer-white-supremacy-20190315-story.html; KeithDB, "The El Paso Walmart Shooter's Manifesto and Donald Trump," Daily Kos, August 4, 2019, https://www.dailykos.com/stories/2019/8/4/1876640/-The-El-Paso-WalMart-Shooter-s-Manifesto-And-Donald-Trump; Tim Arengo, Nicholas Bogel-Burroughs, and Katie Benner, "Minutes before El Paso Killing, Hate-Filled Manifesto Appears Online," *New York Times,* August 3, 2019, https://www.nytimes.com/2019/08/03/us/patrick-crusius-el-paso-shooter-manifesto.html; Phillips and Friauf, "The World That Made the El Paso Shooter."

65. Lillianna Byington, "Black Americans Are Still Victims of Hate Crimes More than Any Other Group," *Texas Tribune,* August 16, 2018, https://www.texastribune.org/2018/08/16/african-americans; Bruce Glasrud, "Twenty-First Century Texas Race Relations," in Glasrud, *Anti-Black Violence,* 190–91.

5

GANG VIOLENCE IN TEXAS

Urban Dynamics over Time

Mike Tapia

Perhaps because its number of large cities, its high poverty rate, and its lengthy border with Mexico, Texas is perceived by many to have a high level of gang activity. The number of organized youth and adult gangs operating in the state was once ranked third in the nation, according to a survey of law enforcement in all fifty states.[1] However, the scope of the "gang problem" has been a poorly understood and politicized issue for decades, mainly leading to its overstatement in most places. Even in what appears to be a gang-abundant state like Texas, the amount of violence attributable to these groups is actually far less than most would expect. This chapter identifies some of the salient contexts for the gang violence nexus in Texas from roughly the mid-1960s to 2020. The data examined show that gang crime and crime in general are currently at record low levels in Texas. Moreover, virtually all the data presented, regardless of time period, show that gangs account for a very small proportion of total violence in the state. We see this low rate despite the conflation that is known to occur with official crime data, which overextend gang crime motives into more normative episodes of violence. While gang culture certainly promotes violence, it is also evident that high levels of violence are not constant among gangs as a whole over the last seven decades and that not all gangs share the same cultural values. Since the 1980s, gangs proliferated in Texas, but that proliferation also led to diversification. Currently, some gang cultures are more accepting of violence, while evidence suggests other gang cultures actually disavow and limit widespread violence. This difference in gang cultural acceptance of violence has contributed to the overall decline in gang-related violence since the 1990s.

Before delving into the history of gang-related violence in Texas, an understanding of the problems criminologists and historians face when evaluating gang violence is necessary. There is no doubt that gang activity is a potent context for violence. However, the amount of violence in society attributable to gangs is often grossly overestimated.[2] It is easily conflated with mundane incidents of violence involving spouses, intimate partners, other family members, and acquaintances. Domestic violence, sexual assault, and simple or aggravated assault, for example, are rather prevalent events in the general population.[3] Because gang members are enmeshed within these normative contexts for violence in their daily lives, the amount of violence attributable to gangs alone is difficult to measure and, in turn, not well understood.[4] Furthermore, like non-gang violence, the amount of gang-related violence is dependent on a number of societal factors and is therefore prone to fluctuate over time.

Gang crime data are notoriously unreliably coded, and estimates vary depending on whether counts of gang-related incidents are restricted to those that are clearly gang motivated (e.g., drive-by shootings) or are extended to include all criminal activities (e.g., sex crimes, theft, domestic violence) that simply *involve* documented gang members.[5] The reporting of gang crimes is not a requirement of the FBI in its annual collection of official data from agencies across the United States. Therefore, many police departments do not make a distinction between gang crimes and other reported criminal activities. The records that do exist are often not available to the general public, making it difficult for researchers to obtain information on gang violence unless they have an established rapport with police officials and their data gatekeepers.

Historically, the unreliability of information on gangs is not strictly tied to overreporting. Some scholars have noted that the categorization of crime incidents as gang related can be a political process, especially in places where tourism is vital to the local economy or politicians have touted public safety as a campaign promise.[6] In the past, such places were more prone to underestimate or downplay the emergence of gangs in their community. Once it became clear that the federal government was willing to fund anti-gang efforts in large sums to law enforcement and public safety agencies, however, more places were willing to admit publicly the existence of gang violence.

Adopting a universally accepted definition of a "gang" further complicates the study of gang-related violence. As of 2019, the Texas Penal Code defined a gang as "three or more persons . . . who continuously or regularly associate in the commission of criminal activities."[7] However, the debate on how to define gangs is more than a century old in the scholarly literature, and while the modern law enforcement definition is functional for statutory and prosecutorial purposes, it has oversimplified the matter for documentation purposes on the street, leading to a broadened and often misconstrued view of the gang problem.[8] The literature on the counting of gangs and gang members clearly shows that it is an inexact process.[9] Newspaper archive data from the 1950s in several Texas cities shows wildly divergent estimates of the existing number of youth gangs operating in the state.[10] Gangs are secretive and dynamic by design, so that a precise identification of them, their structures, and their activities is elusive, and therefore, any official estimates regarding the precise number of gangs operating in Texas is questionable.

The lack of consistency in reporting gang-related violence notwithstanding, it is possible to draw larger conclusions about the frequency and prevalence of gang violence over time. This chapter debunks several common misperceptions about the gang violence "problem" in Texas and highlights those contexts where this nexus is pronounced. Gang-related violence saw an overall increase from the 1950s to the 1980s as gangs expanded in response to the increased demand for drugs in the United States, competition over territory and drug markets, the availability of more lethal weaponry, and mass incarceration associated with the war on drugs. However, since the peak of the 1980s and early 1990s, gang-related violence decreased across the state as drug markets became more regulated by the gangs themselves and reliance on and support for violence dissipated among those gangs that established control over those drug markets.

In the 1950s and 1960s, gangs were less lethal than modern ones owing to two main factors. First, despite that gangs during this time accepted the murder of a rival or snitches, those incidents of violence remained sporadic and aimed at specific individuals involved in personal disputes.[11] Second, violence was limited because of the rudimentary nature of the "tools of the trade" available to gang members during this era, especially youth gangs. For example, most teenage gang members in the 1950s and 1960s used homemade zip guns as their most lethal weapons.[12] While potentially dangerous in an up-close encounter, the weapon was generally not accurate and it frequently malfunctioned due to faulty construction. Therefore, intended victims were more likely to survive an adversary's attack. In addition to zip guns, younger gang members used an assortment of switchblades, brass knuckles, and other crude weapons characteristic of the era.[13]

Of the brand of street crime seen in South and Central Texas through the early 1960s, Wilson McKinney wrote that its cities were "accustomed at worst to the violence of the juvenile street gangs and Saturday night barroom brawls."[14] There is limited empirical data on gang violence in Texas for eras prior to the 1980s. Ramiro Martinez provides an important exception, having studied homicides in San Antonio over time. He concludes that violence was more prominent for Chicano males between the ages sixteen and twenty-four in the 1950s than in the 1960s. This demographic group accounted for a large portion of murder victims in the city in both decades, but levels in the 1950s were slightly higher. Furthermore, intra-ethnic homicides of young Chicano males were much higher than that of whites and blacks during this same period. In the decades after the 1960s, Chicano rates fell, becoming more aligned with those of whites and blacks.[15]

The late 1960s and early 1970s, however, ushered in a new embrace of extreme and violent tactics to accompany a higher volume of drug trafficking and thus higher stakes in that business. This period is commonly known as the Carrasco era, as the Laredo/San Antonio-based drug cartel headed by Fred Carrasco set a new standard for drug-related

Figures 5.I. the types of weapons frequently used by juvenile gangs in the 1950s and 1960s. Courtesy of University of Texas, San Antonio Institute of Texan Cultures

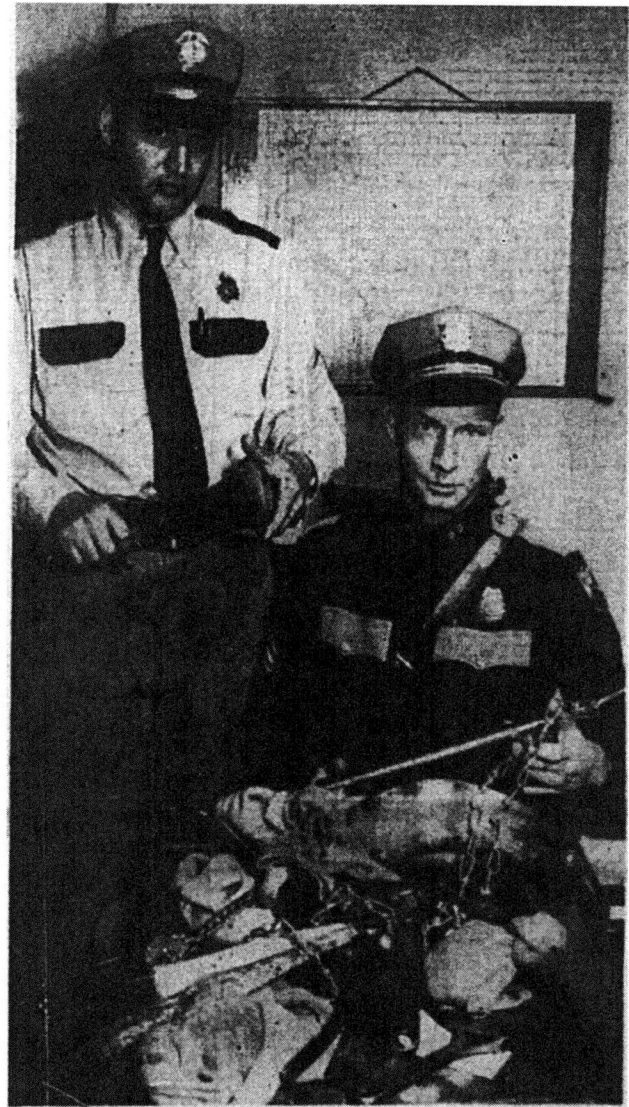

TEEN WEAPONS—Radio Patrol Sergeants Rudy Trevino, left, and Frank Gorman examine a pile of weapons seized by police who halted a juvenile gang fight.

Figure 5.2. Officers with weapons confiscated from youth gangs operating in San Antonio and El Paso in the mid-1950s. Courtesy of *El Paso Herald* (February 25, 1958).

violence in its operations that many feared and that future generations would emulate.[16] The Carrasco era marked an important chapter in South and Central Texas's modern drug-smuggling and violence history. Indeed, the violence and related drama that accompanied it on barrio streets and in Texas prisons represented a critical transformation in underworld politics that would govern those settings for the next several decades. The South Texas border region became one of the most active drug smuggling corridors, or "plazas," in the United States, earning it a designation by the federal government as a High Intensity Drug Trafficking Area (HIDTA).[17] This designation allows for an infusion of drug and human smuggling interdiction resources to enter the region in the name of homeland security. Similarly, in far West Texas, certain El Paso gangs have been influenced by hyper-violent drug cartels in Ciudad Juárez, Chihuahua, Mexico just across the border, making it one of the most militarized border zones in the United States.[18]

The numbers of homicides among young males in San Antonio plummeted in the 1980s but surged dramatically in the early 1990s.[19] While murders of young black males reached new highs during this period, rates for young Chicano males did not exceed recorded homicides of the 1950s and 1960s. Based on the available evidence, it appears that acceptance or use of violence among gangs was at least partially predicated on race. Given that San Antonio's demographic and socioeconomic composition is similar to that of other large cities in Texas, it is highly likely that this gang violence trend by race was also observed across the state.[20] Although Martinez's work lends insight to the question of which decade produced the most violent deaths among barrio and ghetto youth, his 1950s and 1960s data do not capture whether homicide motivations were gang-related activities. Thus, we are left to infer that the 1950s gang scene was more violent—but it is a very reasonable assumption.[21]

The emergence of prison gangs in Texas in the 1980s was largely due to the drastic growth of the prison population and the inmates' need to develop a form of self-governance in the wake of a failing system of institutional control.[22] This marked the beginning of a qualitatively different type of violent era in the history of Texas gangs. The sources of violence attributable to prison gangs are the "blood in" initiations (near-fatal to fatal attacks on rivals), prison riots and small wars among prison gangs of different races, clashes between rival gangs (intra-race) on the street and in prison, and the killing of a gang's own members for transgressions against the group (real, perceived, and politicized).[23] Upon expanding to the street, these groups began terrorizing Texas communities and menacing the youth gangs to cooperate with them or face violent consequences.

Since forming in the 1980s, the Aryan Brotherhood of Texas, a prison gang devoted to the cause of white supremacy, has been regarded as one of the state's most violent groups, with about one hundred murders to its credit from its founding to 2014.[24] While it tends to be somewhat more rural than other prison gangs, it has a significant presence, along with another white supremacists gang called Aryan Circle, in Ft. Worth, Houston, and Odessa.[25] However, like other prison gangs, its members can be found in most locations across Texas. Historically, its clashes have more often been with black prison gangs, namely the Mandingo Warriors and the Self-Defense Family, than with Latino prison gangs.[26]

Chicano prison gangs are noted for extorting independent drug dealers and street gangs out of a portion of their profits with the threat of violent consequences for resistance.[27] Collecting "the dime" (i.e., the street tax on non-mafia drug dealers) is enforced, initially, with a verbal threat, a *calentada* (roughing-up), and may include the taking of the cash, drugs, and weapons on site if the enforcement action occurs at the dealer's home. When such incidents are reported to the local police, law officials and the media usually define the crime as a home invasion.

Many places throughout Texas, especially the state's seven major metro areas, have a Chicano prison gang.[28] Reflecting national trends in violence, the activities of Chicano prison gangs yielded a high body count from the 1980s through the 1990s. Veteran Texas prison gang investigator Johnny Santana counted about seventy homicides between 1980 and 1999 involving the notorious Texas Syndicate alone.[29] Nonetheless, it is difficult to know the net effect of prison gang activity on levels of violence over a longer timeframe. On one hand, these groups have committed hundreds of murders since their inception. On the other hand, their existence suppresses violence levels because it organizes the underground drug market with fear and intimidation.[30] Texas prison gangs have also enacted a number of "peace treaties" over time, both within and across racial groups, which suppresses violence to maintain order.[31]

The emergence of prison gangs provides a clear demarcation point for comparing gang violence norms across several generations. Yet, the main distinction is not so much related to acceptance or use of violence but that the violence is more widespread and less restricted in terms of victims or when the use of violence is deemed acceptable. The murdering of a rival or a snitch was certainly part of the subculture of the 1940s and 1950s gangsters in Texas cities, but the main difference is that incidents were sporadic and aimed at specific individuals in personal disputes.[32] By comparison, such activities in the era of prison gangs became systematic.

These changes might be referred to as period effects—that is, evolution or sign of the times—since the United States experienced a widespread surge of gang activity and homicides beginning in the 1980s.[33] Unlike modern gang violence, the weapons and methods used in violent confrontations during the 1950s were designed for close, personal attacks. By contrast, Texas prison gangs emerged in an age of technological advance on all fronts, and once they branched out into the community, advanced weaponry enabled them and their junior affiliates on the street to threaten and harm their victims from greater distances. Prison gangs also became a selection mechanism for the most calculating, ruthless individuals within the criminal subclass of street gangs and Texas prison inmates.[34]

The typical recruit in a Texas prison gang comes from a street-oriented family and generally has a violent or lengthy criminal history that began with their involvement in juvenile street gangs. These individuals were not marginal members of their youth gangs but usually held leadership positions or were loyal soldiers with lucrative skills in auto theft, burglary, armed robbery, and other felonies. A willingness to and reputation for meting out violence against rivals is one of the most valuable assets to a street or prison gang, even if it is the individual's only skill.

At their height of power and influence, the level of brutality among prison gangs represented a clear break from the norms of earlier gangs, creating notoriety for their genre. Prison gangs of all races were considered volatile, reckless, and vindictive. However, it appears that in the long term, such levels of brutality and elitism were not sustainable, perhaps due to broader violence norms in the Texas Chicano community in particular. Prominent research on this topic shows that Latino/as and Mexican American populations in the United States experience lower levels of violence than their black counterparts.[35] Violence levels among African American gangs remain high, especially in high-poverty neighborhoods. Several salient contributors to elevated violence among gangs in these contexts include drug-crew turf disputes interlaced with those that involve mutual taunting by rap music artists in lyrics and on social media.[36]

There is widespread fear and resentment of prison gangs in the Chicano community. As violent as barrio gangs are reputed to be, the 1950s and 1960s groups "stood for something," because they were often viewed as defenders of local neighborhood turfs and traditions.[37] Compared to those groups and to the non-gang population, the extreme levels of violence among Chicano prison gangs may be pathological, as they violate long-held community value systems of respect for the barrio.[38] That is, such violence may be unnatural in the order of barrio processes because it violates "true" neighborhood norms when prison gangs extort money from individuals, local businesses, and even other illegal groups.

Gang-related violence in Texas peaked in the 1970s and 1980s but saw a precipitous decline beginning in the mid-1990s that continued into the first two decades of the twenty-first century. The beginning of the mass incarceration era, increased flow of drugs into the state, and more lethal weapons utilized by gangs contributed to the increase in gang-related violence in the 1970s and 1980s. Yet, during the 1990s, the gang disputes were more or less settled and territories well defined and under control. As a result, rates of gang-related violence went down. Although gang subculture did not completely disavow violence during this era, the realities of gang life limited the necessity of widespread violence.

In the 1990s, San Antonio, the third-largest city in Texas at the time, reportedly had the largest number of gangs of any major urban area in the state.[39] In terms of gang versus non-gang episodes, law enforcement generally codes the motives of homicides accurately. Figure 5.3 contains the proportion of homicides that were gang related for an eleven-year period.[40] Gang-related homicide was highest in 1993, mirroring the national trend. On average, about 16 percent of San Antonio homicides were gang related throughout this decade, which was a comparable estimate to the national rate for that time period and similar to the 19 percent in Dallas.[41]

Another crime that is almost always gang related is drive-by shootings. Figure 5.4 contains counts of these events in San Antonio from 1993 to 2003. Whereas there is some fluctuation over time, as in the case of homicides, the number of drive-by incidents seemed to have stabilized at a much lower level after a significant drop in incidents in 1994 and again in 1997. The peak of 1,262 drive-bys in 1993, when the county's population size was about one million, produced an alarming drive-by rate of 126.2 per 100,000 in that year, earning the city the moniker, the "drive-by capitol" of the United States.[42] The rate of drive-bys in San Antonio is decidedly extraordinary when compared to the rate of 36.6 per 100,000 in Los Angeles in the early 1990s, a time generally considered the height of the gang epidemic in California's most populated city.[43]

Violent episodes, both fatal and nonfatal, are less reliable as a measure of gang-related crime than homicides or drive-by shootings. This

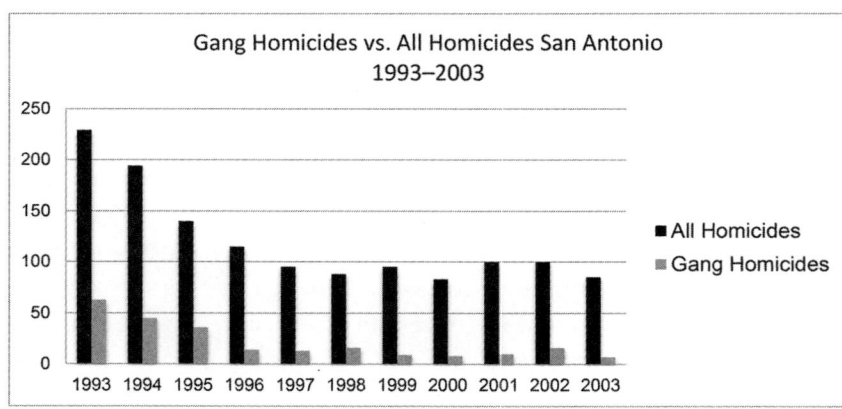

Figure 5.3. Gang homicides vs. all homicides, San Antonio, Texas, 1993–2003.

category is flawed for a number of complex reasons, including the investigating officers' skill and discretion (i.e., conflation with non-gang motivations), witnesses' fear of retaliation, and the subcultural street-code

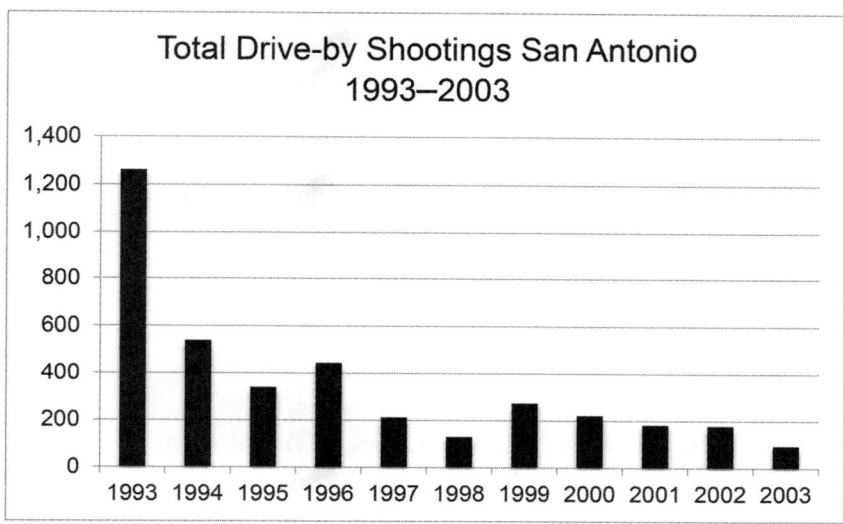

Figure 5.4. Total drive-by shootings, San Antonio, Texas, 1993–2003.

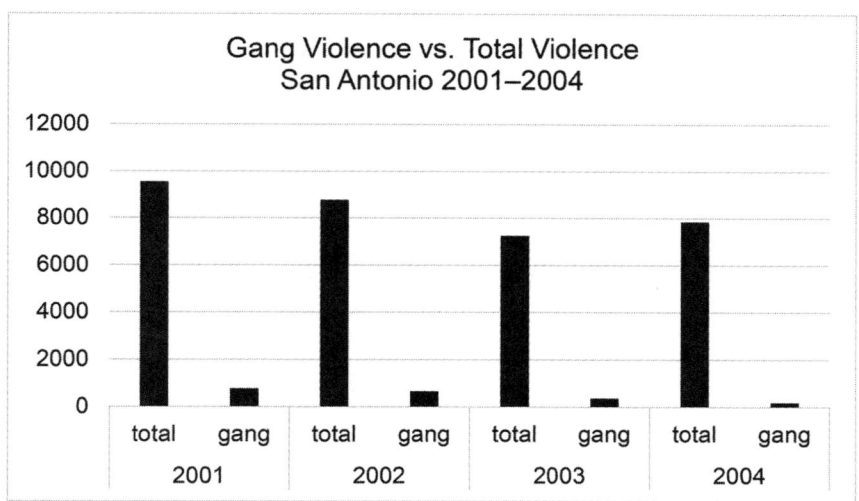

Figure 5.5. Gang violence vs. total violence, San Antonio, Texas, 2001–2004.

norm that prohibits "snitching" by cooperating with authorities, among other numerous factors. Nonetheless, the data for San Antonio, presented in fig. 5.5, is available for a restricted number of years.

In keeping with the national trend of falling violent crime rates, the number of gang-related violent incidents in San Antonio drastically decreased (by 76 percent) from 778 in 2001 to 188 in 2004.[44] These incidents were a small percentage of the city's total violent crimes. In 2001, only 8.1 percent of all violent crime was attributable to gangs, diminishing to a mere 2.4 percent in 2004. An estimate obtained with statewide gang database information for 2018 collected by the Texas Department of Public Safety indicates that gang crime has since remained at this extremely low level.[45]

Despite the overall decline of gang-related violence in the late 1990s and 2000s, several acts of violence remained pervasive. The senseless victimization of innocent bystanders in episodes of street gang violence and the intentional targeting or collateral killing of a gang member's kin are examples of the decline in values or unwritten rules that once forbade such behaviors.[46] The resentment toward prison gang brutality was also evidenced in the widespread rebellion against prison gangs by the mass of Texas gangsters for the past few generations. This revolution was primarily initiated by younger members of hybrid street-prison gangs called *Tangos,* and the leaders of this new movement have reorganized the structure of the Texas gang hierarchy in its jails, prisons, and streets.

The widespread emergence of Tango factions across the state is one of the most significant violence-generating gang activities in Texas over the past two decades. Tango factions represented a younger generation of former prison gang hopefuls that developed a fierce resistance to the prison gangs after several decades of being a critical part of their hierarchy.[47] In all major cities, these Tangos developed a collective disdain for the prison gangs' norms and methods of governance, leading to widespread, routine violence within Texas' jails and prisons. The self-proclaimed *raizon de etre* of the various Tango factions in Texas is in rebellion against overbearing prison gangs by employing a "power in numbers" strategy against their oppressors with violent attacks and resistance in lockup facilities.[48] The Tangos, primarily Latino based, are also somewhat "post-racial" in that they accept white and black members to increase their numerical strength.[49]

Outlaw motorcycle gangs (OMGs) represent another element among violent organizations within the state. Compared to traditional street or prison gangs, their status as violent groups is slightly ambiguous because their members tend to have more conventional roles in society than the typical gang member. For "one-percenter" biker gangs with a self-proclaimed affinity for and proven track record of violence, their status is less ambiguous, but there are only a handful of them across the United States, and most make efforts to camouflage themselves in daily life.[50]

Historically, the principal OMG in Texas is the Bandidos, considered one of the nation's potentially most dangerous groups with a strong presence in El Paso and San Antonio. In recent years (through 2019), the Cossacks, the Kinfolk, the Mongols, and the Vagos have emerged to challenge the Bandidos' dominance in various locales across the state. Like traditional gangs, biker gangs in Texas are involved in all forms of crime, including drug trafficking and violence. Their involvement in these activities is consistent over time but is seemingly infrequent because they are less abundant in the population than traditional gang members, who emerge from the underclass and who are less selective in their membership.

As with most serious adult gangs, there are a handful of high-profile incidents involving biker gangs in Texas, in addition to less visible incidents known mainly to law enforcement. A recent melee between disputing OMGs in Waco, Texas, was the single-most violent episode exclusively involving biker gangs in Texas. On May 19, 2015, more than two hundred members of the Bandidos and the Cossacks had a violent clash at a restaurant after a planned meeting to settle a turf dispute. The meeting ended with nine dead and more than twenty injured. Interestingly, there were no criminal convictions stemming from that event.[51]

Gang migration is thought to be a key mechanism involved in the spread of modern gang subculture, to include its types and levels of violence. When a local street gang adopts the name of a "nation" such as the Crips, the Bloods, or the Latin Kings, the implication is that they are connected to the larger group. Whether such claims are true is a topic that has been debated in the street gang literature for several decades.[52] The most authoritative voices on the gang migration topic once found little support for its role in the spread of gangs over long distances, but others have since found that it *is* a significant cause of such gang proliferation, particularly in places with newly emerging gang problems.[53]

As large as Texas is, with its seven major metro areas, its gang subculture is influenced by some of the nation's most potent gang locales. California gang subculture has affected West Texas primarily, while the Houston area is most influenced by Louisiana, Florida, and other southern states, which tend to have higher violent crime rates. Most recently, mass evacuations of New Orleans' poorest ghetto residents after Hurricane Katrina into Houston likely exacerbated the spread of hardcore gang subculture (see New Orleans' violent crime rate in table 5.1).[54]

For decades, Central Texas' main external influences have been the midwestern states. While such gang connections between the two regions are logical, given the normative migration stream of Chicanos between them, it became most evident in Dallas and San Antonio in the 1980s and 1990s. Importation of hyperviolent gang subcultures from cities like Chicago and Los Angeles and influence from the dominant gang subculture in that era seem to drive these effects.

For some context on Texas' levels of violence in general, Table 5.1 contains violent crime rates per 100,000 population for sixteen Texas cities in 2013. The data for a random set of large American cities is also included for comparison. Odessa, Texas, a city of about 165,000 people, had the highest violent crime rate in the state at 806 per 100,000. Although Midland, Texas, is part of Odessa's metro area, it has a much lower rate (286.3). Lubbock and Amarillo were tied for the second-highest violent crime rate, at about 660, with Houston ranked third at 560. Corpus Christi had the fourth-highest at 523. All other Texas cities were below 500 with some under 400 and two under 300. The violent crime rate for the state capital of Austin (not shown) was among the lowest at 360.

According to official FBI crime statistics, as of 2020, cities on the Texas-Mexico border are among those with the lowest levels of violence

Table 5.1. Violent crime rates per 100,000 population of Texas's large cities (bold) and in other large US cities in 2013.

Corpus Christi	523	McAllen	283	San Antonio	460	Abilene	399
Larado	431	Odessa	806	Brownsville	240	Amarillo	661
Lubbock	658	Midland	286	Fort Worth	362	Dallas	333
Houston	559	El Paso	347	Arlington	485	Waco	403
Baltimore	633	Las Vegas	678	Philadelphia	937	New Orleans	782
Boston	503	Los Angeles	375	Riverside, CA	333	Albuquerque	742
Sacramento	415	Miami	655	San Diego	348	S.F. / Oakland	570
Denver	328	Fresno	510	Tucson	433	Oklahoma City	821
Detroit	780	Kansas City	468	Tulsa	970	Mobile	1,413

FBI Uniform Crime Report at https://www.ucrdataool.gov/Search/Crime/Local/RunCrimeOne
YearofData.cfm

(see table 5.1).[55] In thinking about the structural and cultural mechanisms creating these low violence rates, there is no doubt that some of it is rooted in the fact that these cities are highly saturated by Latino/as, ranging between 80 and 90 percent of inhabitants.[56] Numerous criminological studies show that violence levels in US Latino communities (i.e., immigrant communities) are significantly lower than that of black communities.[57] Prominent research on this topic shows that Mexican American communities are particularly low in violence, and in some studies even less violent than white communities.[58] To the extent that gangs are a reflection of the broader ethnic community, this helps to explain low levels of violence in Latino communities despite their abundance of gangs. One illustrative case study is that of El Paso, the largest city on the Texas-Mexico border.

To investigate the prominence of juvenile gangs (so-called rat packs) in El Paso during the mid-twentieth century, city officials assembled a grand jury in June 1950.[59] In the impoverished South El Paso area, a shooting in August 1951 was attributed to a gang war that had broken out between the 7-X, 2-N, and [Lucky] 13 gangs.[60] Gangs have been a prominent part of the El Paso landscape ever since, even developing violent black gangs despite their low number in the population.[61]

Today, the Barrio Azteca (BA) is one of a dozen or so Texas Chicano prison gangs to emerge over time, with its geographic home base of El Paso as its main distinction. What distinguished the BA from most other Texas prison gangs was its unique geographic placement with Ciudad Juárez as its neighbor. Juárez's hyperviolence per its drug cartels allowed the BA to flourish in the underworld very quickly and in a way that perhaps no other US Chicano gang ever has.[62] Ironically, among large US cities, El Paso in particular has had one of the lowest violent crime rates for decades, most recently ranked as the third safest using FBI crime data.[63] Its gang subcultures are therefore over-vilified, but they are not completely benign. A paradox is identified wherein police claimed "gang crime is at a record high" in 2017, yet in 2020, the city's violent crime rates continued to be among the lowest in the United States. The same can be said of all of Texas' border cities in terms of gang violence for that year, evidencing a lack of "spillover" effects from Mexican drug cartel violence.[64]

Even older research on Latino/a enclaves in other Texas cities, including smaller border cities, have seen these protective effects as well. Nestor Rodriguez wrote that the constant influx of Mexican migrants to large southwestern cities, such as Houston, in the 1980s made the poverty experience in Latino/a areas different from that of poor populations in other US regions.[65] He noted that Latino/a immigrants tended to harmoniously mix into established Chicano communities in Houston, which we now know dilutes the effects of violence and other negative outcomes usually associated with concentrated poverty.[66] Valdez made a similar assessment for the border town of Laredo, Texas.[67]

For border cities such as Laredo, El Paso, and those in the Rio Grande Valley, poor Latino/as adjusted to high community-level rates of poverty by relying more on the informal economy, which is abundant in those regions.[68] Although the drug addiction, sex work, criminal activity, and welfare dependency that is normally associated with underclass subculture among gangs is present in all US regions, drug trafficking and its availability are more abundant in the Southwest, especially in border cities. This remains an important distinction from the traditional underclass scenario that disproportionately affects black and

Latino/a communities in Dallas, Houston, and San Antonio (i.e., large, non-border cities). Perhaps as a result, violent crime rates in those cities were usually higher than in those large Texas cities that border with Mexico in the 2010s (per fig. 5.4).

Countless contemporary writers have noted the ubiquity of drugs in El Paso/Juárez and other Texas border regions.[69] Whereas the drug trade can be a main cause of violence where the demand is high and supply is relatively low, as in non-border regions with more diverse populations, El Paso, Laredo, and cities in the Rio Grande Valley do not experience this phenomenon. The cost of drugs is relatively low, and the products are readily available, seemingly reducing the need for gang conflicts over the street markets. Moreover, prison gangs enforce the drug tax in all border cities.[70] Few dealers are known to challenge the edict, but there are certain gangs from which it is not always enforceable, and these tend to lead to isolated cases of gang violence.

For more context on the topic of gangs, race, and violence in Texas, consider the case of San Antonio, which is often likened to El Paso due to its similar size and socioeconomic makeup. San Antonio's gang patterns and Latino gang culture, while similar to El Paso's early gang activities, experienced a cultural shift away from traditional barrio gang norms in the 1980s and 1990s.[71] Although it is along Interstate 35, a major drug corridor from Laredo, San Antonio is a full two and a half hours from the Mexican border; thus, the drug economy and local gang culture are quite different from that of "border towns."[72] Eventually, many of San Antonio's Latino street gangs began to mimic black gangster subculture due to the influence of Chicago, Houston, Dallas, and even San Antonio's own black gangs, who are historically more violent than its Latino youth gangs.[73] The violent crime rate in San Antonio, while often lower than El Paso's from 1980 to 2000, far surpassed it thereafter. Perhaps El Paso's proximity to Mexico (i.e., as a perpetually Latino-saturated place) keeps its Latino gang subculture more traditional (ethnocentric) as compared to the ethnically hybridized ones in Texas cities of other regions. If so, it is possible that this relative insulation from black gang cultural influences has implications for its rates of violence.

Gang violence in Texas has a long and interesting history due, in part, to the state's size and diversity. In Texas, one of the United States' largest territories and population centers, delinquent and criminal subcultures have flourished in the modern era. With a total current population of 29 million and sixty-eight cities with population exceeding fifty thousand people, Texas' capacity for hosting these subcultures as they morph and adapt to societal change continues. The state has a violent history that began even before the formation of modern gangs. It has served as the "frontier" in westward expansion, and its binational nature on the border with Mexico has contextualized a tense area of struggle for hegemony among various groups. As some have argued, this set the tone for subcultures of violence to emerge. For gangs in the state, however, violence seems to have been influenced by more contemporary and external factors. Essentially, the midsize and larger cities further from the Mexican border had the highest violent crime rates and, by extension, the emergence of violent gang activities. Cities on the Texas-Mexico border consistently have the lowest violent crime rates despite alarmist claims of politicians that Mexican drug cartels are responsible for increasing violence along the southern border. In these regions, the high levels of Chicano gangs and the disavowal of extremely high levels of violence by those gangs (once drug markets were established) contributed to lower rates of gang-related violence. Yet, over the last two and a half decades, even among those groups considered to be the most violent, paradoxical findings were conveyed about the countervailing effects prison gangs have with outlawing drive-by shootings, signing peace treaties among themselves, and suppressing drug trade violence with street tax enforcement. In sum, gangs are undoubtedly embroiled in violence. Yet, broad assumptions about acceptance and encouragement of that behavior at all times and in all contexts overlook more nuanced understandings of who gang members are and what values they collectively promote. The history of gang-related violence in Texas demonstrates that both internal and external factors contribute to shifts in violence and the ways in which gangs decide to embrace or discourage those actions.

Notes

1. Walter Miller, *The Growth of Youth Gang Problems in the US 1970–1998,* Report (Washington, DC: Office of Juvenile Justice and Delinquency Prevention, 2001), 1–81.

2. Judith Greene and Kevin Pranis, *Gang Wars: The Failure of Enforcement Tactics and the Need for Effective Public Safety Strategies* (Washington, DC: Justice Policy Institute Report, 2007).

3. Steven Sumner et al., "Violence in the US: Status, Challenges, and Opportunities," *Journal of the American Medical Association* 314, no. 5 (August 2015): 478–88.

4. For example, in 2014, the police chief of Odessa, Texas (which has the highest violent crime rate in the state), revealed to the press that due to various factors, it is "nearly impossible to quantify" the proportion of crimes in the city that are gang related. See Audris Ponce, "DPS Assessment Reports 12 Gangs, Cliques in West Texas," *Odessa American,* May 24, 2014.

5. Greene and Pranis, "Gang Wars"; Malcolm Klein, *The American Street Gang* (New York: Oxford University Press, 1995); Malcolm W. Klein, *Gang Cop: The Words and Ways of Paco Domingo* (Walnut Creek, CA: Alta Mira Press, 2004); Cheryl Maxson and Malcolm Klein, "Defining Gang Homicide: An Updated Look at Member and Motive Approaches," in *The Modern Gang Reader,* 2nd ed., ed. Jody Miller, Cheryl L. Maxson, and Malcolm W. Klein (Los Angeles: Roxbury, 2001).

6. C. Ronald Huff, "Youth Gangs and Public Policy," *Crime and Delinquency* 35, no. 4 (October 1989): 524–37; Associated Press, "Arlington Wants Gangs Away from City's Theme Parks, Stadiums" *Odessa American,* December 25, 2007; Gini Sikes, *8-Ball Chicks* (New York: Doubleday, 1997).

7. Texas Constitution and Statutes, Penal Code, tit. 11, § 71.01(d) (2019) (criminal street gang definition), https://statutes.capitol.texas.gov/Docs/PE/htm/PE.71.htm.

8. Richard A. Ball and G. David Curry, "The Logic of Definition in Criminology: Purposes and Methods for Defining 'Gangs,'" *Criminology* 33, no.2 (May 1995): 225–45.

9. Ball and Curry, "The Logic of Definition in Criminology," 225–45. G. David Curry and Scott Decker, "What's in a Name? A Gang by Any Other Name Isn't Quite the Same," *Valparaiso University Law Review* 31, no. 2 (Spring 1997): 501–14; Finn-Aage Esbensen et al., "Youth Gangs and Definitional Issues: When Is a Gang a Gang and Why Does It Matter?" *Crime and Delinquency* 47, no. 1 (January 2001): 105–30; James B. Jacobs, "Gang Databases," *Criminology & Public Policy* 8 no. 4 (2009): 705–9; David M. Kennedy, "Constructing and Deconstructing Gang Databases," *Criminology & Public Policy* 8, no. 4 (2009): 710–16.

10. Robert Duran, *Gang Paradox: Inequality and Miracles on the US–Mexico Border* (New York: Colombia University Press, 2018); Mike Tapia, *The Barrio Gangs of San Antonio, Texas, 1915–2015* (Ft. Worth: Texas Christian University Press, 2017); Mike Tapia, *Gangs of the El Paso–Juarez Borderland* (Albuquerque: University of New Mexico Press, 2020).

11. Tapia, *Barrio Gangs;* Tapia, *Gangs of the El Paso–Juarez Borderland.*

12. Duran, *Gang Paradox;* Klein, *Gang Cop;* David Montejano, *Quixote's Soldiers: A Local History of the Chicano Movement, 1966–1981* (Austin: University of Texas Press, 2010); Tapia, *Barrio Gangs;* Tapia, *Gangs of the El Paso–Juarez Borderland.*

13. A 1953 newspaper article highlighted recent changes in the weaponry used by juvenile street gangs in Ft. Worth, Texas. It referred to these groups as "chain gangs" for the new trend of carrying and swinging large chains against their enemies and other non-gang victims. See Jud Dixon, "'Chain Gangs' Cause Plenty of Headaches," *Odessa American,* November 11, 1953.

14. Wilson McKinney, *Fred Carrasco: The Heroin Merchant* (Austin, TX: Heidelberg Publishing, 1975), 13.

15. Ramiro Martinez, *Latino Homicide,* 2nd ed. (New York: Routledge, 2014), 154.

16. McKinney, *Fred Carrasco;* Tapia, *Barrio Gangs;* Juan Santana and Gabriel Morales, *Don't Mess with Texas: Gangs in the Lonestar State* (Columbia, SC: Create Space Publishing, 2014).

17. Guadalupe Correa-Cabrera, "Security, Migration and the Economy in the Texas–Tamaulipas Border Region," *Politics & Policy* 41, no. 1 (February 2013): 65–82; Chad Richardson, *The Informal and Underground Economy of the South Texas Border* (Austin: University of Texas Press, 2012).

18. Duran, *Gang Paradox;* Rajeev Gundur, "The Changing Social Organization of Prison Protection Markets: When Prisoners Choose to Organize Horizontally Rather than Vertically," *Trends in Organized Crime* (February 2018): 1–20; Tapia, *Gangs of the El Paso–Juarez Borderland;* US Department of Justice, *West Texas High Intensity Drug Trafficking Area (HIDTA) Drug Market Analysis 2011,* (Washington, DC: National Drug Intelligence Center, 2011), 1–32.

19. Martinez, *Latino Homicide,* 156.

20. Martinez's analysis required meticulous collection of historical homicide data for the city of San Antonio. While replicable for other cities, no other such studies exist outside of those contained in this book.

21. Tapia, *Barrio Gangs.*

22. Robert Fong, "The Organizational Structure of Prison Gangs: A Texas Case Study," *Federal Probation* 54, no. 1 (1990): 36–44; Gundur, "Changing Social Organization."

23. Theodore Davidson, *Chicano Prisoners: The Key to San Quentin* (New York: Holt, Rinehart and Wilson, 1974); Fong, "Organizational Structure"; Robert Fong, Ronald Vogel, and Salvador Buentello, "Prison Gang Dynamics: A Look Inside the Texas Department of Corrections," in *Corrections: Dilemmas and Directions,* ed. Peter J. Benekos and Alida V. Merlo (Cincinnati, OH: ACJS Anderson, 1992), 57–77; Santana and Morales, *Don't Mess with Texas.*

24. Beth Pelz, James Marquart, and Terry Pelz, "Right-Wing Extremism in Texas Prisons: The Rise and Fall of the Aryan Brotherhood," *Prison Journal* 71, no. 2 (September 1991): 23–37; Santana and Morales, *Don't Mess with Texas;* Southern Poverty

Law Center, "Aryan Brotherhood of Texas," accessed March 23, 2020, https://www.splcenter.org/fighting-hate/extremist-files/group/aryan-brotherhood-texas.

25. Associated Press, "More than 70 White Supremacists Imprisoned," *Odessa American,* November 16, 2015; Audris Ponce, "DPS Assessment Reports 12 Gangs, Cliques in West Texas," *Odessa American,* May 24, 2014; Santana and Morales, *Don't Mess with Texas.*

26. Southern Poverty Law Center, "Aryan Brotherhood."

27. Avelardo Valdez, "Mexican American Youth and Adult Prison Gangs in a Changing Heroin Market," *Journal of Drug Issues* 35, no. 4 (October 2005): 843–868; Avelardo Valdez, Alice Cepeda, and Charles Kaplan, "Homicidal Events among Mexican American Street Gangs: A Situational Analysis," *Homicide Studies* 13, no. 3 (July 2009): 288–306.

28. Generally, regionalism governs the formation of such factions. San Antonio is home to the Texas Mexican Mafia, or Mexikanemi. The Texas Syndicate is big in Austin, Houston, and Dallas, while Corpus Christi is the origin of La Raza Unida. The homebase of the Hermandad de Pistoleros Latinos (HPL-45s) is in Laredo, and the Texas Chicano Brotherhood (TCB) is from the Rio Grande Valley.

29. Santana and Morales, *Don't Mess with Texas.*

30. It is a commonly held "fact" by gang unit officers and gang members themselves that Chicano prison gangs in California and Texas are responsible for subduing the early 1990s drive-by shooting phenomenon among street gangs in the barrios by "outlawing" them. The method of enforcement was that anybody who came into a large jail or prison in those states on a charge of committing a drive-by shooting on a family home was to be assaulted repeatedly, especially if innocent victims were hurt in the incident. See Klein, *Gang Cop;* Santana and Morales, *Don't Mess with Texas;* Robert Morrill, *The Mexican Mafia, La Eme: The Story* (San Antonio, TX: Mungia Printers, 2008); Al Valdez and Rene Enriquez, *Urban Street Terrorism: The Mexican Mafia and the Sureño Trece* (Santa Ana, CA: Police and Fire Publishing, 2011).

31. Santana and Morales, *Don't Mess with Texas;* Morrill, *The Mexican Mafia.*

32. Tapia, *Barrio Gangs;* Tapia, *Gangs of the El Paso-Juarez Borderland.*

33. Beth Bjerregaard and Alan J. Lizotte, "Gun Ownership and Gang Membership," *Journal of Criminal Law and Criminology* 86, no. 1 (Fall 1995): 37–58; James Howell, "Youth Gang Homicide," *Crime and Delinquency* 45, no. 2 (April 1999): 208–41.

34. Gundur, "Changing Social Organization," Mike Tapia, "Texas Latino Gangs and Large Urban Jails: Intergenerational Conflict and Issues in Management," *Journal of Crime and Justice* 37, no. 2 (February 2013): 256–74; Mike Tapia, Corey Sparks, and J. Mitchell Miller, "Texas Latino Prison Gangs: An Exploration of Generational Shift and Rebellion," *Prison Journal* 94, no.2 (March 2014): 159–79; Valdez, "Mexican American Youth and Adult Prison Gangs."

35. Ramiro Martinez Jr., *Latino Homicide: Immigration, Violence, and Community* (New York: Routledge, 2002); Martinez, *Latino Homicide;* Robert J. Sampson, Jeffrey

D. Morenoff, and Stephen Raudenbush, "Social Anatomy of Racial and Ethnic Disparities in Violence," *American Journal of Public Health* 95, no. 2 (February 2005): 225–32.

36. John Donnelly, "Two Houston Rappers Killed Outside Strip Club," Fox 26 News Houston, November 27, 2018, http://www.fox26houston.com/news/two-men-killed-in-parking-lot-of-club-onyx; Julian Gill, "Daughter of Houston Rap Artist Killed Inside Studio Speaks Out," *Houston Chronicle*, June 26, 2019.

37. Tapia, *Barrio Gangs.*

38. Robert Durán, *Gang Life in Two Cities: An Insider's Journey* (New York: Columbia University Press, 2013); Nestor Rodriguez, "Economic Restructuring and Latino Growth in Houston," in *In the Barrios: Latinos and the Underclass Debate,* ed. Joan Moore and Raquel Pinderhughes (New York: Russell Sage Foundation, 1993), 101–27.

39. Ruth Triplett, "Youth Gangs in Texas, Part II," *Texas Law Enforcement Management and Administrative Statistics Program* 4, no. 4 (1997): 1–11.

40. San Antonio Police Department, "The Status of Gangs in Our Community," City Manager's Report to Council, April 15, 2004.

41. Greene and Pranis, *Gang Wars,* 1–104; Eric Fritch, Tori Caeti, and Robert Taylor, "A Quasi-Experimental Test of the Dallas Anti-Gang Initiative," in *Policing Gangs and Youth Violence,* ed. Scott Decker (Belmont, CA: Wadsworth, 2003).

42. It is not clear where and when this informal title originated, but it was once the most common phrase uttered in popular or professional discussions of youth gang violence in San Antonio. It was even used to justify the need for federal funds for gang intervention granted to the city by the Office of Juvenile Justice and Delinquency Prevention (OJJDP) in 1996. Bolden also alludes to the city's reputation as the drive-by capitol in a similar context. See Christian Bolden, "Friendly Foes: Hybrid Gangs or Social Networking," *Group Processes & Intergroup Relations* (May 2014): 1–20.

43. H. Range Hutson, Deirdre Anglin, and Marc Eckstein, "Drive-by Shootings by Violent Street Gangs in Los Angeles: A Five-Year Review from 1989 to 1993," *Academic Emergency Medicine* 3, no. 4 (April 1996): 300–303.

44. It is not known whether San Antonio Police Department used motive-based or documented member-based criteria to generate these estimates.

45. Texas Department of Public Safety, 2019 a. TxGang Database, summary statistics, https://www.dps.texas.gov/section/criminal-investigations/texas-gang-intelligence-indexInterested researchers can request access to this database by following the instructions listed on the website.

46. For example, Martinez noted that in the 1950s and 1960s era in San Antonio, 100 percent of Latinos murdered in the sixteen to twenty-four age group were male. No young Latinas were murder victims in this era, and few Latino children or elderly were murder victims. See Martinez, *Latino Homicide.*

47. Tapia, "Texas Latino Gangs."

48. Gundur, "Changing Social Organization."

49. Tango Blast is now a statewide federation of factions, originally based out of Houston, once known as Houstone. Dallas and Ft. Worth Tangos went by D-town and Foritos, and Austin is La Capirucha (i.e., Capitol of Texas). West Texas is known as El Weso ("the bone") or Puro Tango Blast. Only San Antonio's Tango Orejon stands alone in this arrangement, as it remains unaffiliated with the rest of Texas. See Santana and Morales, *Don't Mess with Texas;* Tapia, *Barrio Gangs.*

50. Tom Barker, *North American Criminal Gangs* (Durham, NC: Carolina Academic Press, 2012).

51. Meagan Flynn, "Nine Died in the Nation's Deadliest Biker Shootout. Texas Prosecutors Couldn't Convict a Single Person," *Washington Post,* April 3, 2019.

52. John Hagedorn, *People and Folks: Gangs, Crime, and the Underclass in a Rustbelt City* (Chicago: Lakeview Press, 1988); Cheryl Maxson, "Investigating Gang Migration: Contextual Issues for Intervention," *Gang Journal* 1, no. 2 (1993): 1–8.

53. Cheryl Maxson, Kristi J. Woods, and Malcolm W. Klein, "Street Gang Migration: How Big a Threat?," *National Institute of Justice Journal* 230 (1996): 26–31; Dan Waldorf, "When the Crips Invaded San Francisco: Gang Migration," *Gang Journal* 1, no 4. (1993): 11–16; George Knox et al., "Addressing and Testing the Migration Issue: A Summary of Recent Findings," in *Gangs: A Criminal Justice Approach,* ed. J. Mitchell Miller and Jeff Rush (Cincinnati, OH: ACJS/Anderson Monograph Series, 1996); Mark E. Moreno, "Mexican American Street Gangs, Migration, and Violence in the Yakima Valley," *Pacific Northwest Quarterly* 97, no. 3 (Summer 2006): 131–38; Mike Tapia, "Latino Street Gang Emergence in the Midwest: Strategic Franchising or Natural Migration?," *Crime and Delinquency* 60, no. 4 (June 2014): 592–618; Douglass Yearwood and Alison Rhyne, "Hispanic/Latino Gangs: A Comparative Analysis of Nationally Affiliated and Local Gangs," *Journal of Gang Research* 14 (Winter 2007): 1–18.

54. Alice Cepeda et al., "Patterns of Substance Abuse among Hurricane Katrina Evacuees in Houston, Texas," *Disasters* 34, no. 2 (December 2010): 426–46.

55. "FBI stats show border cities are among the safest," *Axios,* December 1, 2020, https://www.axios.com/2020/12/01/border-cities-safest-fbi-data.

56. For demographic data for Texas border cities, see https://www.census.gov/quickfacts/. Use the search function to look up the different cities demographic profiles.

57. Scott Desmond and Charis Kubrin, "The Power of Place: Immigrant Communities and Adolescent Violence," *Sociological Quarterly* 50, no. 4 (October 2009): 581–607; Jeffrey D. Morenoff, "Racial and Ethnic Disparities in Crime and Delinquency in the US," in *Ethnicity and Causal Mechanisms,* ed. Marta Tienda and Michael Rutter (New York: Cambridge University Press, 2005); Min Xie and Eric Baumer, "Reassessing the Breadth of the Protective Benefit of Immigrant Neighborhoods," *Criminology* 56, no. 2 (February 2018): 302–32.

58. Benjamin Bradshaw et al., "A Historical Geographic Study of Lethal Violence in San Antonio," *Social Science Quarterly* 79, no. 4 (December 1998): 863–78; Martinez, *Latino Homicide;* Sampson et al., "Social Anatomy."

59. Jim McVicar, "EP Juvenile Gang Wars Exist, But Underground," *El Paso Herald Post,* February 16, 1960; Bill Montgomery, "Juvenile Authorities Say 50 Teen-Age Gangs Active," *El Paso Times,* October 20, 1956. Now obsolete maneuvers, such "grand jury probes" were political tools used by the district attorney in large Texas cities to garner support for prosecuting youth gangs in this era. See, for example, similar processes occurring around this time in San Antonio, "Judge Gives DA Credit for Youth 'Gang' Inquiry," *San Antonio Express News,* August 5, 1951.

60. "EP Police Trail Suspect in Gang Shooting of Youth," *El Paso Herald Post,* August 24, 1951.

61. Only 4 percent of El Paso's population is black, yet "modern"-style black gangs such as the Bloods and the Crips have been present in the city for nearly forty years. The dominant narrative regarding black gangs in El Paso is that they stem from gang-involved soldiers from other places who are stationed at Ft. Bliss Army Base located in El Paso. The two predominant black gangs in El Paso are the Bloods and their rivals, the Gangster Disciples (GDs), both imported from other regions. For example, the One-Trey-Five (135) Piru Bloods have New Jersey roots, and 109 Pirus have St. Louis roots. The Georgia Boys was a particularly active set of Gangster Disciples (a midwestern gang) who had violent conflicts with other servicemen and gangs native to El Paso. As of 2015, Bloods members named in a 2010 civil gang injunction were still involved in lethal violence against the Gangster Disciples. See Luis Barajas, "Drive-By Shooting Response Team," El Paso Police Department (2002), 1–14; Daniel Borunda, "223 Arrested in Crackdown," *Las Cruces Sun News,* June 30, 2008; Borunda, "Central El Paso, Freeway Shootings Linked to 'Gang Feud,'" *El Paso Times,* August 13, 2015; Josh Gerstein, "Army Transfers Could Trigger a Gang War," *New York Sun,* March 16, 2006.

62. Barrio Logan of San Diego, California, once had a profile similar to that of the BA, as it was said to have become involved with the cartel in Tijuana for some time in the 1990s, but these ties proved superficial, having weakened soon after the arrests of several key Logan members. See, for example, John Sullivan, "Gangs, Hooligans, and Anarchists," in *Networks and Netwars: The Future of Terror, Crime, and Militancy,* ed. John Arquilla and David Ronfeldt (Santa Monica, CA: Rand Corp, 1999), 99–128; United Gangs, "Barrio Logan Heights," accessed November 5, 2017, https://unitedgangs.com/barrio-logan-heights-gang. Other, less significant links between US-based gangs and Mexican cartels have surfaced in reports involving Texas border cities, but they are few and far between. For example, see Jason Buch, "Zetas and Prison Gang Members Enter Pleas in San Antonio," *San Antonio Express News,* January 11, 2013; Jose M. Martinez and Abel Montilla, "Gangs on the US Border," presentation, Texas Gang Investigator's Association, San Antonio, June 25, 2018; Santana and Morales, *Don't Mess with Texas;* US Department of Justice, "West Texas High Intensity Drug Trafficking Area." There may be other, less significant examples of such collaborations on other parts of the border, but these are some of the few major, publicized cases to date.

Some detached observers have aptly referred to the BA as one of the world's most dangerous gangs. For example, see Nicholas Casey, "Drugs Blocked at Border Fuel Juarez Murders," *Wall Street Journal,* May 22, 2010. While this title is often given to MS-13 by the press and politicians in hyperbolic fashion, by comparison to the BA, it has proven to be a glib misnomer. T. W. Ward illustrated that the roots and evolution of MS-13 are not much different than most US Latino street gangs. See Ward, *Gangsters Without Borders: Ethnography of a Salvadoran Street Gang* (New York: Oxford University Press, 2013). Under the Trump presidency, critics suggested that former Attorney General Jeff Sessions exploited the false sense of danger posed by MS-13 to the general public to further politicize the issue of Latinos and crime.

63. Adrian Mak, "Safest Cities in America," AdvisorSmith, October 11, 2021, https://advisorsmith.com/data/safest-cities-in-america.

64. "FBI stats show border cities are among the safest," *Axios,* December 1, 2020, https://www.axios.com/2020/12/01/border-cities-safest-fbi-data.

65. Rodriguez, "Economic Restructuring."

66. Martinez, *Latino Homicide;* Sampson et al., "Social Anatomy."

67. Avelrado Valdez, "Persistent Poverty, Crime, and Drugs: U.S.-Mexico Border Region," in *The New Barrios: Latinos and the Underclass Debate,* eds. Joan Moore and Raquel Pinderhughes (New York: Russell Sage, 1993), 173-194.

68. Valdez, "Persistent Poverty"; Richardson, *Informal and Underground Economy.*

69. Richardson, *Informal and Underground Economy;* Charles Bowden, *Down by The River: Drugs, Money, Murder, and Family* (New York: Simon & Schuster, 2002); Correa-Cabrera, "Security, Migration"; Howard Campbell, *Drug War Zone: Frontline Dispatches from the Streets of El Paso and Juárez* (Austin: University of Texas Press, 2009).

70. Santana and Morales, *Don't Mess with Texas.*

71. Tapia, *Barrio Gangs.*

72. Street taxes from drug sales also are collected in the barrios of San Antonio by the Texas Mexican Mafia, or "La Eme," but there is competition from the Texas Syndicate and other prison gangs and resistance by their junior affiliates. This is unlike El Paso, where the BA was the only street tax enforcer.

73. Bradshaw et al., "Historical Geographic Study"; Martinez, *Latino Homicide.*

6

VIOLENCE IN TEXAS PRISONS

Mitchel P. Roth

American prisons are inherently violent places. As one convict put it, "Violence has always been a part of prison."[1] Until the arrival of prison gangs in the late 1970s and early 1980s, Texas prison violence was far more predictable. Nowhere was there more violence than in the "tanks," or dormitories, of the state's prison farms, where inmate guards, known as building tenders, ran roughshod over inmates. Whether the Huntsville penitentiary or the farm units, violence appeared in a variety of incarnations, including rapes, riots, guards abusing convicts, inmates assaulting each other, suicides, and even self-inflicted mutilation to avoid picking cotton from dawn to dusk on the farm units.

Prison violence often is the result of private disputes and group conflicts that erupt among large populations of hardened convicts with too much time on their hands and too little room to spend it. One cannot understand prison subcultures without being familiar with the so-called culture of violence rooted inside America's prisons. One study suggests that the main cause of male violence, inside or out of prison, is the belief that one's reputation is on the line. Put another way, violence often results from a "perpetrator's sense of threat to one of his most valued possessions . . . his reputation for strength and toughness," making him unwilling to tolerate any signs of disrespect.[2]

When prisons were less demographically diverse and the prison-guard ratio more congruent, convicts in Texas and other American prisons lived according to a "convict code." This was long before the emergence of the prison gang problem. Up until the 1960s, unwritten rules dictated daily relations and the behavior of prisoners. New inmates were expected to be quickly brought up to speed on what behaviors were acceptable behind bars. Veteran convicts tutored new inmates on the rules of the yard and what forms of violence were acceptable. It was a time when inmates better understood they were all in this together and viewed prison officers, rather than each other, as the enemy. In the mid-1960s, observers noticed that a surge in prison population combined with desegregation was pushing the former convict code into obsolescence. Thus, a new generation of inmates unfamiliar with the convict code increasingly challenged the status quo in prisons across the nation.

The tumult of the 1960s caught up to the Texas prison system (TPS) in the second half of the decade. "Treatment by race" had been one of the most salient features of the system since its inception. This began to change in 1965 when individual prison units were desegregated, paving the way for the hoped-for racial coexistence it was intended to produce. However, inmates were still housed by race in separate dorms and cell blocks within the prison units and for years did not mix in dining halls or even in agricultural hoe squads. It would take another decade for the TPS to actually alter its state-sanctioned system of racial segregation.

After Texas prisons were desegregated, the Texas prison subculture underwent a major transformation. With the spread of race- and ethnic-based prison gangs in the 1980s, white inmates no longer held all the cards and were put on the defensive. As one inmate put it, there was always hatred for "the Man, always white." Solidarity held the historically oppressed minority inmates together, providing a sense of security and protection—"except from each other." Conversely, the Anglo inmates were not just fragmented, but their "symbolic representation of all that the minorities hate [kept] them victims."[3] With less effective control mechanisms and an explosion of the prison population in the state, cycles of retaliatory gang violence pushed inmate-on-inmate violence to frightening levels during the 1980s and early 1990s. The sharp increase of prison violence during this period amplified preexisting cultures of violence that traditionally existed in Texas prisons.

Yet, during the late 1990s and into the twenty-first century, the rate of prison violence decreased. This decline in violence, at least lethal violence, within the TPS mirrored declines in violence outside of prison walls across the state. It resulted from several trends. First, Texas prisons hired more prison guards and trained them more effectively to deal with growing prison populations. Second, prison guards and administrators became more familiar with prison gangs and worked to segregate gangs from each other in different prisons. Finally, an increase in prison guard violence accompanied the rise in prison populations. The use of force suggests that while lethal inmate-on-inmate violence decreased, prison culture still promotes the use of violence against inmates. In a counterintuitive way, violence is utilized to limit violence. Thus, while rates of prison violence seem to be lower in the twenty-first century than in the last two decades of the twentieth, a culture of violence still seems to predominate inside prison walls.

The so-called Texas control model dominated the state's prison philosophy for much of the 1960s and 1970s. The system was maintained in large part thanks to the strategy of using violence-prone inmates, known as *building tenders* (BTs), to control and run penal facilities, maintain order, function as mediators, and use fear and coercion to control the population. It was not unheard of for BTs to permit inmates to settle disputes with fists if conflicting inmates came to the BTs and asked to "settle it like men."[4] During this era before the prison gangs, inmates could count on relative stability when it came to violence and safety.

BTs were part and parcel of the Texas control model during the administrations of the prison directors George Beto (1962–71), who was regarded as its "chief architect,"[5] and James Estelle (1972–83). Beto firmly believed that "either you picked their leaders, or they [did]." The ever-pragmatic prison director was convinced that inmates otherwise would be at the whim of the most violent and aggressive inmates. By selecting inmates who seemed best suited for the role of BT, prison officials could circumvent some of the violence and aggression.[6] Under the regimes of Estelle and Beto, absolute control was achieved thanks to carefully selected BTs. Although both directors tried to restrain the BTs, due to budgeting in Austin, hiring an adequate full-strength civilian guard force was not in the foreseeable future. This compromise, however, allowed the Texas Department of Corrections (TDC) to operate with fewer employees while maintaining a high degree of discipline. The control model offered a predictable and stable environment on a low budget that became the envy of other states.[7]

During the era of the BTs, official guards might have been outnumbered, but they were rarely in danger from the inmates thanks to the ferocity of the BTs. A fixture of southern-themed prison films, such as *Brubaker* and *Cool Hand Luke,* BTs and trusties, or convict guards, were used to maintain control in Texas prisons, particularly the farm units, where without them, the guard-convict ratio as late as the 1970s would have been 6:50. Their impact was felt much more in the bunkhouses, or tanks, on the farm units, where more than one hundred convicts were often jammed into one large room.[8] At one time or another, inmates have been used as guards in most southern prisons. While they were theoretically constrained like the official prison keepers, for most of their existence, especially in Texas, they could be depended on to inflict maximum physical abuse on their charges at their own discretion.

BTs were considered part of an "elite" group of inmates that "directly controlled prisoners in the living area."[9] Evidence for BT violence and physical abuse on the farm units was introduced at a 1974 hearing, where inmates testified about beatings and harassment. In terms of violence and physical abuse by BTs, the Retrieve Unit was regarded as among the worst. During the 1974 hearing, prisoners recounted the "Father's Day incident" that took place on June 17 and 18, 1973.

The incident was put into motion when Warden Bobby Taylor ordered agricultural prison workers out to the fields to harvest a corn crop that was going bad due to heavy rains that had delayed harvesting. Being called out to the fields on a Sunday—and this one was Father's Day—was unusual. Convicts rarely worked en masse on weekends in any event. This particular Sunday was expected, like other Father's Day Sundays, to be a day of heavy visitation. When the hoe squads were taken out to the fields, thirteen of the three hundred men refused to work. Ten of the thirteen were charged with disciplinary infractions and confined to cells.[10]

On Monday, June 18, Director Estelle ordered Taylor to use "whatever force was necessary to put the ten men back to line work in the fields."[11] Warden Taylor selected a group of officers and instructed them to arm themselves in case the convicts refused orders. Eight guards and BTs armed with lead-lined rubber hoses, baseball bats, and axe handles walked to the administrative segregation (adseg) cell block to get the prisoners. As they were released from the cells, they were beaten by the officers as they moved along the main corridor. They suffered lacerations and bruises, and two needed medical treatment. The convicts were warned not to mention this to anyone. Ultimately, word leaked out and the disciplinary actions against the inmates were withdrawn.[12]

Out on the farm units, the BTs remained the dominant force, the "acknowledged rulers." In this era, inmates, usually black, could be punished on the word of a single BT. There are several accounts of trusties holding down recalcitrant inmates while guards whipped them with the "bat," a twenty-four-inch- long, four-inch-wide leather strap with a wooden handle.

Conversely, thanks to the existence of the BTs, correctional officers operated in a safer environment, as their inmate counterparts prowled the tanks like sharks, wielding extraordinary power. BTs controlled not only inmates but also much of the illegal activities. As one historian put it, the BT "was a vital cog in the BT machine."[13] Their dark side is rarely mentioned, but there is ample evidence that they were heavily involved in prostitution (both consensual and nonconsensual sex). It has been often reported that Beto rejected one BT due to his reputation for aggressiveness, suggesting "he would rape a snake through a brick wall." Sexual violence was clearly under the purview of the BTs, who "made sexual assault a sport" and had first choice of young, vulnerable inmates to use for cooking, laundry, cleaning, and sex.[14]

During the era of the BTs, inmates rarely fought with prison-made shanks. Thanks to the intelligence network the convict guards maintained, it was difficult for prisoners to make and keep weapons in their cells without the BTs knowing about it. Ultimately, until the 1980s, inmate fights were rarely lethal, typically consisting of fist fights, gang brawls, or violent rapes.[15] The BTs were mostly white convicts, and when it came to a dispute between whites and blacks or Hispanics, he usually sided with the white inmate. BTs tended to be older, violent repeat offenders who maintained a prisoner's compliance with his orders through a combination of physical and mental "superiority." Although there were black and white BTs, the power was not equally distributed.

BTs were able to control prison violence for the most part but there were always one-of-a-kind events that no one, neither prisoners nor officers, was prepared for. One cannot discuss violence in Texas prisons without mentioning the bloodiest day in Texas prison history in terms of lives lost. Since 1965, there has been no instance of Texas prison violence to match what transpired during the eleven-day hostage-taking siege at the Huntsville State Prison. Between July 24 and August 3, 1974, ringleader and drug kingpin Fred Carrasco, also known as the Heroin Merchant, and two other inmates held eleven hostages in a bid to break out of the prison.[16] The hostages were a mixture of inmates, guards and other prison employees, as well as a member of the clergy. Carrasco was known for his violent reputation on the streets of San Antonio and was credited with killing or ordering the executions of dozens of associates and competitors when he ran the state's largest drug trafficking operation out of South Texas.[17]

While the authorities wanted a peaceful ending, due to prison policy there was no chance that any of the prisoners would be allowed out of the prison alive. All personnel who worked inside were aware of a written TDC policy that said, "In the event any officers or employees on duty that have been seized as hostages, no officers or employees on duty shall disregard, alter, modify, or change in any manner the prescribed duties, obligations, or responsibilities of his position on demands of the prisoners. Or pleas from the hostages regardless of the consequences."[18]

Coming as it did in the wake of New York state's bloody Attica Prison siege in 1971 that resulted in thirty-nine deaths, Texas prison officials were intent on preventing a bloody replay, although things did not work out as planned. The inmates had three guns smuggled into them, a rare event in prison. Rather than the usual knife or sharpened instrument, the presence of guns created a much more complicated scenario for the authorities, one that they were unprepared for. In a violent end to the standoff eleven days after it began, Carrasco and one of his accomplices were killed and two of the hostages were shot dead by their captors as they tried to leave the building in the so-called Trojan horse, which observers called the "Trojan Taco."[19] Another hostage, Father Joseph J. O'Brien, survived a serious bullet wound.

The motivations of inmates at Attica and Huntsville differed, but in both instances, lethal violence was used either by inmates or law enforcement at the climax of each episode. According to one report, "With the exception of the Indians massacred in the late nineteenth century, the State Police assault [on Attica] which ended the four-day prison uprising was the bloodiest one-day encounter between Americans since the Civil War."[20] Referring to the Huntsville debacle, critics would later note that the authorities "sacrificed real flesh and blood individuals to a principle which is dubious," referring to the hardline policy against opening the gates for hostage-taking prisoners under any circumstances, even at the cost of hostage lives.[21]

One of the more interesting observations about prison violence during the BT era was made by Huntsville prison librarian-teacher Aline House, a hostage survivor of the Carrasco siege. In her account of the incident, she wrote, "What a dilemma for eleven individuals who had never participated in, nor been witness to scenes of extreme violence." This comment by a longtime employee gives credence to the notion that Huntsville Prison had rarely experienced "extreme violence" well into the 1970s.[22]

The 1960s civil rights movement impacted the lives of inmates, many of whom familiarized themselves with their constitutional rights. Prison lawyers and writ writers were able to challenge the legality of confinement as prisoners began to accept that "litigation was a better alternative to violence."[23] What followed was an avalanche of litigation that transformed prison conditions for better or worse. But unforeseen consequences would soon include race-based gangs spreading into the new liberal prison environment, leading to black, Hispanic and white gangs battling for supremacy behind bars. Research indicates that inmates historically self-segregated along racial and ethnic lines by choice, perpetuating the de jure segregation that characterized prisons until the 1970s.

One of the last noteworthy violent episodes involving BTs took place on October 24, 1979, when inmate Gus Feist was beaten to death by several BTs in the Retrieve Unit's main hallway. Feist was expected to testify in the 1980 *Ruiz v. Estelle* civil rights lawsuit just two weeks later, but he never made it to court. Feist's family was informed that Gus had died after hitting his head on a concrete floor in a fight with another inmate. His family filed suit charging the unit's warden, David Christian, with ordering a TDC guard and a gang of BTs to beat him for his continued criticism of the TPS. Ultimately, the case was settled out of court for what was described as "a paltry sum."[24]

The *Ruiz* court decision signaled the death knell for the control model and all that went with it. This constitutional lawsuit, brought by prisoner David Ruiz against Texas "helped dislodge traditions of plantation punishment," creating an "equally severe and larger prison system in its place."[25] Writing in 1980, Judge Wayne Justice noted, "The overcrowding at TDC exercises a malignant effect on all aspects of prison life.... Virtually all inmates are exposed to, and many are victimized by the concomitants of assaults, rapes and other violence—for every day of their incarceration."[26]

With the TDC power structure in freefall in the 1980s, convicts began to turn on guards and each other. This resistance had rarely occurred when the BTs were at their apogee. Guards had felt protected, but now the tide had turned, to the point where guards became afraid and leery of inmates. As a result, in contrast to the era of the Texas control model, correctional officers became more concerned for their own safety and were purportedly more likely to accede to convict demands. Guards would trade information with each other on which convicts they should not cross. One veteran sergeant admitted his own compromises, explaining, "I've been struck several times, been bitten by inmates. Some of them, I'm afraid of. I'm afraid to say something to them because I know what I'm going to get if I do say something to them. A lot of times, I avoid [them]—if I see an inmate do something wrong, I just completely ignore it. I just walk off it. And I know it's not right, but a lot of people are doing it, a lot of supervisors are doing it because it—like I say, I'm afraid of certain people here, I'm not going to say nothing to them 'cause I know them."[27]

Once they were removed, guards could no longer count on BTs for backup. Moreover, the ability to administer extralegal physical punishments was restrained. One veteran guard noted that "it's changed because you can't put that boot in their ass. . . . Ain't no fear anymore." With change in policies facilitated by the court cases, between 1983 and 1986, assaults more than quintupled from 733 to 4,144 a year.[28]

During the James Estelle years, the Texas prison underwent a significant increase in overcrowding, rising from sixteen thousand in 1972 to thirty-six thousand in 1982. As a result, prisons resorted to extraordinary measures, including double, triple, and quadruple celling, a situation that became increasingly difficult to maintain, leading to the expansion of the BT system. Under his predecessor, prison work strikes and homicides were rare. They became more frequent under Estelle. Between 1960 and 1975, the number of homicides and rapes rose precipitously.

Once the control model was abolished and the BT system dismantled, "racial animosities, once controlled and contained, became more overt, creating considerable tension."[29] Compared to the former prison model, any violence that took place was officially sanctioned and rarely reported. With the transition to a new paradigm, everyone seemed to be carrying prison-made knives, or shanks, and violence increased.[30] With the BTs out of the way, it was time for inmates to settle old scores, and inmate-on-inmate violence escalated to levels never seen before. Without BTs lording over them, prisoners were able to fashion lethal instruments from almost any material they could find. In 1984 and 1985, there were respectively twenty-five and twenty-seven homicides. The numbers more than doubled the previous highs of twelve in both 1981 and 1982. In addition, the nature of murders changed. Multiple offender attacks became more prevalent, and more than half the assailants in both single offender and multiple offender incidents were identified as prison gang members. The rash of murders ended in the late summer of 1985 when suspected gang leaders were sent into adseg.[31]

Between the late 1960s and early 1980s, despite the continued but unofficial existence of BTs, fights between inmates sometimes took place. As one prison official noted, back then, inmates knew that they not only had to defeat their opponent but also had to be ready to deal with the BTs if they caught them or found out they had been fighting. As the former correctional officer put it, "He had to win quickly because if the BTs intervened, it didn't matter whether the victim needed medical attention or not . . . [the] aggressor, whether he won or not, might end up in the hospital." Before knives became ubiquitous among inmates, when there were fights, they usually "ended decisively and didn't last more than a half dozen punches." [32]

The first five years of the 1980s were among the most violent in the prison system's history. The decade started out with the killings of Ellis Unit Warden Wallace Pack and farm manager, Officer Billy Max Moore, the highest-ranking Texas prison officials to die in the line of duty. Both were killed on April 4, 1981, by convict Eroy Brown, who was being transported in a car by the two officials, when he stole a gun out of the warden's holster. Brown shot Moore in the struggle for the weapon and drowned the warden in a drainage ditch. Brown surrendered meekly to officers when they arrived, and he claimed self-defense. Prior to the *Ruiz* decision, Brown would no doubt have ended up on death row. Surprisingly, he was acquitted during a jury trial. [33]

The killing of the two high-ranking administrators was just the beginning, albeit the incident was unrelated to gang violence. Both lethal and nonlethal stabbings became commonplace, at least compared to the previous era. In 1984, there were 404 nonlethal stabbings, dropping to 168 the following year. Much of the violence was driven by gang animosities. In August 1985, a black inmate was stabbed seventeen times in a recreation room inside the Clemens Unit and died in the prison hospital. Four members of a white supremacist gang surrendered and were placed in isolation. In retaliation, black inmates assaulted four white inmates in the same unit, none fatally. The following month, an inmate in Ramsey II was fatally stabbed to death. Around the same time, an Ellis II Unit inmate was mortally wounded, stabbed seventeen stab times with a sharpened metal spoon, making him the fourth murder at the unit in this time period. [34]

The *Ruiz* decision was a major contributing factor to the development of prison gangs, as it triggered a wave of race violence and disorder in Texas prisons. [35] Inmates were drawn to gangs for protection and the opportunity to have a place in the new power structure. The turmoil set off by federal court decisions (*Lamar v. Coffield* and *Ruiz v. Estelle*) disrupted the prison system, leading to "social change, population displacement, and political disorganization."[36] With the Texas prison units now desegregated, and the BTs abolished, it forced a realignment of the convict power structure. By most accounts, in terms of race, the new power structure had its heaviest impact on white inmates, who found themselves socially and politically displaced "as the formal political alignment with prison officials shifted to allow the emergence of black assertiveness commensurate with the physical plurality of black inmates."[37]

One of the unforeseen results of America's punitive war on crime was a growing racial disparity behind bars. As prison populations rose to unprecedented levels, nationally, the rates of incarceration continued to vary by region, with the South imprisoning more people per capita than other regions.[38] In the racially and ethnically stratified prisons of the modern era, after a new inmate hears the gate of freedom slam behind them, they enter a subculture that few first-timers are prepared for, no matter how much they think they are. Typically, they have to navigate the various inmate cliques. Prison yards are usually broken down into distinct racial categories, where segregation is strictly enforced. In a large state prison complex, the new "fish" is likely to become familiar with the "woods," short for peckerwoods, or the whites; the "kinfolk," or blacks; the "Raza," or Americans born of Mexican descent; the "paisas," or native Mexicans; and in some prisons, the "chiefs," a Native American contingent. It is essential that newcomers become familiar with the unwritten rules of the prison yard pertaining to interracial relations. For example, it is acceptable for individuals from different races to play on the same teams, whereas there is a prohibition against playing individual games, such as chess, outside the prisoner's race.

Inmates can be in a cubicle with another race if the situation warrants it, but they never sit on each other's beds or watch each other's televisions. They can attend the same churches but cannot pray together. However, in case these rules are accidentally broken, the consequences are usually not too grim. Worst-case scenarios include getting a talking to from one of the leaders (who can claim an exception to the rule) or a punch in the face. When it comes to the dining halls, rules are sacrosanct. Races are never supposed to dine together, with violations harshly sanctioned. An inmate could expect a severe beating, and if they eat off the same tray, they will end up in the hospital. Eating from the same piece of food can be viewed as a capital offense as well.

Until the mid-1980s, Texas prisons remained mostly free from gang violence. But bloodshed between the Mexican Mafia and the Texas Syndicate and between the Aryan Brotherhood and the Mandingo Warriors (black prison gang), in 1984 and 1985, resulted in the murders of fifty-two prisoners in a twenty-one-month period.[39] In 1985, the TPS began locking prison gang members in adseg. This move was deemed the first step toward cutting violence, reasoning that allowing members to roam prison yards was too dangerous for the general population.[40] The following are brief descriptions of some of the more prominent Texas prison gangs.

With the appearance of race-based prison gangs in Texas and elsewhere in the 1980s, some observers suggested that historically, white convicts had "not been organizationally minded" because they lacked a heritage of oppression to draw them together like Hispanics and African Americans.[41] The best known and oldest white prison gang in the country is the Aryan Brotherhood (AB), formed in California's San Quentin Prison around 1968. The ABs promote a white supremacist agenda and are known for their deadly attacks on other prison gang members, quite often their own. Active both on the street and behind bars, their activities range from extortion and contract killings to drug trafficking and prostitution.

The Aryan Brotherhood of Texas (ABT) first appeared in Texas in late 1984 or early 1985, and by the end of that year was considered such a threat that the officials placed known members into lockup. It was founded in Texas mainly as a criminal enterprise and does not have ties to the original AB. Despite claims of solidarity, members have been arrested for hurting fellow brothers in and out of prison, going as far as torching tattoos off bodies, hacking fingers off a corpse to keep as a trophy, and ordering the deaths of informants to be as "messy as possible." ABTs reserved some of the harshest violence for its own members and associates. Members are rewarded for these grisly retaliatory acts with sought-after tattoos that include the AB motto, "God Forgives, Brothers Don't."[42]

The growth of the ABT was based on the lost status of white inmates. They had no compunction about killing another inmate in full view of staff and other inmates. While other gangs waited until the appropriate moment when no one was looking, ABT members took a different route that ensured their status and reputation for violence in the prison demimonde. It was common for white inmates to target black inmates for "disrespecting whites." Some accounts report ABTs pursuing black inmates around recreation yards with knives and stabbing others through open food slots.[43]

Gang members were responsible for a disproportionate amount of prison violence in the 1980s. In 1984, they made up only 2 percent of the prison population but committed more than half the inmate-on-inmate murders. What is most surprising from an outsider's perspective is that most attacks involved gang members from the same race and ethnicity. In the words of one observer, "Racial violence always took back seat to the savagery inflicted by gang members on enemies, usually of the same race."[44] In a federal trial targeting the ABTs, it was revealed that "they were mostly killing each other, and when a hit was ordered on an informant, the assassin was ordered to make the death "as messy as possible."[45] According to a study by the Anti-Defamation League (ADL) in 2013, the Aryan Brotherhood was the "most violent extremist group in the United States," responsible for "at least 29 murders between 2000 and 2012." Particularly disturbing is the fact that 41 percent of their murders between 2000 and 2012 were "internal killings."[46] It is not uncommon for a member to target another member suspected of snitching or trying to start a splinter faction.

ABTs are careful to weed out potential informants before they even join the gang. Prospects are required to show government-issued proof of their criminal credentials by providing FBI-issued rap sheets that chronicle arrests, convictions, and sentences. One journalist described these documents as "resumes of bad deeds."[47] In the 1980s, prospects were required to be Texas natives. While it tolerated killers, kidnappers, and drug dealers, by most accounts, child molesters or rapists were regarded with the highest disdain and would do well to avoid ABT members in prison at any cost.

For the rest of the 1980s, the prison administration ratcheted up its pressure on the ABT, leading to internal conflict within the organization. One of the more salient issues between members was the racism implicit in its white supremacist agenda. One member proclaimed, "This racial shit has the heat on us to begin with. . . . Texas Aryan Brotherhood is an organized crime family, not the KKK or Aryan Nations. . . . No more power plays and no more Aryan Nations shit."[48] By 1988, the ABT had splintered into smaller groups and no longer commanded the loyalty it once enjoyed.

According to at least one warden, by the 1980s, the Texas Syndicate (TS) was the most powerful and violent prison gang in Texas. While there is little substantiation for the warden's claims, he asserts it was officially founded at the Retrieve Unit in 1971 by ex-convicts from California.[49] It did not earn its predilection for bloodshed until the mid-1980s, after the demise of the BTs and restraints placed on staff by federal courts. The TS is a Texas-based prison gang that includes mostly Hispanic members and on rare occasions allows Caucasian members to join. More so than other Hispanic gangs, it has been associated or allied with Mexican immigrant prisoners, while the others tend to associate with US-born or raised Hispanics.

The advent of the gang problem, brought about by the rapid organizational changes at TDC, exacerbated the traditional Texas social cleavages and made self-protection the best reason for joining gangs. For more than thirty years, it has been recognized that the emergence of violent prison gangs is closely related to "rapid fundamental changes in prison," especially in Texas.[50]

Between the 1970s and the end of the century, prison gangs adhered to traditional standards of behavior, criminality, and structure. However, as American prisons continued to become more overcrowded with younger inmates unfamiliar with these traditions, the leading prison gangs such as the Mexican Mafia, the TS, and the AB have found themselves on the decline in many prisons due in no small part to the fact that recent gang members refuse to follow the traditional principles, disrespecting other convicts and guards alike. A new generation of gangster has come of age on the streets, where loosely structured street gangs are united more by one's hometown than by racial or ethnic pride.[51]

By most accounts, the new generation is much less likely to adhere to traditions set by older gangs. For example, more traditional prison gangs such as the ABT and the TS expected members to seek authorization from their higher-ranking members before using violence against another prisoner. In stark contrast, many of the younger generation of gang members seem to act on impulse and eschew the longer approval process when they act. One of the newer gangs is the Texas prison gang Tango Blast. One observer compared the gang to "the headless horseman," adding that "Tango will take anybody."[52] Without a true leadership structure or even shot-callers, Tango Blast also creates many more problems because unilateral violence is much harder to control.

In 2015, the Texas Department of Public Safety (TDPS) branded TB as the "top gang threat to Texas," attributing its growth to its lack of a delineated hierarchy, lack of constitution/by-laws, and especially its lack of a "blood in, blood out" mandate. TB membership now outnumbers that of older prison gangs. Further distinguishing TB from its precursors is that when members of Mara Salvatrucha (MS-13) or Southern California affiliated gang members (*Sureños*) enter a Texas prison where none of their fellow members are residing, they can join TB. In any case, "Due to its liberal guidelines and loosely organized structure," Tango membership will continue to exceed other rival prison gangs.[53]

Violence remains a constant presence behind bars in Texas. Yet there is no denying the decline in inmate-on-inmate murders since the 1980s. For one, weapons are not as available. Material for shanks was everywhere in 1980s, from metal spoons in dining halls to metal fans sold in the commissary. A fans could be used to make dozens of shanks from its blades and grill alone. Inmates seemed always armed with razor sharp weapons. However, these materials are harder to get now; inmates eat with plastic cutlery. But the ever-innovative inmates manage to find materials for making lethal knives and cutting instruments nonetheless.[54] Inmate-on-inmate violence is by most accounts probably underreported, as are sexual assaults and suicides. Violent deaths might have declined, but the main factors behind inmate violence remain: racism and intergang conflict.

Between 1995 and 1997, Texas was opening a new prison almost every week. By 1997, it had 112 prisons (compared to California's thirty-three).[55] Most of the prisons were built in rural, mostly white, pro-prison communities. The Terrell Unit opened in October 1994. Most of its guards (75 percent) were white, while the inmate population was more than 80 percent African American and Hispanic. Texas is like other states that have seen prison building as the linchpin to rural economies, offering jobs for mostly white guards who were tasked with policing mostly urban minorities. Not surprisingly, this imbalance often led to clashes, many violent. On another note, Terrell is in East Texas, just sixty miles from where James Byrd Jr. was dragged to his death by white supremacists (and former Texas prison gang members) in Jasper in 1998. One journalist suggested that the level of racial animosity at the prison was "not much different" from other parts of East Texas.[56]

Journalist Joseph T. Hallinan observed the "constant clash" between rural white guards and inner-city inmates, which was attributed to "a lack of understanding of cultural issues."[57] He cites as an example the case of several guards beating a black inmate to death in 1994. One of them went on trial the following year, which Hallinan calls "almost unprecedented, only the second time that a guard was charged with killing an inmate. The guard was a relatively new hire, working in a high-security wing where tensions ran high and the most troublesome inmates were housed. Inmates in this wing and elsewhere in Texas formed "armies . . . reconstituted versions of street gangs from Dallas and Houston [that] consisted almost entirely of black and Hispanic convicts." It was not long before the gangs seized control of their pods in Terrell, "shaking down convicts for money and sex."[58]

Non-gang-affiliated inmates and the rookie guards were on constant alert because of the gangs. Modern studies of correctional officers agree that in the first few months, the new guard is "stunned, dazed and frightened." One 1967 study concluded that new recruits experienced shock equivalent to the "17-hydroxycortico-steroid levels comparable to those in schizophrenic patients in incipient psychosis, which exceed levels in other stressful situations."[59] Perhaps one officer put it best when he testified at trial, "If you're not scared, something's wrong with you."[60]

Ultimately, the aforementioned guard, Joe Boy, was found guilty in the beating death of the inmate, the first time in the 145-year history of the prison system that a civilian guard was convicted of killing an inmate. Sentenced to ten years for manslaughter on March 16, 1995, he was set free after only three months and was happy to change professions to become a truck driver.[61]

In the last decade of the twentieth century, guards in some units were still afraid of approaching known gang members. One officer testified in the 1990s that he had never "stopped a gang member from murdering an inmate." In the words of one officer from Ellis I, "If the opportunity exists, they're gonna make the hit. If you tell them, 'Put that knife down,' he'll look up at you and say, 'I ain't through yet.'" One needs to be familiar with the gang credos to understand that if someone is ordered to kill someone and does not make the hit, they will then become the target somewhere up the line.[62]

In the most exhaustive study of modern Texas prison gangs, two gang scholars identified fifty different prison gangs in the Texas prison system. However, of these, only a dozen fit the "classic profile organizational and violent," while the others mostly lacked structure and leadership. The authors of this study make a strong case that since only about 20 percent of the prison population belongs to gangs, the only way they can hold on to their clout behind bars is through violence, using it to resolve disputes, protect their revenue streams, and discipline members.[63]

In 2003, Travis Trevino Runnels was serving seventy years when he killed thirty-eight-year-old prison supervisor Stanley Wiley in the Clements Unit boot factory. Using the typical weapons of choice inside prison, he used a knife to slice "his neck to the bone." During his subsequent trial, an investigator for the state's Special Prosecution Unit, which handled prison crimes, told the jury "about the danger and violence inside the Texas prison system." In 2003, "the prison system was a violent place."[64] Runnels had a long history of misbehavior behind bars, hitting an officer in the jaw and throwing bodily fluids and lightbulbs at officers. Those who testified against him included several inmate witnesses. They described the murder as premeditated and unprovoked and said that Runnels even told other prisoners he was "going to do something." As for motive—he wanted to work in the barber shop instead of the boot factory. His execution by lethal injection on December 11, 2019, was the ninth in Texas for the year.[65]

One important caveat to the decline in inmate violence in prisons is the likelihood of an increase of force used by prison guards. While it is difficult to track rates of prison guard violence, some studies have suggested an increase. In recent years, three Texas inmates have been killed by prison officers as their "use of force continues to rise." Figures for 2019 indicate 11,000 use-of-force incidents involving staff, compared to 6,624 in 2009, suggesting a dramatic uptick in the use of force by prison officers in those years. Use of force can range from just pushing an inmate up against a wall to spraying the convict with chemical agents. Prison officials attribute the rise in use of force by officers to a variety of issues, including the incarceration of more violent and mentally ill inmates over the past decade.[66] Conversely, physical assaults on guards have fluctuated, rising only 12 percent since 2009 to 106 in 2019, compared to a 66 percent rise in officer use-of-force cases over the same time period.

Violence remains a mainstay in Texas prisons in the twenty-first century. Like its counterparts in the South and other regions of the country, it can best be explained by the inherent qualities of overcrowded and poorly funded prison systems, staff shortages, lack of training, and the high turnover rate of veteran officers. Assaults, rapes, and killings continue to plague the system, yet it is a far cry from the cycle of violence that characterized the Texas prison system following the *Ruiz* decision. For instance, in November 2019, Texas reported its fifth inmate-on-inmate murder of the year. Home to more than a hundred prisons and a population of just over 146,00 prisoners, Texas typically sees only about four inmate-on-inmate homicides a year in its prison system. Inmates are far more likely to die by execution (nine in 2019), suicide, or natural death than to be murdered by another inmate.[67] Despite the decline in violence overall, it is clear that a culture of violence persists in the Texas prison system.

Notes

1. Jorge Antonio Renaud, *Behind the Walls: A Guide for Families and Friends of Texas Inmates* (Denton: University of North Texas Press, 2002), 124.

2. Richard E. Nisbett and Dov Cohen, *Culture of Honor: The Psychology of Violence in the South* (Boulder, CO: Westview Press, 1998), xv.

3. Nisbett and Cohen, *Culture of Honor,* 132–33.

4. Ben Crouch and James W. Marquart, *An Appeal to Justice: Litigated Reform of Texas Prisons* (Austin: University of Texas Press, 1989), 99.

5. John DiIulio, *Governing Prisons: A Comparative Study of Correctional Management* (New York: Free Press, 1987), 105.

6. DiIulio, *Governing Prisons,* 112.

7. Lon Bennett Glenn, *Texas Prison Tales: The Largest Hotel Chain in Texas* (Scotts Valley, CA: CreateSpace Independent Publishing, 2016), 17.

8. David M. Horton and George R. Nielson, *Walking George: The Life of George John Beto and the Rise of the Modern Texas Prison System* (Denton: University of North Texas Press, 2005), 140.

9. David M. Oshinsky, *Worse than Slavery: Parchman Farm and the Ordeal of Jim Crow Justice* (New York: Simon & Schuster, 1996), 85.

10. Steve J. Martin and Sheldon Ekland-Olson, *Texas Prisons: The Walls Came Tumbling Down* (Austin: Texas Monthly Press, 1987).

11. "TDC Inmates Testify," *Huntsville Item,* July 21, 1974.

12. Martin and Ekland-Olson, *Texas Prisons.*

13. Robert Perkinson, *Texas Tough: The Rise of America's Prison Empire* (New York: Metropolitan Books, 2010), 244.

14. Perkinson, *Texas Tough,* 244.

15. Crouch and Marquart, *An Appeal to Justice,* 99.

16. See, for example, Wilson McKinney, *Fred Carrasco: The Heroin Merchant* (Austin: Heidelberg Publishers, 1975); Aline House, T (Waco: Texian Press, 1975); William T. Harper, *Eleven Days in Hell: The 1974 Carrasco Prison Siege at Huntsville, Texas* (Denton: University of North Texas Press, 2004).

17. See Mike Tapia, *The Barrio Gangs of San Antonio, Texas, 1915–2015* (Fort Worth: Texas Christian University Press, 2017); Mike Tapia, "Barrio Criminal Networks and Prison Gang Formation in Texas," *Journal of Gang Research* 25, no. 4 (2018): 45–63.

18. House, *Carrasco Tragedy,* 112.

19. Harper, *Eleven Days in Hell,* 294. The Trojan horse, dubbed the "Trojan Taco" by the press, was central to Carrasco's plan to break out of prison. The apparatus was no more than a makeshift shield built of portable chalkboards taped together and surrounded by a substantial layer of law books. The three inmate captors stayed inside it with four hostages. Eight other hostages were tied to the exterior as a form of protection. The inmates could look out through peep holes as they made their way down the ramp leading to the courtyard.

20. New York State Special Commission on Attica, *Attica: The Official Report of the New York State Special Commission on Attica plus 65 Pages of On-the-Scene Photographs* (New York: Praeger, 1972), xi. For the best account of the uprising, see Heather Ann Thompson, B*lood in the Water: The Attica Prison Uprising in 1971 and Its Legacy*(New York: Pantheon Books, 2016).

21. House, *Carrasco Tragedy*, 112; King Waters, "Won't Give In to Carrasco, Says Prison Official," *Houston Chronicle,* July 25, 1974, 4.

22. House, 82.

23. E. Rotman, "The Failure of Reform," in *The Oxford History of the Prison: The Practice of Punishment in Western Society,* ed. Norval Morris and David J. Rothman (New York: Oxford University, 1998), 172.

24. Glenn, *Texas Prison Tales,* 128.

25. Glenn, 244.

26. Quoted in Martin and Ekland-Olson, *Texas Prisons, 169.*

27. Crouch and Marquart, *Appeal to Justice,* 175.

28. Perkinson, *Texas Tough,* 311.

29. Crouch and Marquart, *An Appeal to Justice,* 238.

30. Perkinson, *Texas Tough,* 312.

31. Crouch and Marquart, *An Appeal to Justice,* 238.

32. Glenn, *Texas Prison Tales,* 96.

33. For the best account of the case, se, Michael Berryhill, *The Trials of Eroy Brown: The Murder Case That Shook the Texas Prison System* (Austin: University of Texas Press, 2012).

34. Glenn, *Texas Prison Tales,* 99.

35. Glenn, 99; Crouch and Marquart, *An Appeal to Justice,* 238.

36. Mary E. Pelz, James W. Marquart, and Terry Pelz, "Right-Wing Extremism in the Texas Prisons: The Rise and Fall of the Aryan Brotherhood in Texas," *Prison Journal* 71, no. 2 (Fall-Winter 1991): 27.

37. Ibid., 23–37.

38. Scott Christianson, *With Liberty for Some: 500 Years of Imprisonment in America* (Boston: Northeastern University Press, 1998), 280.

39. David C. Pyrooz and Scott H. Decker, *Competing for Control: Gangs and the Social Order of Prisons* (New York: Cambridge University Press, 2019).

40. Dane Schiller, "Prisons Work to Cut Use of Solitary," *Houston Chronicle,* August 22, 2016.

41. Pelz et al., "Right Wing Extremism." See also John Irwin, *Prisons in Turmoil* (Boston: Little, Brown, 1980).

42. Dane Schiller, "Feds Target Aryan Gang,'" *Houston Chronicle,* November 26, 2012, A1, A6.

43. Pelz et al., "Right Wing Extremism."

44. Renaud, *Behind the Walls.*

45. Schiller, "Feds Target Aryan Gang."

46. Jon Kelly, "Aryan Brotherhood of Texas: How did Neo-Nazi Prison Gangs become so Powerful?" *BBC News*, April 4, 2013, https://www.bbc.com/news/magazine-22019433.

47. Dane Schiller, "Aryan Brothers: Resume Is Required," *Houston Chronicle*, September 6, 2012, A1, A17.

48. Pelz et al., "Right Wing Extremism."

49. Glenn, *Texas Prison Tales*.

50. Crouch and Marquart, *An Appeal to Justice*, 204.

51. Mike Glenn, "Gang Membership Growing in Texas," *Houston Chronicle*, April 18, 2014, p. 282.

52. Glenn, "Gang Membership Growing in Texas."."

53. Texas Joint Crime Information Center, *Texas Gang Threat Assessment: A State Intelligence Estimate* (Austin: Texas Department of Public Safety, August 2015), 35. https://www.dps.texas.gov/director_staff/media_and_communications/2015/txGangThreatAssessment.pdf.

54. Renaud, *Behind the Walls*.

55. Norval Morris and David J. Rothman, eds., *The Oxford History of the Prison: The Practice of Punishment in Western Society* (New York: Oxford University, 1998), 18–19, 28.

56. Joseph T. Hallinan, *Going Up the River: Travels in a Prison Nation* (New York: Random House, 2001), 87-88.

57. Joseph T. Hallinan, *Going Up the River: Travels in a Prison Nation* (New York: Random House, 2001), 88.

58. Hallinan, *Going Up the River*, 86–88.

59. Peter G. Bourne, "Some Observations on the Psychological Phenomena Seen in Basic Training," *Psychiatry* 30, no. 2 (1967), cited in Ted Conover, *Newjack: Guarding Sing Sing* (New York: Random House, 2000), 12.

60. Hallinan, *Going Up the River*, 89.

61. Hallinan, 90.

62. Robert Draper, "A Guard in Gangland," *Texas Monthly*, August 1991, https://www.texasmonthly.com/news-politics/a-guard-in-gangland.

63. David C. Pyrooz and Scott H. Decker, *Competing for Control and the Social Order of Prisons* (New York: Cambridge University Press, 2019).

64. Keri Blakinger, "Killer of Prison Official Executed," *Houston Chronicle*, December 12, 2019, A3, A4.

65. Blakinger, "Killer of Prison Official Executed."

66. Jolie McCullough, "Three Texas Inmates Have Died at the Hands of Prison Officers as Use of Force Continues to Rise," *Texas Tribune*, February 7, 2020.

67. Keri Blakinger, "State Prisoner's Death Probed as Homicide," *Houston Chronicle*, November 29, 2019, A7.

7

BEYOND THE GUN

A Brief Examination of Mass Shootings in Texas

Kenneth W. Howell

On the morning of August 1, 1966, Charles Whitman, an architectural engineering major and trained Marine sniper, made his way to the observation deck of the University of Texas (UT) at Austin Tower, dragging behind him a footlocker that contained an assortment of weapons, including a high-powered hunting rifle and a small store of supplies. From his perch, Whitman could clearly see a large span of the campus below. Calmly, he peered down the scope of his rifle and at 11:48 a.m., just as classes were being released and students were making plans for lunch, he squeezed off his first round. For more than ninety minutes, Whitman continued to randomly target pedestrians below. By the time Austin police officers were able to breach the assassin's defensive position and stop the massacre by gunning him down, Whitman had wounded more than thirty people and killed fourteen others. As details emerged, authorities discovered that the shooter's killing spree started before he arrived on campus. Sometime during the night before the shooting, Whitman murdered his mother, Margaret, in her Austin apartment and his wife, Kathy, in the couple's home. After arriving on campus and as he made his way to the top of the tower, he murdered a receptionist and two individuals touring the campus with family members. The remainder of the victims were wounded or killed once Whitman began his sniping rampage.[1] At the time, the shooting represented the deadliest mass shooting by a lone gunman in the history of the United States, and it was the first of its kind to take place on a college/university campus.[2]

The tragedy that transpired at the UT campus on August 1, 1966, was the first mass shooting in Texas during the modern era. While most scholars place this event within the category of a large-scale public shooting, they likely differ on their definitions of the term *mass shooting,* especially given that federal and state agencies have slightly different definitions of the term.[3] For consistency, this chapter employs the definition of mass shooting as defined by criminologists Jaclyn Schildkraut and H. Jaymi Elsass: an incident of targeted violence carried out by one or more shooters at one or more public or populated locations. Multiple victims (both injuries and fatalities) are associated with the attack, and both the victims and location(s) are chosen either at random or for their symbolic value. The event occurs within a single twenty-four-hour period, though most attacks typically last only a few minutes. The motivation of the shooting must not correlate with gang violence or targeted militant or terroristic activity.[4]

While the historical record reveals that public shootings occurred prior to the 1960s, the UT Tower shooting was a transformative event because it was larger in scale than previous incidents and received unprecedented coverage in the media.[5] For the first time in the history of journalism, media outlets covered a mass public shooting live from the scene, capturing the chaos of people scrambling for their lives and hiding behind structures that shielded them from the view of the assailant. News cameras recorded Austin police officers as they engaged Whitman and offered aid to those who were wounded in the mayhem. In the days that followed the shooting, the media continued to cover the story. Within one month after the incident, the *New York Times* ran seventeen articles on the event, and the *Dallas Morning News* printed sixty-eight.[6]

The UT Tower shooting occurred at the beginning of a new crime wave in the United States that lasted for more than three decades. Between 1966 and 1991, homicide rates rose drastically, except for a slight downturn in the early 1980s. According to criminologists, the changes in the homicide rates were consistent with other crime statistics. Scholars argue that the changes in crime rates were related to dynamic social changes occurring in the nation, including an expanding workforce. As more people entered the workplace, a consequence of the maturing baby boomer generation and the successes of the women's rights movement, "interactions between individuals became more distant and superficial—people were more likely to look out for themselves and less inclined to watch out for others, particularly people they did not know."[7] Further, changes in the workforce "increased the number of targets (or potential victims) that were available to would-be offenders."[8]

Aware of the growing crime rate, Americans turned to the federal government for solutions. In the early 1980s, President Ronald Reagan and his administration sponsored legislation designed to reduce criminal activities, "including mandatory sentencing, habitual offender laws, reduced judicial discretion, and longer prison terms."[9] Despite these efforts, crime rates continued to rise, peaking in the early 1990s. As the turn of the century approached, however, the continued efforts of the US Congress and state legislatures finally produced notable results. Since the mid-1990s, the crime rate has continually declined.[10]

Between 1966 and 2020, thirty-three mass shootings occurred in Texas. While these incidents shared certain similarities, each episode was unique in terms of the shooters' motives, the number of casualties, the types of weapons used in the shooting, and the attention that the event received from journalists and politicians. These differences notwithstanding, some general trends emerged over the decades. For example, the locations of the shootings have been relatively consistent. The most frequent occurrences of the mass shootings have been in the workplace (seven cases), closely followed by restaurants and bars (five), churches (four), universities and public high schools (three), military bases (three), private homes (three), and retail stores (one). In addition, four random shootings either occurred at multiple locations or took place along highways and busy streets, and in three shootings, police officers were specifically targeted. Another common trend is the number of shootings that have occurred in each decade. Between 1966 and 2010, Texas experienced between three and five mass shootings every ten years. This trend remained consistent until the second decade of the twenty-first century, when the state witnessed nineteen mass shootings, more than the previous four decades combined.

There were also certain similarities between the shooters involved in these incidents. One of the more common characteristics of the shooters was that they had previously been diagnosed and treated for mental health issues, but they also experienced other similar traits, such as financial stress, undiagnosed physical and emotional anguish, domestic disputes with estranged spouses, and a desire to seek revenge against individuals or groups whom allegedly wronged the shooter in some way. Furthermore, all the mass shooters in Texas during the modern era were males, although in at least one case, there was a female accomplice. Despite these similarities, however, the perpetrators of mass shootings are different in many important ways, including age, race, and socioeconomic status.[11] Another major difference is the intended targets of the gunmen. In many cases, shooters targeted a specific individual or group, but in other incidents, their victims were selected at random. Regardless, even in cases where there appeared to be predetermined victims, innocent bystanders were frequently killed or wounded during the melees.

There was less commonality among the victims of mass shootings. In large-scale public shootings, the victims were randomly selected with little regard for age, race, or gender. For example, in the UT Tower shooting, Whitman fired indiscriminately at individuals on campus who crossed his line of sight. In other incidents, the shooters were more familiar with their victims. The targets of these assailants ranged from estranged spouses, employers, coworkers, or classmates. It is the unpredictability of mass shootings that strikes fear in the hearts of the public, causing a sensation that they might be gunned down while shopping at their local grocery store or that their children might be the victims of the next school shooting. Statistically, this fear is unwarranted, but it remains beneath the surface, nevertheless. In some ways, the expectations of being a victim of a mass shooting has become a cultural phenomenon. The only way to deal with these concerns is to be more informed about mass shootings and to identify commonsense approaches to preventing these types of violent incidents in the future.[12]

Mass shootings in Texas during the modern era can be divided into two chronological periods: The first phase covers the years between 1966 and 2011. Unlike other forms of violence documented in this volume, where criminal activities increased until the early 1990s and then declined, the number of mass shootings were virtually nonexistent in the 1960s and 1970s, when the UT Tower was the only mass shooting to occur within the state, but they became more common between the 1980s and the early 2000s with the number of incidents in each decade averaging between three and five episodes. The second phase encompasses the years between 2011 and 2019. Also counter to other forms of violence traced in this collection that continued to decline during this decade, the number of mass shootings increased. There were more mass shootings during this ten-year period than in the previous four decades combined.

Furthermore, unlike the other forms of violence documented in this collection, it does not appear that a culture of violence significantly impacted or shaped mass shootings in Texas. According to some scholars, the cultural identities of regions and states are directly influenced by the amount of violence experienced during their historical development. In certain cases, a culture of violence emerges, leaving a distinct heritage that continues to shape and direct modern social and cultural trends. This theory argues that a culture of violence leads citizens to accept or justify certain types of violent acts and criminal behaviors.[13] If this theory holds true for Texas, it is not overly apparent in the mass shootings that occurred within the state after 1965. Mass shootings are a unique form of violence, and there are too many variables involved with these incidents to claim that a culture of violence is directly responsible for these types of events. While citizens of Texas may have developed an expectation that mass shootings will continue to occur, the vast majority do not condone or justify the actions of assailants involved in these incidents. Without widespread acceptance or justification in society, it is difficult to interpret mass shootings within the context of a culture of violence. Thus, if scholars are going to develop a clearer understanding of mass shootings, it may be beneficial to examine common trends associated with these events.

The period between 1966 and 2011 is significant because common patterns related to mass shootings were established and have remained constant. To identify these baseline trends, it is necessary to examine the shootings in chronological order, according to the decades in which they occurred. The first two decades were relatively calm, as only one incident occurred—the UT Tower shooting. However, beginning in the early 1980s, Texas witnessed an increase in mass shootings with rampages taking place at the First Baptist Church in Daingerfield in 1980, the Western Transportation Company in Grand Prairie in 1982, and the Ianni's Club in Dallas in 1984. Local and national media outlets, including both broadcast stations and newspapers, covered all three events, but nationwide coverage tended to be more limited. While some scholars might attribute the increase in shootings to economic, social, and political changes within the state, circumstances related to the events do not support their conclusions. Only the Western Transportation Company shooting was indirectly linked to economic concerns; the other two incidents were more random in nature. All three events, however, exhibited elements of a personal vendetta against the victims.

The shooter involved in the attack on the First Baptist Church in Daingerfield was Alvin Lee King III, a former math teacher at Daingerfield High School. On Sunday, June 22, 1980, King arrived at the church wearing army fatigues, a flak jacket, and a helmet. He brought with him an AR-15 rifle with a bayonet, an M-1 rifle, two pistols, and a pack filled with 250 rounds of ammunition. At approximately 11:20 a.m. during the church's morning service, King kicked in the front door of the building and shouted, "This is war." He then began firing indiscriminately into the congregation, killing five congregants and wounding ten others. Though some locals claimed King was an atheist, the shooter's motives did not appear to be related to religious convictions. Instead, in the months prior to the shooting, King's daughter had accused him of incest, prompting a criminal investigation and a subsequent indictment. As part of his defense, King had asked several townspeople, many of whom were members of the First Baptist Church, to testify as character witnesses at the pending trial. For a variety of reasons, no one in the community agreed to appear on the defendant's behalf. On the morning of the shooting and the day before his trial was to begin, King overpowered his wife and tied her to a kitchen chair, armed himself, and drove to the church, apparently motivated by a sense of revenge. Following his rampage, King unsuccessfully attempted to commit suicide by shooting himself in the head. Surviving the self-inflected wound, he was charged with five counts of murder and ten counts of attempted murder. However, before his case went to trial, King hung himself in his prison cell.[14]

Two years after the events in Daingerfield, John Felton Parish, a truck driver for Western Transfer & Storage Inc., went on a shooting spree, killing six people and wounding three others, before police shot and killed him. Prior to the incident, the supervisor at the Jewel T distribution center, a client of Western, complained that Parish was a troublemaker and requested that the driver not be sent to their facility again. Western honored Jewel T's request, fearing that they would lose their contract with the distributor. In addition, and perhaps related to being reassigned to other jobs, Parish believed that his paycheck was substantially less than he had calculated. He had a heated argument with his supervisor about the discrepancy in pay. These issues undoubtedly led to Parish entering the Western building on August 9, armed with an M1 carbine and two pistols. Once again, a heated argument ensued, leading Parish to shoot and kill his supervisor as well as a fellow truck driver and an operations manager. Following the initial confrontation, the shooter fled the building and walked down the street to the Western truck yard, where he shot and killed another individual and wounded two others. He briefly held a fourth person hostage before releasing her and stealing one of the company trucks. Next, Parish drove to the Jewel T distribution center, where he killed two more people and wounded another. Near the distribution center, Parish hijacked an eighteen-wheeler truck, which he later crashed into a police barricade, forcing the truck to skid into a nearby building. As he crawled from the damaged truck and tried to escape, police officers shot him multiple times before he fell dead. Like the King shooting, this incident was partly fueled by revenge, but unlike the event in Daingerfield, the rampage in

Grand Prairie was scattered over different locations and resulted from the actions of a disgruntled worker.[15]

The final mass shooting that took place in Texas during the 1980s occurred at the Ianni's Club, a popular nightclub in Dallas. Abdelkrim Belachheb, a Moroccan national, entered the United States through Los Angeles in 1981. He later became a permanent legal resident by marrying an American citizen. After working at a restaurant in Los Angeles for a year, he relocated to Dallas. According to one friend, Belachheb often dressed and acted like a playboy and tried desperately to fit into American society. A former roommate also noted that the thirty-nine-year-old Moroccan frequently suffered from severe bouts of depression. In Dallas, Belachheb worked several jobs before securing a position as the headwaiter at Augustus's Restaurant in Addison. This job proved temporary, however, and on the night of the shooting, he picked up his final paycheck before heading to the Ianni's Club for a night on the town. At the nightclub, he was dancing with Marcelle Ford, when the two engaged in a heated argument on the dancefloor. After the encounter, Belachheb left the club, returning moments later with a pistol he retrieved from his car. He located Ford and shot her multiple times. The shooter fled the club again but returned after he had reloaded his weapon. Once inside, he began firing indiscriminately into a crowd of people. Before fleeing a third and final time, Belachheb had shot six more people, killing five instantly and wounding one. Within a few hours, the murderer called the police and surrendered without further violence. At trial, Belachheb's defense attorney unsuccessfully entered a plea of temporary insanity on behalf of his client, but a jury found him guilty and sentenced him to life in prison because the shooter's crimes were not defined as capital offenses under 1984 legal statues. Following this incident, the Texas Legislature passed House Bill 8 (the multiple murder statue), which classified serial killings and mass murder as capital crimes, closing the loophole that had allowed Belachheb to escape the death penalty.[16]

In the 1990s, Texas witnessed a general decline in crime rates, including homicides.[17] During the same decade, however, the incidents of mass shootings in the state slightly increased. Statistically, the increase was minimal and did not appear to be a major shift from the previous decade. In other words, the shootings were not the result of major changes in the state's economic, social, or political environment. Instead, the number of mass shootings occurred at approximately the same rate as during the previous and subsequent decades. Also, the shootings in the 1990s followed trends associated with earlier incidents, especially in relation to the location of the events (i.e., workplace, churches, schools, restaurants, or bars). Further, many of the shooters suffered from mental illnesses, such as depression, and were motivated by a sense of revenge. There was one general trend that began to emerge in the 1990s that counters one of the modern myths associated with mass shootings—the shooter's choice of weapons. Most media and political pundits argue that AR-15 rifles (a semiautomatic rifle that has the appearance of a military-style weapon) are commonly used in mass shootings.[18] However, the shootings in Texas in the 1980s and subsequent decades demonstrate that the weapons most frequently used in mass shootings were semiautomatic pistols.

The first mass shooting of the 1990s occurred at a Luby's Cafeteria in Killeen, a small rural town in Central Texas. On October 16, 1991, this violent rampage began when George Hennard drove his pick-up truck through the front window of the cafeteria. Believing an accident had occurred, diners in the restaurant approached the vehicle to see if they could provide aid to the driver. As they drew closer, Hennard opened fire with two pistols. The assailant left his truck and calmly walked through the cafeteria shouting at the patrons and targeting random individuals, particularly women. The event lasted for approximately ten minutes before police arrived on the scene and exchanged gunfire with the shooter, hitting him twice. Severely wounded, Hennard moved to the bathroom hallway in the back of the restaurant, where he used his final bullet to commit suicide.[19] This incident left twenty-three dead and twenty-seven wounded. The shooter's apparent motives in this case are difficult to define but undoubtedly were related to troubled affairs with women, a strained relationship with his parents, a history of drug abuse, and mental health issues.[20]

At the time, the Luby's massacre was the worst public mass shooting in the history of the nation.[21] Given the scale of the event, it is not surprising that the shooting received extensive media coverage. As

Texans learned more about the bloody incident, they began to demand changes to the state's gun statutes. One of the staunchest advocates for revising existing gun laws was Suzanna Gratia Hupp, a survivor of the shooting who lost both of her parents in the incident. In the months that followed, Hupp expressed her frustrations that she legally owned a handgun but had to leave the weapon in her car outside the restaurant to comply with Texas' concealed weapons statutes. She argued that if her gun had been in her purse on the day of the shooting, she might have been able to limit the carnage and possibly save her parents. During the years following the Luby's massacre, Hupp became a staunch advocate for Second Amendment rights, testifying at hearings across the nation in favor of concealed-carry laws, and between 1996 and 2006, she served in the Texas House of Representatives, advocating for the Second Amendment and supporting changes to the state's gun laws. In part, her efforts led Texas Governor George W. Bush to sign a new concealed weapons bill in 1995.[22]

The second mass shooting of the decade occurred at Palo Duro High School in Amarillo, Texas, on September 11, 1992. It represented the first of two high school shootings in the state during the modern era. The day of the incident began like any other Friday morning at the school during the fall semester. Students gathered at a pep rally in the school's activity center to show support for their football team, which was scheduled to play later that day. As students began to return to class after the rally, Randy Earl Matthews, a seventeen-year-old transfer student from Memphis High School, pulled a small caliber pistol and began targeting classmates in the hallway. Kevin Dockery, the liaison officer at the school, was in the front office when he heard the shots. After calling 911, the officer, accompanied by a teacher, began to search for the shooter. They located Matthews and chased him through the hallway, forcing him from the building. Dockery and the teacher continued their pursuit a few blocks from the school, where they found the assailant hiding between two houses with another student. Matthews drew his weapon but did not use it against his pursuers. The other student, who was also armed, threw his gun under a nearby parked car. Matthews surrendered without further incident, and Dockery placed both students under arrest, holding them until police officers arrived at their location and took custody of the youths. In the end, Matthew had shot and wounded six male students, and another student suffered injury as a result of being trampled in the hallway by his classmates as they fled the building.[23]

Unlike in many school shootings, all of the victims survived. On the Monday following the incident, Matthews was arraigned on one count of attempted murder, five counts of aggravated assault, and one count of unlawfully carrying a weapon on a school campus. Later, he was convicted of the charges and sentenced to eight years in prison for his crimes. While the motive was unclear, some speculated that the shooting spree was associated with gang activity, though others claimed that Matthews had been bullied by his peers and had been in a fight with another student before school on the morning of the shooting. Matthews had attended Palo Duro High School for only nine days before the incident and was deemed an outcast by many of his classmates, especially the athletes. The episode saw limited coverage in local news outlets but virtually none in the national press. Interestingly, the community and school officials took immediate action to strengthen security on their campuses with the hopes of preventing similar incidents from occurring in the future. They increased the number of liaison officers throughout the district, enacted a student Crime Stoppers phone number where suspicious behaviors can be reported anonymously, initiated crisis management procedures, and fostered programs designed to educate students about the consequences of bullying.[24]

The next two mass shooting to occur in Texas were incidents of workplace violence. On April 3, 1995, James Daniel Simpson entered the front door of the Walter Rossler Company, a refinery inspection firm in Corpus Christi, Texas. Armed with two pistols, Simpson methodically moved from one office to the next, shooting and killing the owner of the company, the owner's wife, and three employees. Having moved through the building, Simpson exited through a back door and shortly afterward used one of his pistols to commit suicide. The twenty-eight-year-old assailant had previously worked at Walter Rossler Company as a metallurgist but quit eight months prior to the shooting over work-related disagreements with the owner. It remained unclear, however, whether Simpson's previous dispute with his employer was the motive in the case. At least one forensic psychiatrist speculated that Simpson suffered from depression and paranoia even though the shooter had no history of mental health issues. Others familiar with the case claimed that the shooting was the result of workplace violence and vengeance.[25]

Six months after the shooting in Corpus Christi, Charles Lee White entered the ProtoCall store, a paging company in San Antonio, Texas, and killed his girlfriend and another employee. A second coworker was wounded in the melee before Lee turned his rifle on himself and committed suicide.[26] This act of violence differed from other workplace shootings because the motive for the murders were more related to domestic violence than the actions of a disgruntled employee. Unlike the Walter Rossler Company murders, the media provided virtually no coverage of the ProtoCall shooting. Given the lack of media coverage, the actual number of recorded mass shootings is brought into question. While the number of shootings in the 1990s appears to be nearly double that of the previous decade, it is possible that incidents like the ProtoCall murders might have been officially reported in the 1980s as homicides instead of mass shootings and that media outlets might have covered the incidents in a similar fashion. It is just as likely that subsequent decades witnessed more shootings than law enforcement agencies reported or than media coverage would otherwise indicate.[27]

The last high-profile shooting in Texas during the 1990s happened at the Wedgewood Baptist Church in Fort Worth on September 15, 1999. This event took place a few months after the Columbine High School shooting in Littleton, Colorado, on April 20, 1999, and while the shootings were unrelated, coverage of the Wedgewood First Baptist Church incident received wider national scrutiny, especially given that several of the victims were high school students.[28]

On the evening of the Wedgewood Baptist Church shooting, approximately 150 teenagers assembled for a social program that was the culminating activity for the annual "See You at the Pole" event, where young Christian students gathered at the school's flagpole, affirmed their faith in God, and prayed about problems confronting society. Around seven o'clock, Larry Gene Ashbrook, a jobless loner who suffered from schizotypal disorder, abruptly entered the church sanctuary where students were gathered. Armed with two pistols, Ashbrook, slowly and methodically, targeted those inside, murdering seven people, including three adults and four students, and critically wounding seven others. At one point, the gunman lit a pipe bomb and rolled it down an aisle; however, no one was harmed when the bomb exploded. The event last approximately eight minutes, ending when the assailant sat down in one of the pews and turned his gun on himself. Ashbrook had no affiliation with the church or any of its members. While the shooter shouted antireligious obscenities, it was theorized that he suffered from a psychotic episode related to the death of his parents (his mother had died nine years earlier and his father died two months before the shooting) and financial stresses related to his inability to maintain employment.[29] The Wedgewood Baptist Church shooting was the second mass shooting to occur at a Texas church in the modern era, however, unlike the Daingerfield shooter, Ashbrook apparently was not motivated by revenge.

In the first decade of the twenty-first century, Texas witnessed four mass shootings. While these events followed the same general trends established in previous decades regarding location, each shooting had unique characteristics that set them apart. For example, the Mi-T-Fine Car Wash shooting in Irving, Texas, proved more complex, combining the motives of workplace violence and theft. Robert Wayne Harris, who had worked at the car wash for ten months prior to the shooting, noticed that an armored car picked up cash receipts from the business every day except Sunday. Therefore, Harris knew a large amount of cash would be in the company's safe on Monday morning. On Wednesday, March 15, 2000, Harris engaged in sexual misconduct in front of a female customer, leading to his arrest and termination of employment. On Sunday, Harris barrowed a car from one friend and a pistol from another. The next morning, Harris returned to the car wash before it opened for business. He led the manager, assistant manager, and cashier into the main office at gunpoint, where he forced his former boss to open the company safe. Once he had secured the money from the safe, Harris shot the three employees and cut the throat of the manager with a knife. Before he could make his escape, he shot three more employees who had arrived for work, killing two of them and leaving one permanently disabled. Law enforcement officers later apprehended Harris at the home of friend. After being detained, he confessed to the murders. In addition to the murders at Mi-T-Fine Car Wash, Harris confessed to abducting and murdering another woman in November 1999. Prior to these events, Harris had been involved in numerous criminal acts, including three previous convictions for burglary of a building, a history of assault and battery, and dealing illegal drugs. Harris was convicted of capital murder and sentenced to death by lethal injection. During the sentencing phase of the trial, the prosecutor in the case stated that Harris was motivated by "hatred, revenge and greed, nothing more."[30]

Mass shootings in the Lone Star State continued to demonstrate the complexities often associated with workplace violence. Like the Proto-Call shooting, the AMKO Trading Store shooting in Houston, Texas, resulted from issues related to domestic violence. However, the case also involved economic grievances waged against a rival businessowner. On January 9, 2001, a northwest Houston convenience store owner, Ki Yung Park, killed his estranged wife and placed her in one of the coolers at their store before traveling to AMKO Trading Store, a wholesale business in southwest Houston, where he entered the store with two pistols in hand and shot the owner, his wife, and their daughter, killing all three. After police arrived on the scene, Park used one of his weapons to commit suicide. Park had apparently worked with the owner of AMKO Trading Store years prior to the shooting and had a cordial relationship with him and his family. However, their friendship deteriorated when Park became stressed over business losses and marital problems. Park blamed the wholesaler for his economic problems and accused him of having an affair with his wife.[31]

While the causes of the AMKO Trading Store shooting were multi-faceted, investigators were able to piece together Park's motives in the killings. However, the Century 21 shooting in San Antonio, Texas, left investigators puzzled over the apparent motives linked to the violent rampage. On July 23, 2003, Ron G. Thomas walked into the Century 21 real estate office where he worked as a liaison between management and trainees, cleared off his desk and the walls in his office, then pulled out a concealed pistol and shot three of his coworkers, killing two and wounding one. The shooter fled the scene in his vehicle, traveling northeast along Interstate 35. After driving approximately 130 miles, police officers were able to catch up with Thomas at a location north of Temple, Texas. As they closed in on his position, the assailant used his weapon to commit suicide. According to investigators, Thomas was a former Army recruiter but had worked for Century 21 for several years. He had not been under any psychiatric counseling or taking any medications. The investigators claimed to have uncovered evidence that Thomas was a control freak who disliked the idea that his supervisors were females. However, this was not consistent with the testimony of the shooter's coworkers nor family members of victims who stated that he was a top salesman and a good office mentor. Of those who knew Thomas, none could point to a motive for the rampage. However, according to investigators, others claimed the real estate agent had a violent streak. Like many mass shootings, this case left survivors and investigators with more questions than answers.[32]

Not all shootings in Texas prior to 2011 took place at civilian locations. Two mass shootings at the end of the decade occurred on military bases—Fort Hood on November 5, 2009, and Fort Bliss on September 20, 2010. The incident at Fort Hood, a US Army base located in Killeen, Texas, does not fit neatly within the definition of mass shootings because it had possible ties to terrorism and targeted military personnel. However, some scholars have defined the incident as a workplace mass shooting, especially considering that the event involved a single shooter and multiple casualties. On November 5, 2009, Nadal Malik Hasan, a US Army major serving as a psychiatrist, entered the Soldier Readiness Center, where Army personnel received routine medical treatment immediately prior to and on return from deployments overseas. Armed with two handguns, Hasan opened fire, targeting soldiers in uniform. As he was leaving the building, a local civilian police officer employed at the base arrived on the scene and engaged the shooter. The officer wounded Hasan and restrained him in handcuffs, bringing an end to the rampage. During the incident, which lasted approximately ten minutes, Hasan fired more than two hundred rounds, killed thirteen individuals, and left thirty others wounded. As the shooting progressed, Hasan was shot four times. The final shot damaged his spinal cord, leaving him paralyzed from the chest down.[33] Even though Hasan's rampage was confined to the base, the community of Killeen was reminded of the bloody event that had transpired during the Luby's cafeteria massacre the previous decade.

Subsequent investigations found that Hasan was in direct communications with known terrorists, but Army investigators and government officials avoided discussing the shooter's motives and refused to bring charges of terrorism against him. Instead, the Army officially charged Hasan with thirteen counts of premeditated murder and thirty-two counts of attempted murder on July 20, 2011, under the Uniform Code of Military Justice. At trial, Hasan was found guilty on all counts on August 23, 2013, and five days later, a US military court sentenced him to death. Believing that government officials failed to properly identify the shooting as an act of terrorism, the families of the victims filed a wrongful death claim against the US government, Hasan, and the estate of Anwar al-Awlaki (*Manning et al v Esper et al,* US District Court, District of Columbia, No. 12–01802). A federal judge, however, dismissed the suit in early 2019.[34]

Fort Bliss, located in El Paso, was the scene of the second shooting on a military base. On September 20, 2010, Steven Kropf, a sixty-three-year-old citizen of El Paso and retired Army sergeant, entered the Shoppette Convenience Store and shot two females, killing one and critically wounding the other. The women were civilian employees of the Army & Air Force Exchange Service, which operates merchandise stores on military bases, including fast-food restaurants and convenience stores. Following the shooting, Kropf left the store and was in his vehicle when military police arrived at the scene and confronted him. Having prepared for active-shooter scenarios in the wake of the events at Fort Hood, the officers responded to the incident in less than three minutes. Following a brief gun battle with the assailant, the officers shot and killed him. The FBI found no apparent motive for the case, especially considering that the victim who was killed worked at another store on the base and only stopped at the Shoppette location to pick up more Halloween candy to restock the shelves at her location. In the days following the shooting, the incident received widespread news coverage, which is not surprising considering it occurred less than a year after the

Fort Hood massacre. However, media outlets quickly dropped the story, leaving the public to draw their own conclusions about the shooter's motives.[35]

The second phase of mass shootings in Texas occurred between 2011 and 2019. This period was characterized by a rapid increase in the number of large-scale shootings as well as noticeable changes to the general trends established in incidents that transpired in the previous decades. Aside from shootings occurring more frequently, there were subtle changes in the locations where some of the incidents took place. Four of the shootings occurred at random locations where the shooter had little or no connection to the area. These types of shootings often began along highways, but in one case, the assailant initiated his attack from a building because the location apparently provided an ideal vantage point for a gun battle with authorities. Regarding the latter location, the shooter had traveled from outside of the state to commit his heinous crime. In addition, some of the mass shootings occurred within residential homes, and one incident happened at a large retail store. Though some locations of the shootings changed during this period, other locales were consistent with attacks in previous decades, including two church shootings, three at restaurants and bars, and one at a public high school. Surprisingly, given the number of workplace shootings that occurred between 1982 and 2003, only two of the shootings between 2011 and 2019 can be considered an act of workplace violence, and one of those occurred on a military base.

Another noticeable change was related to the motives of the shooters. In some cases, no motive could be established aside from a random act of violence committed against citizens or law enforcement officers, while in other incidents, the motives were directly related to domestic violence and familicide. In many of the cases, however, the motives remained closely aligned to those associated with previous shooters, especially regarding the mental health of the shooter. At least one new aspect emerged during this period. In several of the shootings, the gunman was a young military veteran or active-duty soldier who had previously been diagnosed with posttraumatic stress disorder (PTSD). In part, the increase in the number of veterans involved in these incidents might be attributed to the nation's continued involvement in foreign wars and the multiple deployments that modern military personnel endure.

Between 2011 and 2019, nineteen mass shootings occurred in Texas. While some of the events were limited in scope, others represented some of the deadliest cases since the UT Tower shooting. Because of the large number of shootings occurring during a relatively short period of time, it is necessary to group the incidents according to shared characteristics, focusing on the types of shooting, the victims who were targeted, or the locations where the incidents occurred. While these categories serve as a useful way to organize these episodes, the groupings also provide insights into the general trends associated with mass shootings in Texas during the second decade of the twenty-first century.

The largest category of shootings took place at restaurants, clubs, or retail stores. These types of incidents tended to have the most diverse motives, ranging from revenge, mental health issues, domestic violence, and in one case, racial hatred. The first of these episodes occurred on March 14, 2015, when Richard and Desiree Castilleja were involved in an altercation with the staff at Dad's Sing Along Club in San Antonio, forcing the employees to escort the couple from the pub. The Castillejas went to a nearby convenience store and waited for the bar to close. As patrons were leaving the club, the man returned with a handgun and began firing into the crowd, wounding two individuals. There likely would have been more victims, but an officer working a nearby traffic accident heard the shots and raced to the scene. Fearing for the safety of the crowd, the officer shot and killed Castilleja. Desiree was apprehended and charged as an accomplice to the crime.[36] A similar incident took place in Brownsville, Texas, where Marco Antonio Hernandez shot four people in the parking lot of the Chaparral Night Club. Fortunately, all the victims survived the ordeal. Hernandez fled the scene but later turned himself in to authorities. He was charged with four counts of aggravated assault with a deadly weapon and unlawful possession of a firearm by a felon. At trial, Hernandez was sentenced to fifteen years in prison.[37]

As in previous decades, some of the shootings during this period took place at restaurants or at retail stores. One such incident occurred in Seminole, Texas, on March 4, 2017, when Jacob Groening and his wife became embroiled in an argument at Perika's Terrace, a local bar and restaurant. Groening had been drinking heavily throughout the day and continued to drink excessively once they reached Perika's Terrace. He became enraged when his wife refused to continue drinking with him. The argument moved to the parking lot, and when the couple attempted to return to the bar, the owner refused to allow them to reenter the building. Groening shouted that he would kill the owner and left the parking lot on foot, leaving his wife behind. After hitching a ride home, he returned to Perika's Terrace, where the restaurant owner, the owner's wife, and a male patron were sitting on the back patio. Recognizing Groening when he pulled into the parking lot, the two men moved off the patio toward the assailant, who shot them with a small caliber pistol, killing one and critically wounding the other. Groening then returned to his vehicle and left the scene, returning to his residence, where he fired his weapon at his wife and her mother who were in a car parked outside the Groening home, killing his mother-in-law and injuring his wife. Groening's wife escaped while her husband reloaded his weapon and drove to the local Sheriff's office. Law enforcement officers apprehended the shooter the next morning. The excessive amount of alcohol that Groening had consumed throughout the day undoubtedly contributed to the incident, as did the murderer's desire to avenge perceived wrongs.[38]

One of the largest attacks in the period from 1965 to 2020 occurred at the Walmart Supercenter in El Paso on August 3, 2019. Patrick Crusius, a twenty-one-year-old college student from Allen, Texas, drove 650 miles to El Paso, parked his vehicle outside the Walmart store, and began firing an AK-47 semiautomatic rifle at individuals in the parking lot before entering the crowded store, where he continued firing at shoppers and employees. The gunman primarily targeted Hispanics, killing twenty-three people and injuring twenty-three others. The shooting represented one of the deadliest anti-Latino/a attacks in the United States since 1965. Prior to the shooting, Crusius posted an anti-Hispanic, anti-immigrant manifesto online, claiming that he was inspired by the 2019 Christchurch mosque shooting in New Zealand that killed fifty-one people. Crusius listed grievances related to environmental ruin, cultural and ethnic issues, and a perceived Hispanic invasion of the

United States. First responders, including members of the El Paso Police Department, Texas Rangers, Federal Bureau of Investigation, US Customs and Border Protection, paramedics, and an off-duty police officer, descended on the scene within six minutes of the initial 9-1-1 call. The assailant fled the scene in his vehicle but was quickly apprehended by law enforcement officers.[39]

While state officials and lawmakers did not enact major legislative reforms following the shooting, federal and state prosecutors pursued justice for the victims of the shooting.[40] Crusius faced twenty-two counts of "hate crime resulting in death" and twenty-three counts of "hate crime involving the attempt to kill" as well as twenty-two counts of "use of a firearm to commit murder" and twenty-three counts of "use of a firearm during and in relation to a crime of violence." The El Paso County district attorney also sought the death penalty in the case. Despite the legal and political aspects of this case, the event victimized the entire Tejano community in El Paso and beyond, leaving Hispanics with uneasy questions about their place in American society.[41]

Mass shootings related to domestic violence between estranged spouses also proved more common during the 2010s. Three high-profiled domestic shootings occurred between 2014 and 2017. On July 9, 2014, the first incident happened in Spring, Texas, a suburb of Houston, when Ronald Lee Haskell initiated his plan to kill his ex-wife and all the members of her family. Haskell's wife had divorced him the previous year after enduring several years of domestic violence. She, along with her four children, left their family home in Utah to live near her family in Spring, while her husband moved to Southern California to live with his family. For a brief period, Haskell received treatment for mental health issues, but after the couple's divorce was finalized, his condition worsened. A week before the shooting, Haskell was involved in a violent domestic dispute with his family in California that apparently prompted him to travel to Texas, where he appeared at the home of his ex-wife's sister. Although his ex-wife and children were not present, Haskell forced his way into the home and shot and killed his former sister-in-law, her husband, and four of their five children with a pistol. Though wounded, the couple's oldest daughter miraculously survived the attack and called the police once the shooter left the family's home. Police officers found Haskell at the residence of another relative and pursued him in a high-speed car chase that lasted twenty minutes before cornering him in a cul-de-sac. After a three-hour standoff, the assailant surrendered without further incident. Haskell's motive in the attack seems to have been revenge against his ex-wife, but he also suffered from mental health issues, including depression and uncontrollable anger. Haskell was convicted on six counts of murder and received the death penalty for his murderous rampage.[42]

A similar incident occurred just thirteen months later in a northern suburb of Houston, when David Ray Conley shot and killed his former girlfriend, her common-law husband, and six children. Though this case involved unusual circumstances, the shooter's motive was similar to Haskell case. Conley remained in close contact with his former girlfriend, living with her during times when she was separated from her common-law husband. Conley was apparently the father of two of her six children. On August 8, 2015, Conley became enraged when he learned that his girlfriend and her husband had reconciled their differences. He was also troubled by the way the two were raising their children, including the two he had fathered. He broke into the family's home, held the two adults and the children at gunpoint, and forced them into the master bedroom where he bound them. For the next nine hours, Conley methodically killed each family member, including his own children. After exchanging gunfire with officers who arrived on the scene, Conley surrendered. The district attorney charged the suspect with multiple counts of capital murder. Conley's attorney's entered an insanity plea and delayed their client's trial on the basis of psychiatric evaluations that suggested their client was incompetent. Given Conley's criminal history and the inclusive results of the psychiatric evaluations, it is likely that he will eventually stand trial for the murders.[43]

The last high-profile mass shooting involving domestic violence took place in Plano, Texas, on September 10, 2017. After binge drinking all day, Spencer Hight confronted his estranged wife on the porch of her home armed with a semiautomatic rifle, a shotgun, and a pistol. She was hosting a party for friends and coworkers, who gathered to watch the Dallas Cowboy's football game. When Hight's wife turned to reenter the house, he pulled one of his weapons and shot her. Hight then entered the house and killed six more people. The assailant was still at the scene when the first police officer arrived. Hight pointed his weapon at the officer, who shot and killed him, ending the rampage. A few months before the incident, Hight's wife had filed for divorce based on allegations of physical abuse and alcoholism. Complicating the matter, Hight had recently lost his job as a contractor at Texas Instruments. Unable to find work, he became increasingly isolated and began to consume alcohol excessively. The fact that the shooting took place the day after the couple's wedding anniversary likely added to the shooter's troubled state of mind.[44]

In the years after 2011, four mass shootings in Texas occurred at random locations, where the shooter had little or no connection with the community or their victims. The motives of these types of shootings are the most difficult to ascertain and often leave investigators with few answers. In at least two of these cases, the assailants lived outside of the state and traveled to Texas only a day or two prior to their attacks. For example, Dionisio Garza III, a decorated Army veteran who served in Afghanistan and suffered from PTSD, broke into the Memorial Drive Tire & Auto shop in Houston, Texas, on May 30, 2016. The following morning, Garza shot a customer who had pulled up to the shop prior to its opening and then proceeded to shoot at passing cars. Once police officers arrived at the scene, an intense shootout erupted. Using an AR-15, the shooter fired more than two hundred rounds, killing one individual and wounding six others. The rampage ended when a Houston Police Department sniper shot and killed Garza. Aside from suffering bouts of depression and showing signs of PTSD, no motive was determined in the shooting.[45]

Other random shootings during this period occurred along busy highways and streets. On May 26, 2013, US Marine Esteban J. Smith engaged in a two-hour shooting spree that began at 4:30 a.m. in Concho County and extended into McCulloch County. Armed with a semi-automatic rifle, a handgun, and hundreds of rounds of ammunition, Smith traveled between the towns of Eden (Concho County) and Brady (McCullough County), randomly firing at five different vehicles from his pickup, killing one person and wounding five others. The location of the shooting puzzled law enforcement because Smith had no known connection to the region. He was raised near Bakersfield, California, and was stationed at Camp Lejeune in North Carolina. Prior to the shootings, Smith apparently stabbed his wife to death at a hotel in Jacksonville, North Carolina, before driving to Texas. The highway rampage ended when Smith was killed in a shootout with law enforcement officers from different agencies. No motive was attached to the shooting nor was there a clear explanation of why Smith had traveled the fifteen hundred miles to randomly shoot motorists in Central Texas.[46]

A comparable incident occurred in southwest Houston on September 25, 2016, when a disgruntled lawyer, Nathan DeSai, parked his vehicle at an intersection outside a Randalls Supermarket and randomly fired toward the building and passing cars. During the shooting spree, DeSai wounded nine people. Members of the Houston Police Department arrived on the scene and engaged the shooter in a running gun battle. After several exchanges of gunfire, officers shot and killed the suspect. Again, no clear motive was associated with the incident, but it was discovered that the shooter collected historic military relics, including several Nazi artifacts. Furthermore, investigators determined that DeSai's law firm was in financial disarray. Authorities, however, were unable to determine if the assailant's interest in military history or his financial problems contributed to the shooting.[47]

Twenty-eight days after the Walmart shooting in El Paso, one of the bloodiest highway shootings occurred in the twin West Texas cities of Midland and Odessa on August 31, 2019. The rampage began when a Texas Highway trooper stopped Seth Aaron Ator, a loner who lived in West Odessa and had a criminal past and a history of mental health issues. The situation quickly turned violent when the suspect grabbed a semiautomatic rifle and shot at the police unit through his back window. He wounded one of the two officers inside the police cruiser, then fled the scene. Traveling on the interstate through Midland and Odessa, Ator shot another individual before abandoning his vehicle and hijacking a US Postal Service worker's van, killing the driver and continuing his attack. The rampage came to an end when police officers cornered the assailant in a movie theater parking lot and shot and killed him. During the incident, Ator randomly fired his weapon at residents and other motorists, killing seven individuals and wounding more than twenty others. Prior to the shooting, Ator's employer had fired him, which may have contributed to his motives for the shooting.[48]

Between 2011 and 2015, police officers fell under heavy scrutiny amidst claims that law enforcement agencies perpetrated racial injustices against minorities. In the wake of these accusations, three mass shootings in Texas targeted law enforcement officers. The exchange of gunfire in one of these assaults appeared to be a spontaneous reaction to an officer approaching the home of the assailant to serve him with a court order, but the other two assaults were premeditated and resulted in the ambush of on-duty officers. On August 13, 2012, the first incident occurred when a local constable approached the home of Thomas Alton Caffall III in College Station, Texas, to serve him an eviction notice. Caffall shot and killed the officer as he walked toward the front door of his residence and then took the lawman's sidearm and used it to shoot a nearby neighbor. College Station police officers quickly arrived on the scene and exchanged gunfire with the suspect, killing the shooter. During the engagement, Caffall wounded three officers and killed a bystander. According to Caffall's family members, the assailant suffered from mental health issues, which seemed to grow worse due to a recent divorce and several months of unemployment. Likely, the prospect of becoming homeless further added to Caffall's mental anguish. Aside from these issues, however, no clear motives were associated with the case.[49]

The next two attacks on law enforcement officers took place in Dallas. The first attack occurred on June 13, 2015, when James Boulware planted explosive devices outside the Dallas Police Department headquarters and fired shots at the building before retreating to an armored vehicle that he had purchased from a Georgia-based company that specialized in converting passenger vans into what they referred to as a "Zombie Apocalypse Assault Vehicle and Troop Transport." During the attack, the assailant had called the police and identified himself, stating that the police were responsible for taking his child away from him. Prior to the event, the courts had granted Boulware's wife custody of their son after a bitter court battle. Apparently, police officers had provided testimony that favored his ex-wife's accusations of domestic abuse.

Following the initial shots fired at the police headquarters, Boulware drove his vehicle to the parking lot of a fast-food restaurant, approximately ten miles from the initial scene of the incident. While he was there, officers cornered the suspect. After lengthy negotiations failed to deescalate the situation, a police sniper shot and killed Boulware. Surprisingly, the shooter was the only fatality in the rampage. Boulware's parents later confirmed that their son suffered from mental illness and was delusional. Other relatives stated that the assailant had threatened to kill all the adult members of the family and commented that he might shoot up schools and churches, because they were easy targets of opportunity. They also recalled that Boulware claimed to have dreams about the Sandy Hook Elementary School shooting in Newton, Connecticut, as well as other infamous mass shootings. In the hours before the shooting, Boulware's father reported that his son made negative comments about a police officer in McKinney, Texas, who was captured on video pushing down a young black girl at a pool party. According to his father, Boulware commented that the police were the ones responsible for taking his son away. As a result of numerous incidents of domestic violence prior to the shooting, the court required a psychiatric evaluation of Boulware before he could see his son. According to local records, the attending psychiatrist declared Boulware sane despite the claims of family members that he suffered mental health issues.[50]

The second attack on Dallas police officers proved more devastating. Micah Xavier Johnson, a troubled Army veteran of the war in Afghanistan and supporter of black nationalist organizations, carried out an ambush-styled assault against officers who were assigned to monitor an organized protest in downtown Dallas. The protesters gathered at Belo Garden Park in response to police killings of two African Americans, Alton Sterling in Baton Rouge, Louisiana, and Philando Castile, Falcon Heights, Minnesota. To bring attention to their cause, protesters organized peaceful marches in major cities across the nation, including Dallas, for July 7, 2016. Johnson saw the gathering as an opportunity to attack law enforcement personnel, stating that he wanted to kill white people, especially white police officers. Near the end of the protest march, Johnson launched his attack and engaged officers in a running battle that lasted for more than six hours, leaving five officers dead and seven others injured. Two civilians were also wounded. The rampage came to an end when Johnson fled to a parking garage, where police were able to corner him. After negotiators failed to secure the shooter's surrender, a remote-controlled robot was used to deliver and detonate an explosive devise near the suspect. The explosion killed Johnson instantly. Nationwide, the attack had been the deadliest single day for law enforcement since the terrorist attacks of September 11, 2001.[51]

The targeting of law enforcement officers in mass shootings was unique to the 2010 to 2020 era, as animosity toward law enforcement rose in response to several incidents of police shootings of unarmed black men and women during this period. Activist groups claimed that police departments were tainted by systemic racism and that officers frequently harassed and killed minorities. Even though the vast majority of protesters were opposed to the use of violence, the targeting of law enforcement officers seemed to be directly related to the growing concerns of police brutality toward racial minorities.[52]

While new motives were associated with the mass shootings occurring during the second decade of the twenty-first century, other incidents followed the same trends as witnessed in previous decades, including shootings in workplaces, churches, and schools. During a second shooting at Fort Hood on April 2, 2014, Ivan Lopez went on a ten-minute rampage at various locations on the base, killing three people and wounding twelve others. However, this shooting was different from the 2009 episode at Fort Hood, because it resembled more closely an act of workplace violence. Within an hour before the shooting, Lopez visited the Forty-ninth Transportation Battalion office and requested a ten-day leave to attend to a family issue. When his request was not immediately granted, he became belligerent. In apparent distress, Lopez left the building but returned shortly with a semiautomatic pistol and opened fire on the soldiers inside. He then drove to two separate buildings, firing his weapon at Army personnel at both locations as well as in places along the route between the buildings. The rampage ended when a military police officer confronted the gunman in a parking lot. At this point, Lopez turned his weapon on himself and committed suicide. Later investigations determined that Lopez suffered from PTSD, depression, and anxiety. In addition, he experienced financial troubles and was emotionally disturbed by the death of his grandfather and his mother five months prior to the shooting. Finally, there were allegations that Lopez may have been bullied by other soldiers on the base.[53]

A second workplace shooting occurred in Katy, Texas, at Knight Transportation on May 4, 2016. Marrion Guy Williams, a sixty-five-year-old employee who had been fired the previous month, entered the company's office with a shotgun and pistol and began firing at his former coworkers, killing one and wounding two others, before using his weapon to commit suicide. The motive associated with the case was determined to be solely linked to the company's dismissal of Williams.[54]

Two Texas shootings took place at Texas churches between 2017 and 2019. On November 5, 2017, Devin Patrick Kelley, who was dressed in tactical gear and armed with a semiautomatic rifle and two pistols, pulled his Ford Explorer into the parking lot of the First Baptist Church at Sutherland Springs, Texas, parked, and exited the vehicle. While still outside, Kelley shot and killed two people before entering through a side door of the church and methodically targeting members who had gathered for Sunday service. For more than ten minutes, the gunman walked up and down the aisle of the rural church shooting people who were trying to find cover between the pews. During the assault, Kelley fired nearly seven hundred rounds, killing twenty-six people and wounding twenty others. Kelley then fled. A neighbor and another man pursued Kelley on the highway until the suspect's vehicle crashed into a field. Once the police arrived at the site of the crash and secured the area, they discovered that Kelley had committed suicide.[55]

Following this episode, investigations into the background of the shooter painted a picture of a deeply troubled individual who engaged in numerous acts of domestic violence, animal cruelty, disregard for authority, and an apparent obsession with mass murders. He had even spent time in a mental health facility in 2012 after expressing suicidal thoughts to a coworker. Investigators also discovered that Kelley should have never been able to legally own a firearm because he had been dismissed from the Air Force with a bad conduct discharge. During his time in the Air Force, Kelley was brought before a general court-martial on four charges of assault in incidents involving his first wife and stepson. He pleaded guilty to two counts of domestic violence. Unfortunately, the Air Force failed to enter Kelley's court-martial convictions into the FBI's National Crime Information Center database. Therefore, the assailant was able to easily falsify documents necessary for the legal purchase of firearms. As a civilian, Kelley's pattern of violence against women continued. Investigators theorized that the motive for the shooting at Sutherland Springs was Kelley's intention to kill his estranged second wife and her family. Because his wife and her mother sometimes attended the First Baptist Church, he must have calculated that she would be present on the day of the shooting. However, neither woman was in attendance at the time of the attack, but his wife's grandmother was among those killed during the shooting.[56]

At least two new issues emerged from this incident that led to new gun legislation designed to mitigate mass shootings in the future. First, citizens pushed Texas lawmakers to allow concealed weapons to be carried in gun-free zones, including churches. As a result, the Texas Legislature passed Senate Bill 535 that allows citizens to carry firearms into churches, synagogues, and other places of worship unless the property owners specifically prevent firearms with posted signage. Second, national lawmakers called for closer communication between the military and federal agencies, especially regarding court-martial convictions. The debates grew more serious after the family of one of the Sutherland Springs victims sued the US Department of Defense, including the US Air Force, for negligently, recklessly, carelessly, and/or egregiously failing to report the criminal conviction of Kelley to the proper federal authorities.

On November 15, 2017, Senator John Cornyn introduced the Fix NICS Act of 2017 (S.2135) that addressed deficiencies in the process of reporting military convictions to federal agencies. The final version of Senator Cornyn's bill was passed as part of the Consolidation Appropriations Act and signed into law on March 23, 2018.[57] Despite these actions, the people of Sutherland Springs were left to pick up the pieces of their community and try to put them back together again. Understandably, the tragedy had opened old wounds of all the survivors of past mass shootings, bringing a certain despair that such events seemed to be occurring with a greater frequency than in any time in the modern era.[58]

The second church shooting occurred on December 29, 2019, at the West Freeway Church of Christ in White Settlement, a suburb of Fort Worth. During Sunday services, Keith Thomas Kinnunen, a transient drifter who had a history of mental health issues and a criminal record that spanned across three states, pulled a concealed shotgun from underneath his trench coat and randomly fired at other congregants, killing two of them. Immediately, the head of the voluntary church security detail responded and shot and killed the assailant, ending the rampage within six seconds after the first shot was fired and preventing another incident like the one witnessed at Sutherland Springs First Baptist Church. Following the passage of Senate Bill 535 in 2018, the Freeway Church of Christ established an armed security team to protect their members. Church leaders believed that the added security measures were necessary after a series of homicides had occurred earlier that year near their sanctuary. In addition, Texas legislators had passed a law that permitted licensed gun owners to carry concealed weapons to churches and other places of worship that did not specifically bar such practices. Because the church livestreamed its morning services, investigators were able to review the details of the shooting. They noted that several of the congregants had unholstered their concealed weapon, but the shooting had ended before they could take further action. Kinnunen's motives for the attack were unclear. The minister of the church commented after the incident that he had talked with the suspect on more than one occasion and had provided him with food. The shooter's family members and friends commented that he had never fully recovered from the loss of his brother, who had committed suicide ten years before the incident. The day of the shooting was the birthday of the deceased brother, a fact that likely added to Kinnunen's agony. Aside from mental health issues and a lengthy criminal record, no other motives were established in the shooting.[59]

The final mass shooting between 2011 and 2020 occurred at Santa Fe High School in Santa Fe, Texas, in northern Galveston County. On the morning of May 18, 2018, Dimitrios Pagourtzis, a seventeen-year-old student at the school, entered the school's art complex armed with a pump shotgun and a revolver. Once inside, Pagourtzis began firing at classmates and teachers, killing ten individuals (eight students and two teachers) and wounding thirteen others. The shooting represented the deadliest high school shooting in Texas history and was the third deadliest in the United States, following close behind the murderous rampages at Columbine High School (Littleton, Colorado) in April 1999 and Stoneman Douglas High School (Parkland, Florida) in February 2018. Pagourtzis likely would have killed more individuals had it not been for the prompt intervention of two school resource officers on campus and a Texas State Trooper who accompanied them once he arrived at the scene. Pagourtzis fired several rounds at the officers, critically wounding one of them, before surrendering. In addition to the shotgun and pistol, investigators discovered explosive devices stashed on the campus as well as in a nearby neighborhood. Some claimed that the shooter had been bullied by classmates as well as some of the school's coaches, speculating that this might have been the motive for the incident. Others described Pagourtzis as quiet but friendly. In addition, he was a member of the school's junior varsity football team and an honor roll student. However, there were subtle signs that the teenager was suffering from undiagnosed mental health issues. After the shooting, investigators discovered that Pagourtzis had posted several images on social media that showed him wearing a T-shirt with the words "born to kill" written across the front. They also found a digital journal on his computer and phone in which the teenager had written about the shooting and indicated that he planned to commit suicide at the end of the attack. Following his arrest, Pagourtzis was charged with capital murder. However, at the time of publication, his case has yet to be tried because court-ordered psychological evaluations determined that he was not fit to stand trial in his current mental state.[60]

Given the scale of the shooting, it is not surprising that media outlets provided extensive coverage of the event. Reporters converged on the scene and immediately began interviewing students, teachers, school officials, members of the community, and law enforcement officers. As expected, the students were emotionally distraught, questioning why their school had endured such a tragic event. Many residents of Santa Fe called on the government to ban guns or to add regulations to existing laws governing the purchase of firearms. Others were focused on improving school security.[61] Ironically, in the weeks following high school shooting in Parkland earlier that year, Santa Fe High School experienced a false alarm of an active-shooter situation. The campus was locked down, and the emergency response system seemingly worked as designed. In fact, the school received an award for its safety procedures. The school was also in the process of training volunteer staff members to carry weapons, joining more than 170 other school districts in the state that had adopted similar plans. However, the latter decision had been approved only the month before the shooting and had yet to be implemented. In the end, school officials determined that their safety program had worked by preventing an even greater loss of life but pledged to continue to find improved ways to protect their students. In the final analysis, the school board president commented that their efforts realistically could only mitigate, not prevent, such incidents from occurring.[62]

Following the Santa Fe shooting, Texas Governor Greg Abbott called for a meeting at the capitol with various stakeholders to discuss what policies were needed to improve school safety. After three days of discussion, the Governor Abbott issued a forty-three-page report that addressed issues such as mental health screenings, expanded school protection programs, and new measures for regulating the use of guns. Governor Abbott used a similar tactic following the Sutherland Springs shooting to prompt legislators to ease gun restrictions in places of worship and hoped lawmakers would respond once again with the passage of new legislation designed to make schools safer. Ultimately, the Texas legislature answered the governor's request and passed sweeping legislation, including Senate Bill 11, designed to prevent, or at least mitigate, future mass school shootings. While gun control advocates argued that the new laws were insufficient, many Texans applauded the efforts of their elected officials, arguing that they had taken steps in the right direction to protect school children across the state.[63]

For more than fifty years, mass shootings have tragically plagued Texas, resulting in approximately 200 deaths and nearly 250 more wounded.[64] Texans have dealt with these events in myriad ways, suggesting that the larger cultural views in the state do not approve of these acts of violence. Yet, the legislation that came out in the uptick of mass shootings in the 2010s typically emphasized easing gun restrictions that, proponents argued, would protect residents from these tragic events. However, their efforts will likely only mitigate the problem, not prevent future incidents from occurring. While some critics of these efforts decry these moves and suggest that they are indicative of a larger cultural embrace of violence, it appears that the actions of state officials are more closely aligned to a "gun culture," where the ownership of firearms is highly valued as a right of citizenship. In this regard, a distinction must be made between a culture of violence and a gun culture because the two are not necessarily synonymous, even though fears associated with the different cultures may be linked. For example, a fear of becoming a victim within a perceived culture of violence may lead to increased support for a gun culture where law-abiding citizens believe the ownership of firearms is necessary to protect themselves. It should be noted that some mass shootings blur this distinction.

Those incidents of mass murder associated with domestic and racial violence seem to reflect the remnant an of an older culture that found these acts acceptable. Thus, there may be evidence to support the presence of a small subculture that still accepts these forms of violence, even in cases of mass shootings, but these views do not align with that of the majority of Texas residents. Instead, the cases examined in this chapter suggest that mental health issues, the design of school campuses and commercial buildings, domestic violence, stresses of financial and social pressures, PTSD that affects many veterans who return home from incessant foreign wars, and political, racial, and ethnic antagonism seem to drive mass shooting incidents more so than a larger cultural embrace of those actions. Although Texas, and the United States more broadly, grapples with the legacy of the historic "culture of violence," the reactions of residents, law enforcement, and legal officials in Texas suggest that mass shootings extend beyond a cultural acceptance of this type of violence. While the motives of mass shooters may never be fully understood, especially given the number of variables associated with each incident, perhaps the combined scholarly efforts of social scientists and criminologists in the future will present new insights into these types of crimes and offer different methodologies for predicting and preventing these senseless and heinous acts.

Notes

1. Joan Neuberger et al., "Behind the Tower: New Histories of the UT Tower Shooting," project of the Public History Seminar at UT Austin, 2016, http://behindthe tower.org; Pamela Colloff, "96 Minutes," *Texas Monthly,* August 2006, https://www.texasmonthly.com/articles/96-minutes; Jaclyn Schildkraut and H. Jaymi Elsass, *Mass Shootings: Media, Myths, and Realities* (Santa Barbara, CA: Praeger, 2016), 33–34. For more information on the UT Tower shooting, see Gary M. Lavergne, *A Sniper in the Tower: The Charles Whitman Murders* (Denton: University of North Texas Press, 1997), and Monte Akers, Nathan Akers, and Roger Friedman, *Tower Sniper: The Terror of America's First Active Shooter on Campus* (Houston: John M. Hardy Publishing, 2016).

2. The UT Tower shooting is now listed as the eleventh deadliest mass shooting in the nation since 1966. For more information, see Dave Lawler and Orion Rummler, "The Deadliest Mass Shootings in Modern US History," updated May 25, 2022, https://www.axios.com/deadliest-mass-shootings-in-modern-us-history-3b2dfb67-7278-4082-a78c-d9fdbef367f1.html.

3. For more information on the various definitions of mass shootings, see Schildkraut and Elsass, *Mass Shootings,* 13–28. Another valuable source is Jaclyn Schildkraut, ed., *Mass Shootings in America: Understanding the Debate, Causes, and Responses* (Santa Barbara, CA: ABC-CLIO, 2018), xxii–xxii. The latter source includes a succinct but valuable discussion on the differences between the definitions that state and federal agencies use to identify what constitutes a "mass shooting." The definitions are important because, depending on how mass shootings are defined, overreporting or underreporting of these events occurs.

4. Schildkraut and Elsass, *Mass Shootings,* 28.

5. Schildkraut and Elsass, 29–33; Schildkraut, *Mass Shootings in America,* vxxiv–xxv. These works are two of the best general accounts on mass shootings in print. Prior to 1900, many of the acts of violence occurred in frontier settings and were associated with conflicts between Native Americans and Anglo settlers. Interestingly, many of the deaths and injuries related to these incidents did not involve the use of firearms but instead resulted from hand-to-hand combat. However, there were some events, especially in the late 1800s, that fall into the category of mass shootings (at least by today's standards). For example, in the summer of 1880, Charles Berhues attacked his cousin at a school where the latter was serving as an attendant, resulting in the death of one individual and the wounding of four others. On March 30, 1891, an unknown shooter wounded fourteen individuals who were attending an event in Liberty, Mississippi. The next month, James Ferguson fired shots at a group of students who were playing outside in Newburg, New York. Fortunately, none of the children were killed, but five of them were wounded. At the end of the decade, a shooter fired on a group of people gathered at a school exhibition in Charleston, West Virginia, killing five individuals and wounding two more. During the tumultuous times of the early twentieth century, economic

conditions coincided with the first wave of mass murders recorded in American history. Many of the homicides committed during this period, however, were familicides and often occurred in rural areas. Sadly, during this period, fathers who suffered financial ruin murdered their families, attempting to save them from ravages of the Great Depression. Many of the familicide victims died from fatal gunshot wounds. However, shootings also took place outside of the home during this period. For example, on March 14, 1912, family members of Floyd Allen, who was on trial for various criminal acts, opened fire at the Carroll County courthouse in Hillsville, Virginia, killing the local judge, prosecutor, sheriff, and two bystanders, including one of the prosecutor's key witnesses. During the mayhem, seven others were wounded, including the defendant. While the Allen incident was perpetrated by outlaws, other public shootings resulted from financial distress and personal vendettas. One case involved Monroe Phillips, who suffered financial ruin after a failed real estate venture. In retaliation, Phillips killed five and wounded twenty others before a local lawyer in the community shot and killed him. Three decades later, in September 1949, Howard Unruh, a twenty-eight-year-old resident of Camden, New Jersey, went on a shooting spree, apparently seeking revenge for derogatory remarks made against him by his neighbors. Before local authorities were able to apprehend him, Unruh killed thirteen and wounded several others. In addition to these type of events, numerous shootings took place on the campuses of public schools, including shootings at Honolulu, Hawaii (1913); Valdosta, Georgia (1922); South Pasadena, California (1940); and Washington, DC (1956). Institutions of higher education also witnessed several noted shootings, including incidents at the University of California (1919) and the New York City hospital and medical school (1935). While these private and public shootings might not have received the same media coverage as modern incidents, they serve as a precedent to what some scholars have defined as the second wave of mass murders, which began in the 1960s. Schildkraut and Elsass cover these incidents in more detail. To save space, I have only mentioned these shootings to show that shootings at public schools and institutions of higher learning are not limited to the modern era.

6. Schildkraut and Elsass, *Mass Shootings,* 34.

7. Schildkraut and Elsass, 34.

8. Schildkraut and Elsass, 34.

9. Schildkraut and Elsass, 36.

10. Schildkraut and Elsass, v36–41. While the declining crime rate across the nation resulted from multiple financial and social factors, some scholars argue that President Reagan's decade-long campaign against crime (as well as the policies of his successor, President George H. W. Bush) began to produce results. Furthermore, schools throughout the United States began to witness a general decline in violence. Despite these downward trends, there were several mass shootings in the nation during the 1990s, including several that took place on public school campuses: Moses Lake, Washington (1996); Bethel, Alaska (1997); West Paducah,

Kentucky (1997); Jonesboro, Arkansas (1998); Springfield, Oregon (1998); and Little-ton, Colorado (1999). Beyond these events, a shooting on a New York commuter train in 1993 left six dead and nineteen wounded, and six years later, a shooting occurred at the offices of Momentum Securities and the All-Tech Investment Group in Atlanta, Georgia, resulting in nine people killed and twelve wounded. Texas also suffered several mass shootings during the 1990s, doubling the number of episodes occurring in the previous decade.

11. The common myth that mass shooters are young white males does not hold true for shootings that took place in Texas. While a slight majority of the shooters were white males, there were almost as many nonwhite shooters. In addition, the average age of the shooters is just over thirty years old.

12. Schildkraut and Elsass, *Mass Shootings,* 71–92. Schildkraut and Elsass discuss the "usual suspects" (causal factors) associated with mass shootings across the nation. The authors claim that politicians, the media, various organizations, and the general public tend to blame the shootings on the same causal factors, such as guns, mental health, and violent media (movies and video games). While it is natural to look for such causal factors, the authors point out that many of the usual suspects highlight another common trend in mass shootings, stating, "In the wake of mass shootings, the discourse focuses on blaming everyone and everything but the person who pulled the trigger." Further, they find that in cases where the shooter can be held responsible for their actions (meaning they did not commit suicide), the actions of the assailant "often are reasoned away by emphasizing issues such as mental health, which takes the lead in the blame game." In conclusion, the authors argue, "While we may never fully understand 'why' these events take place, we are able to gain an understanding continuing a comprehensive discus-sion about the individual, community-level, and sociocultural causes of this type of violence" (p. 92).

13. For an example of this argument, see Edward L. Ayers, "Legacy of Violence," *American Heritage* 42, no. 6 (October 1991), https://www.americanheritage.com/legacy-violence.

14. Jan Reid, "Blood of the Lamb," *Texas Monthly,* March 1983, 140–47, 191–206; Murderpedia, s.v. "Alvin Lee King III," accessed September 29, 2020, https://murderpedia.org/male.K/k/king-alvin-lee.htm; "Alvin Lee King III, Charged with Storming a Church," UPI, accessed September 9 and 28, 2020, https://www.upi.com/Archives/1982/01/19/Alvin-Lee-King-III-charged-with-storming-a-church/4408380264400; Glenn Evans, "Daingerfield Church Reflects on 1980 Shooting," June 22, 2015, https://www.news-journal.com/news/local/daingerfield-church-reflects-on-1980-shootings/articles_c8cecfab-88c4-5376-b9e0-20d25c82d5c2.html; Greg Bischof, "Area Man Pens Book about 1980 Church Shooting in Daingerfield," October 29, 2009, https://www.texarkanagazette.com/news/texarkana/story/2009/oct/29/arempens-book-about-1980-church-shooting-dain/133575; Manny Fernandez, "Two Texas Churches, Linked by Tragedy Amid the Pews," November 21,

2017, https://www.nytimes.com/2017/11/21/us/texas-church-shootings-daingerfield-sutherland-springs.html; "Never Forgotten: Survivors Reflect on Daingerfield Church Shooting 40 Years Later," November 20, 2019, https://www.easttexasmatters .com/news/top-stories/never-forgotten-survivors-reflect-on-daingerfield-church-shooting-40-years-later.

15. Jay B. Lewis, "'Yes, I Know, He's Killing People,'" August 9, 1982, https://www .upi.com/Archives/1982/08/09/Yes-I-know-hes-killing-people/2899397713600; "Disgruntled Driver Slays Six in Texas, Dying in Shootout," *New York Times,* August 10, 1982; Murderpedia, s.v. "John Felton Parish," accessed October 8, 2020, https://murderpedia.org/male.P/p/parish-john.htm; Robert Francis, "In Market: Remembering a Violent Event," *Fort Worth Business Press,* August 9, 2019, https://fortworthbusiness. com/opinion/in-market-remembering-a-violent-event.

16. Gary M. Lavergne, *Worse Than Death: The Dallas Nightclub Murders and the Texas Multiple Murder Law* (Denton: University of Texas Press, 2003); Murder pedia, s.v. "Abdelkrim Belachheb," accessed January 30, 2021, https://murderpedia. org/male.B/b/belachheb.htm; David Barron, "The Estranged Wife of Accused Murderer Abdelkrim Belachheb Testified," UPI, November 8, 1994, https://www .upi.com/Archives/1984/11/08/The-estranged-wife-of-accused-murderer-Abdelkrim-Belachheb-testified/3858468738000.

17. Disaster Center, "Texas Crime Rates, 1960–2019," accessed January 20, 2021, http://www.disastercenter.com/crime/txcrime.htm; Alexia Cooper and Erica L. Smith, Homicide Trends in the United States, 1980–2008 (Washington, DC: US Department of Justice, 2011).

18. Schildkraut and Elsass, *Mass Shootings,* 65. Schildkraut and Elsass argue, "A very common misconception is that mass shooters prefer these types of weapons —semiautomatic, military-style rifles. Yet a study done by Fox and DeLateur (2014) clearly shows that mass shooters' weapon of choice overwhelmingly are semiautomatic handguns. In the 142 shootings examined, 68 were committed with semiautomatic handguns, 35 with semiautomatic, military-style rifles; 20 with revolvers; and 19 with shotguns." Based on Schildkraut and Elsass's findings, it seems evident that Texas mass shootings were consistent with similar incidents throughout the United States. Schildkraut and Elsass also describe the differences between a semiautomatic rifle that is available to the general public and a military-style rifle. According to the authors, "A true assault rifle is fully automatic, thereby continuing to shoot bullets as long as the trigger is engaged, resulting in multiple rounds per trigger pull. Also, they dispel the idea that AR, as in AR-15, stands for assault rifle—it actually stands for ArmaLite, the name of the original developer of the weapon in the 1950s.

19. Carol Dawson and Carol Johnston, *House of Plenty: The Rise, Fall, and Revival of Luby's Cafeterias* (Austin: University of Texas Press, 2006), 175–82; Schildkraut and Elsass, *Mass Shootings,* 39; Gur Tirosh, "The Story of Luby's Shooting," accessed September 29, 2020, https://historybyday.com/human-stories/the-story-of-lubys-shooting;

Paula Chin, "A Texas Massacre," *People* 36, no. 17, updated November 4, 1991, https://people.com/archive/a-texas-massacre-vol-36-no-17; Jack Keyes, "28 Years after a Forgotten Mass Shooting in Texas, a Survivor Looks Back," *Reporting Texas,* June 7, 2019, https://reportingtexas.com/28-years-after-a-forgotten-mass-shooting-in-texas-a-survivor-looks-back; Phillip Jankowski, "Survivors Reflect on Oct. 16, 1991, Luby's Shooting" *Killeen Daily Herald,* October 16, 1991, https://kdhnews.com/news/survivors-reflect-on-oct-16-1991-lubys-shooting/article_e2660bfc-d24a-5566-a65f-a67a9fe6365b.html; "Shooting Rampage at Killeen Luby's Left 24 Dead," *Houston Chronicle,* August 11, 2001, https://www.chron.com/life/article/Shooting-rampage-at-Killeen-Luby-s-left-24-dead-2037092.php; "Texas City Official: Mass Shooting Left Scars, but Killeen 'Resilient,'" CNN, March 11, 2009, http://www.cnn.com/2009/US/03/11/killeen.mass.shooting/index.html; Robert L. Kelley, "EMS Revisited: October 1991 Luby's Shooting," *EMSWorld,* March 30, 2010, https://www.emsworld.com/article/10319733/ems-revisited-october-1991-lubys-shooting; "Where'd They Get Their Guns?: An Analysis of the Firearms Used in High-Profile Shootings, 1963 to 2001," Violence Policy Center, accessed September 29, 2020, https://www.vpc.org/studies/wgun911016.htm; Murderpedia, s.v. "George Jo Hennard," accessed September 29, 2020, https://murderpedia.org/male.H/h/hennard-george-jo.htm.

20. Murderpedia, "George Jo Hennard." Interestingly enough, the *Dallas Morning News* and the *Philadelphia Daily News* reported that Hennard had a movie ticket among his possessions when police searched his body. The movie stub was for the movie *The Fisher King,* which includes as part of its storyline a massacre in a New York restaurant.

21. Tirosh, "Story of Luby's Shooting." According to Tirosh, the Luby's Cafeteria shooting now ranks as the sixth deadliest mass shooting in US history.

22. AOAV, "15 Shootings That Changed the Law: Killeen, 1991," Action on Armed Violence, April 17, 2014, https://aoav.org.uk/2014/killeen-1991; Schildkraut and Elsass, *Mass Shootings,* 40.

23. "Seven Students Injured in School Shooting," UPI, September 11, 1992, https://www.upi.com/Archives/1992/09/11/Seven-students-injured-in-school-shooting/8553716184000; "Student Wounds 6 at High School," *New York Times,* September 12, 1992, https://www.nytimes.com/1992/09/12/us/student-wounds-6-at-high-school.html; "Teen-Ager Shoots 6 in School after Fight, 2 Seriously Hurt," *Los Angeles Times,* September 12, 1992, https://www.latimes.com/archives/la-xpm-1992-09-12-mn-275-story.html; John Mark Beilue, "'Kind of Chaos': Witnesses Recall 1992 Palo Duro High School Shooting," *Amarillo Globe-News,* September 10, 2012, https://www.amarillo.com/article/20120910/news/309109718.

24. Beilue, "'Kind of Chaos': Witnesses Recall 1992 Palo Duro High School Shooting." The actions of Palo Duro Independent School District became more commonplace nationwide following the Columbine High Shooting in Littleton, Colorado. For more details on the Columbine shooting, see Schildkraut, *Mass Shootings in America,* 118–21.

25. "Texas Gunman Kills 5, Self," UPI, April 3, 1995, https://www.upi.com/Archives/1995/04/03/Texas-gunman-kills-5-self/5437796881600; Kelley Shannon, "Six Killed in Workplace Shooting," *News & Record* (Greensboro, NC), April 3, 1995, updated January 23, 2015, http://greensboro.com/six-killed-in-workplace-shooting/article_5b0f2020-5c38-54c7-b871-e88460a6cbc8.html; "6 Die in Texas Office Shooting," *New York Times,* April 4, 1995; "Gunman Kills Five, Himself," *Journal Times* (Racine, WI), April 4, 1995, https://journaltimes.com/article_08c70f4e-ba81-5a8e-9d78-7e0930c3c367.html; "Police Report They've Found No Motive in Texas Shooting/Gunman killed 5, Self at Former Office," SFGate, April 5, 1995, https://www.sfgate.com/news/article/Police-Report-They-ve-Found-No-Motive-in-Texas-3038633.php; Kelley Shannon, "Gunman Kills Five, Then Himself, at Refinery Inspection Company," AP News, April 4, 1995, https://apnews.com/article/43e3a1 68e8024ac986b4794bea137e07; Murderpedia, s.v. "James Daniel Simpson," accessed February 4, 2021, https://murderpedia.org/male.S/s/simpson-james-daniel.htm; Violence Policy Center, "Where'd They Get Their Guns."

26. Schildkraut, *Mass Shootings in America,* 115.

27. While this shooting conforms to the definition discussed in footnote 3, the lack of media coverage of this incident suggests that the public is sometimes unaware of mass shootings occurring in the state. This might indicate that more shootings have occurred during the decades prior to 1960s as well as afterwards. Given this probability, we must consider that mass shootings in Texas throughout the 1990s are consistent with national trends. Many of these incidents may simply have been reported as homicides by local law enforcement and local media.

28. Schildkraut and Elsass, *Mass Shootings,* 37–39. According to Schildkraut and Elsass, the Columbine High School shootings had a significant impact on the way mass shootings were perceived by the American public and by the media. Although other school shootings occurred in the 1990s, Columbine became a watershed event by which all subsequent shootings, including those that occurred beyond school campuses, were judged. Despite a spate of news stories, such as the Gulf War; terroristic bombings at the World Trade Center, the Alfred P. Murrah Federal Building in Oklahoma City, and at the Olympics in Atlanta, Georgia; suicides associated with the Heaven's Gate cult, the Branch Davidian standoff in Waco, Texas; and other newsworthy events, coverage of the Columbine shooting was eclipsed in its coverage only by the 1992 Rodney King verdict and the 1996 crash of TWA Flight 800. Sixty-eight percent of Americans said they closely followed the media coverage of the Columbine shooting. This likely resulted from the fact that news coverage of the event changed, especially given that cable news stations devoted significant airtime to covering the incident in order to capture higher ratings. vAdditionally, the scope of the shooting likely piqued viewer interest. vFinally, the Columbine shooting initiated a national discourse on issues related to mass shootings, including public debates on school violence and gun control. However, media coverage of the Wedgewood Baptist Church shooting should not

be overstated because it still did not reach the same level of coverage as did similar shootings in Texas during the first two decades of the twenty-first century.

29. "Jim Yardley, "Gunman Kills 7, and Himself, at Baptist Church in Fort Worth," *New York Times,* September 16, 1999, https://www.nytimes.com/1999/09/16/us/gunman-kills-7-and-himself-at-baptist-church-in-fort-worth.html; Paul Duggan, "Gunman Kills 7 and Self in Texas Church Shooting," *Washington Post,* September 16, 1999, https://www.washingtonpost.com/wp-srv/national/daily/sept99/texas16.htm; "Teen Struggles after Killings," CBS News (48 Hours), December 16, 1999, https://www.cbsnews.com/news/teen-struggles-after-killings; Stefani G. Kopenecs, "8 Dead in Texas Church Shootings," AP News, September 16, 1999, https://apnews.com/article/612b3b5ef911ee60dbofe183c6a150d0; David K. Li, "Church Killer Made Dad's Life Hell–Horrified Neighbors Hid during Rampages," *New York Post,* September 17, 1999, https://nypost.com/1999/09/17/church-killer-made-dads-life-hell-horrified-neighbors-hid-during-rampages; *TCU Daily Skiff,* September 21, 1999, https://skiff.tcu.edu/SkiffWeb092199/FRONT.html; Dan R. Crawford, *Night of Tragedy, Dawning of Light: The Wedgewood Baptist Shootings* (Colorado Springs: Shaw Books, 2000); Murderpedia, "Larry Gene Ashbrook," accessed October 1, 2020, https://murderpedia.org/male.A/a/ashbrook-larry.htm; Christopher Connelly, "'It Still Hurts, But It Hurts a Little Less': 20 Years after a Fort Worth Church Shooting," KERA News, September 12, 2019, https://www.keranews.org/news/2019-09-12/it-still-hurts-but-it-hurts-a-little-less-20-years-after-a-fort-worth-church-shooting.

30. Murderpedia, s.v. "Robert Wayne Harris," accessed February 4, 2021, https://murderpedia.org/male.H/h/harris-robert-wayne.htm; "National News Briefs; Ex-Employee Arrested in Car Wash Shooting," *New York Times,* March 22, 2000, https://www.nytimes.com/2000/03/22/us/national-news-briefs-ex-employee-arrested-in-car-wash-shootings.html; "Suspect Arrested in Texas Car Wash Slayings," UPI, March 21, 2000, http://www.upi.com/Archives/2000/03/21/Suspect-arrested-in-Texas-car-wash-slayings/4317953614800; Susan Parrott, "Texas Car Wash Slay Trial Begins," September 25, 2000, https://abcnews.go.com/US/story?id=95636&page=1; Clay Morton, "Texas Executes Man Who Murdered 5 at Irving Car Wash 12 Years Ago," *Dallas Morning News,* September 20, 2012, https://www.dallasnews.com/news/2012/09/20/texas-executes-man-who-murdered-5-at-irving-car-wash-12-years-ago; Violence Policy Center, "Where'd They Get Their Guns?."

31. Murderpedia, s.v. "Ki Yung Park," accessed February 4, 2021, https://murderpedia.org/male.P/p/park-ki-yung.htm; Joshua Borelli, "AMKO Trading Store Attack: More Often than We'd Like to Admit, Active Shooters Kill in More than One Location during a 'Single' Event," Officer.com, December 8, 2020, http://www.officer.com/active-shooter/article/21202833/amko-trading-store-attack; Juan Lozano, "4 Killed in Houston Shooting," January 9, 2001, https://apnews.com/article/25acfe0209f7a9f53a1ebff4908fd048; "Five Dead In Houston," CBS News, January 9, 2001, https://cbsnews.com/news/five-dead-in-houston; "5 Dead in Shootings At Houston Businesses, *New York Times,* January 10, 2001, http://www.nytimes.com/2001/01/10/

us/national-news-briefs-5-dead-in-shootings-at-houston-businesses.html; "Korean Shoots 3 to Death, Kills Self in US," *Dong-A-Ilbo,* January 11, 2001, https://www.donga.com/en/article/all/20010111/204801/1/Korean-shoots-3-to-death-kills-self-in-U-S.

32. Jim Vertuno, "Police Say Shooter Was 'Control Freak,'" MyPlainview, July 23, 2003, https://www.myplainview.com/news/article/Police-say-shooter-was-control-freak-08866921.php; "Two Women Dead, One Hurt in San Antonio Office Shooting," Fox News, accessed February 4, 2021, https://www.foxnews.com/story/two-women-dead-one-hurt-in-san-antonio-office-shooting; "More Violence at Work: Texan Kills Two before Shooting Self," *Industrial Safety & Hygiene News,* July 25, 2003, https://www.ishn.com/articles/85646-more-violence-at-work-texan-kills-two-before-shooting-self.

33. Murderpedia, s.v. "Nidal Malik Hasan," accessed October 8, 2020, https://murderpedia.org/male.H/h/hasan-nidal.htm; Robert D. McFadden, "Army Doctor Held in Ft. Hood Rampage," *New York Times,* November 5, 2009; "Gunman Kills 12, Wounds 31 at Fort Hood," NBC News, November 5, 2009, https://www.nbcnews.com/id/wbna33678801; Elise Hu, "TribBlog: Fort Hood Shooting," *Texas Tribune,* November 5, 2009, https://www.texastribune.org/2009/11/05/13-dead-30-wounded-at-fort-hood; Helen Pidd and Ewen MacAskilll, "Fort Hood Gunman Shouted 'Allahu Akbar' as He Opened Fire," *The Guardian,* November 6, 2009, https://www.theguardian.com/world/2009/nov/06/fort-hood-shooter-alive; "10 Minutes of Gunfire 10 Years Ago Left 13 Dead, More than 30 Injured," KWTX News, November 4, 2019, https://www.kwtx.com/content/news/10-minutes-of-gunfire-10-years-ago-left-13-dead-more-than-30-injured-564365711.html; "The Mass Shooting at Fort Hood Was 10 Years Ago, on Nov. 5, 2009," *Army Times,* November 5, 2019, https://www.armytimes.com/news/your-army/2019/11/05/the-mass-shooting-at-fort-hood-was-10-years-ago-on-nov-5-2009; Army Internal Review Team, *Fort Hood: Army Internal Review Team: Final Report* (Washington, DC: US Department of the Army, August 4, 2010). As a result of the shooting, the US Army's Internal Review Team issued a 118-page report on improving security and active-shooter response times at the base to prevent another mass shooting or to increase response efficiency to reduce the number of casualties if such an event did occur again.

34. James C. McKinley Jr., "Texas: Hearing in Fort Hood case," *New York Times,* November 21, 2009, https://www.nytimes.com/2009/11/21/us/21brfs-HEARINGINFOR_BRF.html; Nathan Koppel, "Hasan Found Guilty in Fort Hood Shooting: Army Psychiatrist Faces Sentence of Life in Prison or Death," *Wall Street Journal,* August 24, 2013, http://www.wsj.com/articles/SB10001424127887323665504579030933574360364; Billy Kenber, "Nidal Hasan Sentenced to Death for Fort Hood Shooting Rampage," *Washington Post,* August 28, 2013, https://www.washingtonpost.com/world/national-security/nidal-hasan-sentenced-to-death-for-fort-hood-shooting-rampage/2013/08/28/aad28de2–offa-11e3-bdf6-e4fc677d94a1_story.html; Jonathan Stempel, "US Judge Dismisses Claims over 2009 Fort Hood Massacre," Reuters, January 23, 2019, https://www.reuters.com/article/usa-shooting-fort-

hood/u-s-judge-dismisses-claims-over-2009-fort-hood-massacre-idUSKCN1PH 29M.

35. "FBI: Gunman was retired sergeant," *Courier of Montgomery County* (TX), September 20, 2010, https://yourconroenews.com/neighborhood/moco/news/ article/FBI-Gunman-was-retired-sergeant-9273348.php; "FBI Identifies Fort Bliss Shooter," CNN, September 9, 2010, https://www.cnn.com/2010/CRIME/09/21/texas .base.shooting/index.html; Michael Martinez, "Ft. Bliss Shooting Investigated by FBI," FBI–El Paso Division, September 21, 2010, https://archives.fbi.gov/archives/ elpaso/press-releases/2010/ep092110.htm; "FBI: Fort Bliss Gunman Was Retired Army Sergeant," *San Diego Union Tribune*, September 21, 2010, https://www.sand iegouniontribune.com/sdut-fbi-fort-bliss-gunman-was-retired-army-sergeant-2010sep21-story.html; David E. Poe, "Bliss Shoppette Shooting Leaves 2 Dead, 1 Injured," *Fort Bliss Monitor*, September 22, 2010, https://www.army.mil/article/45531/ bliss_shoppette_shooting_leaves_2_dead_1_injured.

36. Chris Quinn and David Hendricks, "SAPD Officer Shoots, Kills Gunman outside North Side Club," MySA, March 14, 2015, https://www.mysanantonio.com/news/ local/article/SAPD-officer-shoots-kills-gunman-outside-North-6133965.php; "Police Fatally Shoot Man Who Fired into a Crowd outside San Antonio Bar," accessed February 4, 2021, https://ktxs.com/news/texas/police-fatally-shoot-man-who-fired-into-a-crowd-outside-san-antonio-bar-; Jessica Soto, "SAPD Officer Shoots, Kills Man Who Opened Fire at North Side Bar," KSAT News, March 14, 2015, https://www.ksat.com/ news/2015/03/14/sapd-officer-shoots-kills-man-who-opened-fire-at-north-side-bar.

37. Schildkraut, *Mass Shootings in America*, 174; "4 People Transported to Hospital after a Shooting Near Brownsville Nightclub," CBS4 News, November 22, 2015, https://www.valleycentral.com/news/local-news/4-people-transported-to-hospital-after-a-shooting-near-brownsville-nightclub; "Brownsville Night Club Shooter Wanted," *Valley Central Daily News* (Harlingen, TX), December 1, 2015, https://www .valleycentral.com/news/local-news/brownsville-night-club-shooter-wanted.

38. "4 Injured in Seminole Shootings, Suspect in Custody," KCBD News, March 5, 2017, https://www.kcbd.com/story/34668372/4-injured-in-seminole-shootings-suspect-in-custody; "UPDATE: Two Dead After Four Shot in Seminole, Gaines County," everythingLubbock.com, March 6, 2017, https://www.everythinglubbock. com/news/update-two-dead-after-four-shot-in-seminole-gaines-county; Lucinda Holt, "Document: Suspect Warned 'You're a Dead Man' before Double Slaying," *Lubbock Avalanche-Journal*, March 10, 2017, https://www.lubbockonline.com/crime-and-courts/local/news/2017-03-10/document-suspect-warned-you-re-dead-man-double-slaying; Eleventh Court of Appeals, No. 11-19-00007-CR, *Jacob R. Groening v. The State of Texas*, on appeal from the 106th District Court, Gaines County, Texas, Trial Court Case No. 17-4718 (January 14, 2021), 2–6.

39. City of El Paso, Texas, "City of El Paso Issues Disaster Declaration," news release, August 4, 2019; Samuel Gaytan et al., "El Paso Shooting Updates: 22 Killed in El Paso Walmart Shooting Near Cielo Vista Mall," *El Paso Times*, August 3,

2019, https://www.elpasotimes.com/story/news/crime/2019/08/03/el-paso-police-report-shooter-walmart-cielo-vista-mall/1910012001; Jim Schaefer and Tresa Baldas, "Inside the El Paso Shooting: A Store Manager, a Frantic Father, Grateful Survivors," *El Paso Times,* August 10, 2019, https://www.elpasotimes.com/in-depth/news/2019/08/10/walmart-el-paso-shooting-survivors-victims-timeline/1962337001; Alejandro Martines-Carera and Mary Huber, "'Texas Grieves': 20 Killed, 26 Injured in El Paso Shooting," *Austin American-Statesman,* August 2, 2019, https://www.statesman.com/news/20190803/texas-grieves-20-killed-26-injured-in-el-paso-shooting; Julián Aguilar and Bobby Blanchard, "Horror in El Paso: 20 Dead, 26 Wounded in Mass Shooting at Walmart," *Texas Tribune,* August 3, 2019, https://texastribune.org/2019/08/03/el-paso-police-say-mass-shooter-active-cielo-vista-mall; Chris Francescani et al., "Mass Shooting That Killed 20 in El Paso Investigated as 'Domestic Terrorism': Officials," ABC News, August 4, 2019, https://abcnews.go.com/US/police-el-paso-issue-report-active-shooter/story?id=64753896; Chas Danner, "Everything We Know about the El Paso Walmart Massacre," *Intelligencer,* August 7, 2019, https://nymag.com/intelligencer/2019/08/everything-we-know-about-the-el-paso-walmart-shooting.html; Lois Beckett and Sam Levin, "El Paso Shooting at Walmart Leaves 21 People Dead," *The Guardian,* August 3, 2019, https://www.theguardian.com/us-news/2019/aug/03/el-paso-shooting-texas-walmart; Simon Romero, Manny Fernandez, and Meriel Padilla, "Day at a Shopping Center in Texas Turns Deadly, *New York Times,* August 3, 2019, https://www.nytimes.com/2019/08/03/us/el-paso-walmart-shooting.html; Erin Ailworth, Georgia Wells, and Ian Lovett, "Lost in Life, El Paso Suspect Found a Dark World Online," *Wall Street Journal,* August 8, 2019, https://www.wsj.com/articles/lost-in-life-el-paso-suspect-found-a-dark-world-online-11565308783; Simon Romero, Manny Fernandez, and Meriel Padilla, "Massacre at a Crowed Walmart in Texas Leaves 20 Dead," *New York Times,* August 8, 2019, https://nytimes.com/2019/08/03/us/el-paso-shooting.html; Tim Arango, Nicholas Bogel-Burroughs, and Katie Benner, "Minutes before El Paso Killing, Hate-Filled Manifesto Appears Online," *New York Times,* August 3, 2019, https://www.nytimes.com/2019/08/03/us/patrick-crusius-el-paso-shooter-manifesto.html; Agence France-Presse, "Gunman Kills 20 at Texas Walmart Store in Latest US Mass Shooting," accessed November 20, 2020, https://go.gale.com/ps/i.do?p=GIC&u=txshracd2489&id=GALE|A595476358&v=2.1&it=r&sid=ebsco; "Death Toll Rises to 22 in Mass Shooting in El Paso, US Texas," accessed November 20, 2020, http://go.gale.com/ps/i.do?pGIC&u=txshracd2489&id-GALE/A595610930&v=2.1=r&sid=ebsco.

40. Kim Krisberg, "Austin's Fight against Gun Violence," *Austin Monthly,* November 2019, https://www.austinmonthly.com/austins-fight-against-gun-violence; Jenna Johnson, "Two Versions of Texas Collide over Gun Measures and Mass Shootings," *Washington Post,* November 8, 2019; Faith Karimi and Allen Kim, "Texas Loosens Firearm Laws Hours after the State's Latest Mass Shooting Left 7 Dead," CNN, September 1, 2019, https://www.cnn.com/2019/09/01/us/texas-new-gun-laws-trnd/index.html; "How Gun Laws in Texas Have and Haven't Changed

Following Mass Shootings in the State," NPR, August 6, 2020, https://www.npr.org/2019/08/06/748811018/how-gun-laws-in-texas-have-and-havent-changed-following-mass-shootings-in-the-st; Ross Ramsey, "Mass Shootings Appall Texas Politicians. So Do the Solutions," *Washington Post,* August 4, 2019; Chandelis Duster, "Texas Gov. Greg Abbott Issues 8 Executive Orders Aimed at Preventing Mass Shootings," CNN, September 5, 2019, https://www.cnn.com/2019/09/05/politics/texas-greg-abbott-executive-orders-mass-shootings/index.html; Cassandra Pollock, "Texas House Speaker Dennis Bonnen Asks Lawmakers to Study Strengthening Laws That Keep Firearms from Felons," *Texas Tribune,* September 4, 2019, https://www.texastribune.org/2019/09/04/dennis-bonnen-appoints-members-house-committee-mass-violence; Patrick Svitek, "Texas Safety Commission Discusses Guns, Terrorism and Social Media at Post-El Paso Roundtable," *Texas Tribune,* August 22, 2019, https://www.texastribune.org/2019/08/22/greg-abbotts-texas-safety-commission-meets-after-el-paso-shooting; Cassandra Pollock, "Gov. Greg Abbott Issues Eight Executive Orders Aimed at Stopping Potential Mass Shooters," *Texas Tribune,* September 5, 2019, https://www.texastribune.org/2019/09/05/texas-gov-greg-abbott-releases-executive-orders-after-mass-shootings; Office of the Texas Governor, "Governor Abbott Forms Domestic Terrorism Task Force in the Wake of El Paso Shooting," August 14, 2019, https://gov.texas.gov/news/post/governor-abbott-forms-domestic-terrorism-task-force-in-the-wake-of-el-paso-shooting.

41. "Texas Mass Shooting Treated as Domestic Terrorism Case: US Attorney," August 5, 2019, https://www.globaltimes.cn/content/1160344.shtml ; "Texas Mass Shooting Treated as Domestic Terrorism," *Cyprus Mail,* August 5, 2019, https://cyprus-mail.com/2019/08/05/texas-mass-shooting-treated-as-domestic-terrorism; "The Mass Shooting in Texas Is Putting New Focus on the Spread of Hate Online," *Today,* August 6, 2019, https://www.today.com/video/el-paso-shooting-puts-new-focus-on-spread-of-online-hate-65399365558; Elizabeth Findell, "Accused El Paso Shooter Patrick Crusius Pleads Not Guilty," *Wall Street Journal,* accessed October 9, 2020, https://www.wsj.com/articles/accused-el-paso-shooter-patrick-crusius-pleads-not-guilty-11570739840; Molly Smith, Aaron Montes, and Daniel Borunda, "90 Federal Charges Filed against El Paso Walmart Mass Shooting Suspect," *El Paso Times,* February 6, 2020, https://www.elpasotimes.com/story/news/crime/2020/02/06/el-paso-walmart-shooting-patrick-crusius-faces-hate-crime-charges/4673136002; Daniel Conrad, "El Paso Shooting Suspect Faces New Murder, Hate Crime Charges," Courthouse News Service, June 25, 2020, http://www.courthousenews.com/el-paso-shooting-suspect-faces-new-murder-hate-crime-charges; Aaron Martinez, "Suspect Faces New Federal Charges in El Paso Walmart Mass Shooting," *El Paso Times,* July 9, 2020; Julián Aguilar, "Who Should Prosecute the El Paso Walmart Shooting Suspect? A Year after the Massacre, Local and Federal Prosecutors Still Face Hard Decisions," *Texas Tribune,* July 31, 2020, https://www.texastribune.org/2020/07/31/el-paso-walmart-shooting-prosecute; "Mexico to Take Legal Action after Mass Shooting," accessed November 20, 2020, http://www

.xinhuanet.com/english/2019-08/06/c_138285969.htm; "'It's Real. It's Violent': After El Paso, Latinos across America Live in Fear," *USA Today,* August 16, 2019, August 16, 2019, https://www.usatoday.com/story/news/nation/2019/08/16/el-paso-texas-mass-shooting-latino-hispanic-reaction/2027932001; Stephen Sawchuk, Denisa R. Superville, and Héctor Alejandro Arzate, "Schools Face Latino Kids' Fears after Shooting," *Education Week* 39, no. 1 (August 21, 2019): 5–6; Julián Aguilar, "'Forgiveness Isn't Given Lightly': El Pasoans Balance Healing with Anger a Year after Walmart Massacre," *Texas Tribune,* August 3, 2020, https://www.texastribune.org/2020/08/03/el-paso-walmart-shooting-anniversary; "Walmart to Limit Ammunition Sales after Mass Shooting in Texas Store," *International Business Times,* September 4, 2019; Vera Bergengruen and W. J. Henningan, "Special Report: The Terror Within," *Time,* August 19, 2019: 22–27.

42. Murderpedia, s.v. "Ronald Lee Haskell," accessed October 8, 2021, https://murderpedia.org/male.H/h/haskell-ronald-lee.htm; "6 Dead in Texas Shooting; Suspect Surrenders after Standoff," ABC News, July 9, 2014, https://abcnews.go.com/US/kids-dead-texas-home-shooting/story?id=24496951; David Stout and Laura Stampler, "Prosecutors: Houston Shooting Suspect First Bound His 6 Victims," July 9, 2014, https://time.com/2971288/six-dead-shooting-spring-houston-texas; Jeremy Rogalski, "Court Records Reveal Haskell Planned and Plotted Shooting Rampage," KENS5 News, September 9, 2014, https://www.kens5.com/article/news/investigations/court-records-reveal-haskell-planned-and-plotted-shooting-rampage/285-259152518; "Authorities: Gunman Tied Up Family before Executing Them," CBS News, July 10, 2014, https://www.cbsnews.com/news/rampage-in-suburban-houston-home-leaves-6-dead; "Prosecutor: Gunman Shot 7 Relatives Execution Style," *USA Today,* July 10, 2014, https://www.usatoday.com/story/news/nation/2014/07/10/houston-shooting-multiple-fatalities-suspect-identified/12466251; Brian Rogers, "Man Accused in Spring Family Massacre Will Face Death Penalty," *Houston Chronicle,* August 26, 2016, https://www.chron.com/neighborhood/spring/news/article/Death-penalty-trial-set-for-man-accussed-in-Spring-9186401.php; "Timeline: 6 Members of Stay Family Killed in Their Home in Spring," ABC13 News, August 28, 2019, https://abc13.com/stay-family-murdered-execution-style-spring-killed-trial/5493731; "Murder Defendant Told Investigators, 'I'm Just Not Right in the Head,'" ABC13 News, August 28, 2019, https://abc13.com/stay-family-trial-murders-spring-killed-ronald-lee-haskell-jr/5498434; Office of District Attorney, Harris County, Texas, "Haskell Sentenced to Death for Family Massacre," October 11, 2019, https://app.dao.hctx.net/haskell-sentenced-death-family-massacre.

43. Murderpedia, s.v. "Ronald Lee Haskell," accessed October 8, 2021, https://murderpedia.org/male.C/c/conley-david.htm; Faith Karmi, "Suspect in Houston Killings Handcuffed 8 Victims, Then Shot Them, Authorities Say," CNN, August 10, 2015, https://www.cnn.com/2015/08/10/us/houston-killings/index.html; Dane Schiller et al., "Suspect Charged with Capital Murder in Death of 6 Children, 2 Adults," *Houston Chronicle,* August 10, 2015, http://www.chron.com/news/houston/

article/Reports-Five-children-three-adults-shot-dead-in-6433574.php; Miya Shay, "Family Massacre Suspect Reportedly Details How Killings Were Planned and Executed," ABC Eyewitness News, August 12, 2015, http://abc7chicago.com/8-dead-david-conley-houston-murders-family-murder/923772; "Victims in Mass Killing in Northwest Harris County Identified," vABC Eyewitness News, August 10, 2015, https://abc13.com/harris-county-sheriffs-office-swat-standoff-mass-shooting/914922; Brian Rogers, "Suspect in Mass Shooting Faked Earlier Psych Tests," *Houston Chronicle,* February 10, 2016, https://www.houstonchronicle.com/news/houston-texas/houston/article/Suspect-in-mass-shooting-faked-earlier-psych-tests-6822123.php.

44. "Texas Shooting: Eight Killed, including Gunman, at House Party," *The Guardian,* September 11, 2017, https://www.theguardian.com/us-news/2017/sep/11/texas-shooting-eight-killed-plano-house-party; Laura Petrecca, "8 Dead, including Gunman, after Shooting in Plano, Texas," *USA Today,* September 10, 2017, https://www.usatoday.com/story/news/2017/09/10/reports-deadly-shooting-8-plano-texas/652379001; Lauren del Valle, "8 Killed in Shooting at Dallas Cowboys Watch Party in Plano, Police Say," CNN, September 12, 2017, https://www.cnn.com/2017/09/12/us/texas-plano-mass-shooting-at-cowboys-watch-party/index.html; Ruth Varghese, "Five UTD Alumni Killed in Mass Shooting at Plano Home," *UDT Mercury,* September 13, 2017, https://utdmercury.com/four-utd-alumni-killed-plano-home-mass-shooting; "Man Who Killed Estranged Wife, 7 Others Had Drinking Problem," *Washington Times,* September 13, 2017, https://www.washingtontimes.com/news/2017/sep/13/man-slays-estranged-wife-friends-in-shooting-at-te; "Plano Mass Shooting: Details Revealed about Gunman Spencer Hight," CBS News, September 14, 2017, https://www.cbsnews.com/news/plano-mass-shooting-details-revealed-about-gunman-spencer-hight. One aspect of this case that emerged in the months after the shooting related to the bartender who served alcohol to Hight after he showed signs of being drunk. For more details on the charges waged against the bartender, see Stephen Young, "Shooter in the Plano Watch Party Massacre Showed Off Weapons at Bar Before Bloodbath," *Dallas Observer,* September 27, 2017, https://www.dallasobserver.com/news/plano-football-party-shooting-newest-details-9914609; Morgan Gstalter, "Bartender Accused of Serving Intoxicated Gunman before 2017 Texas Mass Shooting," *The Hill,* May 7, 2019, https://thehill.com/blogs/blog-briefing-room/news/442453-bartender-faces-jail-time-for-serving-intoxicated-gunman-before; Jamiel Lynch and Hollie Silverman, "A Man Shot and Killed 8 People after Leaving a Bar. The Bartender Who Served Him 5 Drinks Was Arrested," CNN, May 8, 2019, https://www.cnn.com/2019/05/08/us/bartender-arrested-intoxicated-man-shooting.

45. "Police: Houston Shooter Chose Spot for Tactical Advantage," CBS News, May 31, 2016, https://www.cbsnews.com/news/police-houston-shooter-chose-spot-for-tactical-advantage; Lomi Kriel and Will Axford, "Gunman Appeared in Midst of a 'Mental Health Crisis,'" *Houston Chronicle,* May 31, 2016, https://www.houstonchronicle.com/news/houston-texas/houston/article/Houston-news-7955711.php;

"Police: 212 Rounds Fired in Houston Mass Shooting," *USA Today,* May 31, 2016, http://www.usatoday.com/story/news/nation-now/2016/05/31/police-212-rounds-fired-houston/85220390; "Family ID's 'Troubled' Army Veteran as Gunman in Houston Rampage," CBS News, May 31, 2016, https://www.cbsnews.com/news/family-ids-troubled-army-vet-dionisio-garza-as-gunman-in-houston-rampage; "Officer Targeted in 2016 Deadly Mass Shooting Shares Story of Survival," CBS News, June 13, 2017, https://abc13.com/shotting-memorial-day-dionisio-garza-houston/2094601. Some reports attempted to connect Garza with Trump supporters, making it clear how political agendas sometimes enter into the media's coverage of mass shootings.

46. "Mass Shooting—Lance Cpl. Esteban J. Smith (Eden, Texas)," May 26, 2013, https://usgunviolence.wordpress.com/2013/05/26/mass-shooting-lance-cpl-esteban-j-smith-eden-tx; "Marine Killed after Shootout with Police in Texas," UPI, May 28, 2013, https://www.upi.com/Top_News/US/2013/05/28/Marine-killed-after-shootout-with-police-in-Texas/79721369738218; Michael Zennie, "Revealed: Decorated US Marine Who Killed a Woman and Wounded Five in Random Texas Shooting Spree Stabbed His Wife to Death in North Carolina Motel 1,500 Miles Away," *Daily Mail,* updated May 29, 2013, https://www.dailymail.co.uk/news/article-2332383/Esteban-Smith-rampage-Decorated-U-S-Marine-killed-woman-wounded-random-Texas-shooting-spree-stabbed-wife-death-North-Carolina-motel-1-500-miles-away.html; Laura Liera, "Parents of Marine Shooting Suspect Remember Him as Loving, Smart Son," Bakersfield.com, May 30, 2013, updated September 8, 2016, https://www.bakersfield.com/archives/parents-of-marine-shooting-suspect-remember-him-as-loving-smart-son/article_5b37b0e1-6350-5163-9666-eb5cdb9ee46e.html; Alix Bryan, "Marine Shooting Suspect's Wife Found Dead in NC Hotel," WTVR News, May 28, 2013, https://www.wtvr.com/2013/05/28/marine-shooting-suspects-wife-found-dead-in-nc-hotel; Betsy Blaney and Michael Biesecker, "Marine's Mom Doesn't Know What Led to Texas Rampage," *USA Today,* May 28, 2013, https://www.usatoday.com/story/news/nation/2013/05/28/marine-rampage-mom/2368049; "Marine in Texas Shooting Also Killed Wife, Police Say," CNN, May 28, 2013, https://www.cnn.com/2013/05/28/us/texas-marine-fatal-shooting-spree/index.html.

47. "Shooting in Houston: 7 Injured after Shooter Opened Fire in Randalls Supermarket, Suspect Shot Dead," India.com, September 26, 2016, https://www.india.com/news/world/shooting-in-houston-7-injured-after-shooter-opened-fire-in-randalls-supermarket-suspect-shot-dead-1515005; John Bacon, "Houston Gunman's Rampage Ends with Suspect Dead," *USA Today,* September 26, 2019, https://www.usatoday.com/story/news/nation/2016/09/26/houston-police-gunman-killed-after-shooting-several-people/91108136; "Nazi Materials Found in Wake of Houston Lawyer Shooting Rampage," ABC7 News, September 26, 2016, https://abc7.com/houston-shooting-texas-active-police-department/1526727.

48. Acacia Coronado and Alex Samuels, "Death Toll in the Midland-Odessa Mass Shooting Climbs to Eight, including the Shooter, *Texas Tribune,* August 31, 2019, https://www.texastribune.org/2019/08/31/odessa-and-midland-shooting-30-victims

-reports-say; Wesley Lowery and Emily Davies, "5 Killed, 21 Injured in a Mass Shooting in Odessa, Texas," *Washington Post,* August 31, 2019, https://www.washingtonpost.com/politics/5-killed-21-injured-after-suspect-hijacked-a-mail-truck-in-odessa-texas/2019/08/31/f659da2c-cc3c-11e9-be05-f76ac4ec618c_story.html; Dakin Andone, "What We Know about the West Texas Mass Shooting," CNN, September 1, 2019, https://www.cnn.com/2019/09/01/us/texas-shooting-what-we-know/index.html; "Death Toll Rises to 7 in US Texas Mass Shooting," accessed November 20, 2020, http://www.china.org.cn/world/2019-09/02/content_75161606.htm; Perry Vandell, "Texas Shooter Who Killed 7 in Odessa Identified," *USA Today,* September 1, 2019, https://www.usatoday.com/story/news/nation/2019/09/01/texas-shooting-gunman-identified-seth-ator/2188123001; Martin Pengelly and Victoria Bekiempis, "Texas Shooting: Five Dead and 21 Injured Near Midland and Odessa, *The Guardian,* August 31, 2019, https://www.theguardian.com/us-news/2019/aug/31/midland-texas-shooting-odessa; Adrianna Rodriguez and BrieAnna J. Frank, "FBI: Texas Shooter 'on Long Spiral Down.' Here's What We Know," *USA Today,* September 2, 2019, https://www.usatoday.com/story/news/nation/2019/09/02/texas-shootings-midland-odessa-what-we-know-rampage-victims/2190982001; Marco della Cava and BrieAnna J. Frank, "A Lone Gunman Fleeing Texas Police Stalked and Shot People over a Frenzied Hour. Scanner Traffic Reveals the Chaos," *USA Today,* September 4, 2019,, https://www.usatoday.com/story/news/nation/2019/09/04/texas-shooting-midland-odessa-police-scanner-audio-reveals-chase/2197222001; Allison Aubrey, "Texas Gunman Who Killed 7 Had Been Fired Just Hours Before Shootings," NPR, September 2, 2019, https://www.npr.org/2019/09/02/756772750/texas-gunman-who-killed-7-had-been-fired-just-hours-before-shootings-reports; Jake Bleiberg, "Records: Odessa Gunman Had 'Suicidal Tendencies' in 2001," *MRT,* September 10, 2019, updated September 11, 2019, https://www.mrt.com/news/article/Records-West-Texas-gunman-has-suicidal-14430883.php; "Neighbor Says Gunman Was 'Violent, Aggressive,'" YourBasin.com, August 31, 2019, updated December 4, 2019, https://www.yourbasin.com/news/local-news/tragedy-strikes-odessa-here-is-everything-we-know; John MacCormack, "Odessa Gunman Lived in a Dirt-Floor Shack, a Small Dog His Only Companion," *San Antonio Express News,* September 2, 2019, https://www.expressnews.com/news/local/article/Odessa-gunman-lived-in-a-dirt-floor-shack-and-14407506.php.

49. Cindy George, Erin Mulvaney, and Brent Zwerneman, "Eviction Notice Sparked Fatal Shooting in College Station," *Houston Chronicle,* August 13, 2012, https://www.chron.com/news/houston-texas/article/3-killed-including-officer-and-gunman-near-3784724.php; Jim Forsyth, "Three Dead in Shooting Near Texas A&M University," Reuters, August 13, 2012, https://www.reuters.com/article/instant-article/idINDEE87C0G020120814; "3 Killed in Shooting Near Texas A&M University," CNN, August 13, 2012, https://www.cnn.com/2012/08/13/justice/texas-am-shooting/index.html; Manny Fernandez and Michael Schwartz, "3 Dead, including Gunman, in Shooting Near Texas A&M," *New York Times,* August 14,

2012, https://www.nytimes.com/2012/08/14/us/3-including-gunman-are-killed-in-shooting-near-texas-am.html; Erin Mulvaney and Cindy George, "Shooter's Life Was Heading Downhill," MySA, August 14, 2012, https://mysanantonio.com/news/local_news/article/Shooter-s-life-was-heading-downhill-3788635.php; Reeve Hamilton, "A&M Trying to Distance Itself from Shooting Incident," *Texas Tribune*, August 14, 2012, accessed February 4, 2021, https://texastribune.org/2012/08/14/m-trying-distance-itself-shooting-incident.

50. Manny Fernandez and Ashley Southall, "Dallas Gunman Killed after Attack on Police Headquarters," *New York Times*, June 13, 2015, https://nytimes.com/2015/06/13/us/dallas-police-shooting.html; Tom Dart, "Dallas Police Attack: Gunman Confirmed Dead Hours after Opening Fire on HQ," *The Guardian*, June 13, 2015, https://theguardian.com/us-news/2015/jun/13/dallas-police-headquarters-shooting-dead; Jason Hanna and Joe Sutton, "Dallas Police HQ Shooting: Suspect James Boulware Killed during Standoff," CNN, June 13, 2015, 2020, https://www.cnn.com/2015/06/13/us/dallas-police-headquarters-shooting/index.html; Elizabeth Chuck, "Dallas Police Attack: Suspect James Boulware 'Heard Voices' Mom Says," NBC News, June 13, 2015, https://www.nbcnews.com/news/us-news/suspect-dallas-police-ambush-had-history-violence-n374921; Nomaan Merchant, "Man Linked to Dallas Police HQ Attack Had Violent Past," *Detroit News*, June 13, 2015, http://www.detroitnews.com/story/news/nation/2015/06/14/dallas-police-headquarters-attack/71219504; Tristan Hallman and Naomi Martin, "One Year Later: Police in Peril when James Boulware Rained Bullets on Dallas Police Headquarters, It Was the 'Worst of Days,'" *Dallas Morning News*, June 11, 2016, http://interactives.dallasnews.com/2016/dpd-shooting.

51. Manny Fernandez, Richard Pérez-Peña, and Jonah Engel Bromwich, "Five Dallas Officers Were Killed as Payback, Police Chief Says," *New York Times*, July 9, 2016, https://www.nytimes.com/2016/07/09/us/dallas-police-shooting.html; Brendan McGarry and Richard, "Dallas Police Shooter Was Army Reserve Vet Who Served in Afghanistan," Military.com, July 8, 2016, https://www.military.com/daily-news/2016/07/08/dallas-police-shooter-identified-as-former-us-soldier-reports.html; Tessa Berenson and Katie Reilly, "Everything We Know So Far about the Dallas Shooting Suspect," *Time*, July 8, 2016, https://time.com/4398101/dallas-police-shooting-suspects; WSJ News Graphics, "What We Know about the Dallas Attack on Police," *Wall Street Journal*, July 8, 2016, https://graphics.wsj.com/how-a-gunman-killed-five-dallas-police-officers; Dan Frosch, Arian Campo-Flores, and Alexandra Berzon, "Dallas Police Killer Took a Sudden, Violent Turn," *Wall Street Journal*, July 11, 2016, https://www.wsj.com/articles/dallas-police-killer-took-a-sudden-violent-turn-1468199545; Administration of Barack Obama, "Remarks at a Memorial Service for Victims of the Shooting in Dallas, Texas" (July 12, 2016); Marjorie Owens, "7/7 One Year Later: Signs of PTSD, Mental Illness; Search for Treatments," KHOU News, July 7, 2017, updated August 22, 2017, https://www

.khou.com/article/news/local/july-7/77-one-year-later-signs-of-ptsd-mental-illness-search-for-treatments/287-455032034.

52. German Lopez, "How Systemic Racism Entangles All Police Officers–Even Black Cops," Vox, updated August 15, 2016, https://www.vox.com/2015/5/7/8562077/police-racism-implicit-bias; Lydia Denworth, "A Civil Rights Expert Explains the Social Science of Police Racism," *Scientific American,* June 4, 2020, https://www.scientificamerican.com/article/a-civil-rights-expert-explains-the-social-science-of-police-racism; Data USA, "Police Officers," accessed on February 26, 2021, https://datausa.io/profile/soc/police-officers#demographics; Heather Mac Donald, "The Myth of Systemic Police Racism," *Wall Street Journal,* June 2, 2020, https://www.wsj.com/articles/the-myth-of-systemic-police-racism-11591119883. It is interesting to note that those who claim systemic racism exists in police departments across the nation ignore the fact that 44.5 percent of all police officers are nonwhite.

53. Schildkraut, *Mass Shootings in America,* 168; Schildkraut and Elsass, *Mass Shootings,* 49; Mark Thompson, "Hunting for Elusive Answers in the Fort Hood Shooting," *Time,* April 2, 2014, https://time.com/47744/fort-hood-shooting-2; Emily Brown, "Fort Hood Shootings: Breaking Down 2014 and 2009, *USA Today,* April 3, 2014, https://www.usatoday.com/story/news/nation/2014/04/03/fort-hood-shootings-2009-2014-compare-contrast/7258515; Daniel Seduski, "Army Releases Report on 2014 Fort Hood Shooting," Homeland Security Digital Library, January 27, 2015, updated May 20, 2016, https://www.hsdl.org/c/army-releases-report-on-2014-fort-hood-shooting; Department of the Army, *Report of Investigation pertaining to the 2 April 2014 Shooting at Fort Hood, Texas* (June 9, 2014), accessed February 27, 2021, https://www.hsdl.org/?abstract&did=761564; Terri Langford, "Fort Hood Shooting Sparks Calls for Concealed Guns on Military Bases," *Texas Tribune,* April 16, 2014, https://www.texastribune.org/2014/04/16/fort-hood-shooting-sparks-debate-soldiers-conceale.

54. Dale Lezon, "Two Dead in Workplace Shooting at Katy Trucking Company," *Houston Chronicle,* May 4, 2016, https://www.chron.com/neighborhood/katy/news/article/Shooting-prompts-lockdown-at-Morton-high-in-west-7392521.php; "Gunman, Victim in Knight Transportation Shooting Identified," *Truckers News,* May 5, 2016, https://www.truckersnews.com/gunman-victim-in-knight-transportation-shooting-identified; Matt Cole, "Victim, Shooter Identified in Knight Transportation Shooting," *Overdrive,* May 5, 2016, updated May 8, 2016, https://www.overdriveonline.com/business/article/14890243/victim-shooter-identified-in-knight-transportation-shooting; Catherine E. Shoichet, "Texas Shooting: Fired Employee Kills 1 at Transportation Center," CNN, May 4, 2016, https://www.cnn.com/2016/05/04/us/texas-shooting-knight-transportation/index.html; "Two Killed in Texas Trucking Company Murder-Suicide," Fox News, May 5, 2016, https://www.foxnews.com/us/two-killed-in-texas-trucking-company-murder-suicide; L. M. Sixel, "Active Shooters at Work on Rise," *Houston Chronicle,* May 13, 2016,

https://www.houstonchronicle.com/business/article/Active-shooters-at-work-on-rise-7468247.php.

55. "Gunman Kills at Least 26 in Attack on Rural Texas Church," *New York Times,* November 5, 2017, https://www.nytimes.com/2017/11/05/us/church-shooting-texas .html; Jim Vertuno, "26 Killed in Texas Church Attack," Police1, November 5, 2017, https://www.police1.com/active-shooter/articles/26-killed-in-texas-church-attack-N9DRHbO3WDiGEuKZ; Neena Satija, "At Least 26 Dead after Worst Mass Shooting in Texas History at San Antonio-Area Church," *Texas Tribune,* November 5, 2017, https://www.texastribune.org/2017/11/05/reports-multiple-people-dead-following-central-texas-police-shooting; "Scenes from the Ground: The Mass Church Shooting in Sutherland Springs, Texas," NPR, November 5, 2017, https://www .npr.org/2017/11/05/562233957/scenes-from-the-ground-the-mass-church-shooting-in-sutherland-springs-texas; Saeed Ahmed, Doug Criss, and Joe Sterling, "This Man May Have Prevented the Texas Mass Shooting from Getting Any Deadlier," WLS-AM, November 6, 2017, https://www.wlsam.com/2017/11/06/this-man-may-have-prevented-the-texas-mass-shooting-from-getting-any-deadlier; Michael J. Mooney, "The Hero of the Sutherland Springs Shooting Is Still Reckoning with What Happened That Day," *Texas Monthly,* October 27, 2018, https://www.texas monthly.com/articles/stephen-willeford-sutherland-springs-mass-murder. For a more detailed account of the shooting, especially the victims' stories, see Joe Holley's *Sutherland Springs: God, Guns, and Hope in a Texas Town* (New York: Hachette Books, 2020).

56. Silvia Foster-Frau, "Sutherland Springs Gunman Spoke of Mass Shooting Years before Attack," *San Antonio Express-News,* August 25, 2020, https://www .expressnews.com/news/local/article/Sutherland-Springs-gunman-spoke-of-mass-shooting-15514642.php; "Texas Gunman Had History of Violence Years before Shooting," AP News, August 26, 2020, https://apnews.com/article/shootings-tx-state-wire-us-news-religion-96f3275c99658ddbcacf4b65b224f5e2; "Court Documents: Texas Church Shooter Had History of Violence Years before Opening Fire in Suther land Springs," CBS DFW, August 27, 2020, https://dfw.cbslocal.com/2020/08/27/court-documents-texas-church-shooter-had-history-of-violence-years-before-opening-fire-in-sutherland-springs; Alison Kodjak, "In Texas and Beyond, Mass Shootings Have Roots in Domestic Violence," NPR, November 7, 2017, https://www .npr.org/sections/health-shots/2017/11/07/562387350/in-texas-and-beyond-mass-shootings-have-roots-in-domestic-violence; "Texas Church Shooter Once Escaped from a Mental Health Center," *Press-Enterprise,* November 7, 2017, https://www .pe.com/2017/11/07/air-force-admits-fault-in-reporting-shooters-past-crimes.

57. Rebecca Kheel, "Congress Demands Details over How Gunman Got Arms: After Texas Mass Shooting, Lawmakers Raise Questions over Whether Military Has Systemic Problem with Reporting," *The Hill* 24, no. 99 (November 8, 2017): 4; A. C. Thompson and T. Christian Miller, "Will Texas Massacre Finally Push the Military to Improve Its Criminal Reporting System?," *Texas Tribune,* November 7, 2017,

https://www.texastribune.org/2017/11/07/will-texas-massacre-finally-push-military-improve-its-criminal-reporti; Alex Samuels, "Texas House Passes Bill Allowing Handgun Owners to Carry Weapons in Church," *Texas Tribune,* May 20, 2020, https://www.texastribune.org/2019/05/20/texas-handgun-allowed-churches-suther land-springs; Benjamin Fearnow, Texas Allows Guns in Churches, Schools after Firearm Access Law Expands, Effective September 1," *Newsweek,* September 1, 2019, https://www.newsweek.com/texas-gun-laws-september-1-effect-schools-churches-restrictions-1457123; John Cornyn, Fix NICS (National Instant Criminal Background Check System) Act, accessed February 28, 2021, https://www.cornyn.senate.gov/fixnics; Joe Difazio, "After Texas Mass Shooting Dishonorable Discharge Gun Ban Number Spikes," *International Business Times,* February 12, 2018, https://www.ibtimes.com/after-texas-church-shooting-dishonorable-discharge-gun-bans-spike-2652652.

58. Joe Holley, "Holley: I Spent a Year with Mass Shooting Victims. Horror Doesn't Heal," *Houston Chronicle,* August 4, 2019, https://www.houstonchronicle.com/opinion/outlook/article/Holley-I-spent-a-year-with-mass-shooting-14279469.php; Matt Wotus and Emily Smith, "Texas Church Turned into a Memorial after Mass Shooting," CNN, November 13, 2017, https://www.cnn.com/2017/11/13/us/inside-first-baptist-church/index.html; Dakin Andone and Jaide Timm-Garcia, "Texas Church Holds First Service since Mass Shooting," CNN, November 13, 2017, https://www.cnn.com/2017/11/12/us/texas-church-service-memorial/index.html; Joey Palacios, "Texas Baptist Church Opens New Sanctuary after 2017 Mass Shooting," NPR, May 19, 2019, https://www.npr.org/2019/05/19/724851331/sutherland-springs-baptist-church-opens-sanctuary-after-2017-mass-shooting; Steve Thompson, "Survivors of Texas' Luby's Massacre Grieve Anew over Sutherland Springs," *Dallas Morning News,* November 8, 2017, https://www.dallasnews.com/news/crime/2017/11/08/survivors-of-texas-luby-s-massacre-grieve-anew-over-sutherland-springs.

59. "Parishioners Kill Man Who Fatally Shoots 2 at Church," AP News, December 30, 2019, http://apnews.com/article/f254ff50cdaf3c8ec9fc4a2ebf0b8cda; Bill Hutchinson and Josh Margolin, "Armed Parishioner Says He's 'No Hero,' as Details Emerge about the Texas Church Shooter," ABC News, December 31, 2019, https://abcnews.go.com/US/parishioner-gunned-texas-church-shooter-hero/story?id=67982047; Eric Levenson, Konstantin Toropin, and Amir Vera, "Texas Pastor Says He Knew and Helped the Gunman before the Shooting," CNN, December 30, 2019, https://www.cnn.com/2019/12/30/us/texas-church-shooting-monday/index.html; Scott Gordon, "'We Knew He Was Crazy, But Not Like This,' Ex-Wife of Church Gunman Says," NBC DFW, December 30, 2019, https://www.nbcdfw.com/news/local/river-oaks-man-identified-as-shooter-in-white-settlement-church/2283777.

60. Juan A. Lozano, "Governor: 10 Dead, 10 Wounded in Texas High School Shooting," Police1, May 18, 2018, https://www.police1.com/active-shooter/articles/governor-10-dead-10-wounded-in-texas-high-school-shooting-AaIQXKkeaZfxd 7x4; Emma Platoff, "10 Killed, 10 More Injured after Shooting at High School Southeast of Houston," *Texas Tribune,* May 18, 2018, https://www.texastribune

.org/2018/05/18/multiple-fatalies-reported-after-shooting-santa-fe-high-school; Johnny Dodd with Jeff Truesdell, "A Texas School's Darkest Day," *People,* June 4, 2018, 127–30; Jeff Karoub, "Texas Teen Charged in Mass Shooting to Get Psych Evaluation," US News Online (Associated Press), October 23, 2019; Nick Powell, "Attorney: Accused Santa Fe Shooter Declared Incompetent to Stand Trial," *Houston Chronicle,* November 4, 2019, https://www.houstonchronicle.com/news/houston-texas/houston/article/Attorney-Accused-Santa-Fe-shooter-declared-14807798.php.

61. It is interesting to note that the citizens of Amarillo followed this same path after the Palo Duro High School shooting in 1992.

62. Eileen Reslen, "Sant Fe Students Describe the Horrific Scene During Today's School Shooting," *Cosmopolitan,* May 18, 2018, https://www.cosmopolitan.com/life style/a20745962/santa-fe-high-school-shooting-students-quotes; Todd C. Frankel et al., "Santa Fe School Had a Shooting Plan, Armed Officers and Practiced. Ten People Still Died," *Texas Tribune,* May 20, 2018, https://www.texastribune.org/2018/05/20/santa-fe-high-school-had-shooting-plan-armed-officers-and-practice-ten.

63. Emma Platoff and Brandon Formby, "Gov. Abbott Announces School Safety Plan and Proposed Changes to Gun Laws after Santa Fe Shooting," *Texas Tribune,* May 30, 2018, https://www.texastribune.org/2018/05/30/texas-gov-greg-abbott-santa-fe-shooting-school-safety-plan-gun-laws; Alex Samuels, "Texas Senate Passes School Safety Bill Intended to Prevent Mass Shootings," *Texas Tribune,* April 29, 2019, https://www.texastribune.org/2019/04/29/texas-senate-pass-school-safety-mass-shootings; Evie Blad, "Substitute Teacher Shot in Santa Fe High School Attack Says Subs Need Safety Training," *Education Week,* May 15, 2019, https://www.edweek.org/ew/articles/2019/05/15/substitute-teacher-shot-in-santa-fe-high.html; Alex Samuels, "How Santa Fe Rebuilt Itself in the Year after a School Shooting," *Texas Tribune,* May 17, 2019, https://www.texastribune.org/2019/05/17/santa-fe-shooting-recover-year-later; Alex Samuels, "Texas Senate Passes Bill to Give More Teachers Access to Guns in Classrooms," *Texas Tribune,* May 21, 2019, https://www.texastribune.org/2019/05/21/texas-senate-marshal-program-school-safety-hb-1387.

64. Two other shootings occurred between 2011 and 2019 that deserve mention but were not included in the discussion because the incidents did not fit the definition of mass shootings as described in this chapter: the Curtis Culwell Center terrorist attack and the Waco shootout between rival outlaw biker gangs at a Twin Peaks restaurant. The first incident occurred on May 3, 2015, when Elton Simpson and Nadir Hamid Soofi attacked the Curtis Culwell Center in Garland, Texas. The assailants were offended by an anti-Islamic exhibit that was on display at the center. During the attack, the shooters confronted Garland police officers and members of the security detail hired by the host of the event. Despite being heavily armed and wearing body armor, the shooters were the only fatalities. This incident was not defined as a mass shooting because the motives of the suspects were declared an act of terrorism. The second event occurred fourteen days later in Waco, Texas, when rival outlaw motorcycle gangs met at Twin Peaks for a regularly scheduled

regional meeting of the Texas Confederation of Clubs and Independents, the statewide biker club coalition that establishes the political rights of its members as well as resolves issues between rival clubs. During the meeting, an altercation occurred that led rival gang members to draw their weapons and begin firing at one another. Despite police presence at the scene before the outbreak of violence, nine bikers were killed, and eighteen others were wounded. While this incident has many of the hallmarks for a mass shooting, it does not fit the definition because the shooting was gang related.

SELECTED BIBLIOGRAPHY

Adler, Jeffrey S. *First in Violence, Deepest in Dirt: Homicide in Chicago, 1875–1920.* Cambridge: Harvard University Press, 2006.

Akers, Monte. *Flames after Midnight: Murder, Vengeance, and the Desolation of a Texas Community.* Austin: University of Texas Press, 1999.

Akers, Monte, Nathan Akers, and Roger Friedman. *Tower Sniper: The Terror of America's First Active Shooter on Campus.* Houston, Texas: John M. Hardy Publishing, 2016.

Alexander, Michelle. *The New Jim Crow: Mass Incarceration in the Age of Colorblindness.* New York: New Press, 2010.

Anderson, Gary Clayton. *The Conquest of Texas: Ethnic Cleansing in the Promised Land, 1820–1875.* Norman: University of Oklahoma Press, 2005.

Arquilla, John, and David Ronfeldt, eds. *Networks and Netwars: The Future of Terror, Crime, and Militancy.* Santa Monica, CA: Rand Corp, 1999.

Ayers, Edward L. *Vengeance and Justice: Crime and Punishment in the 19th-Century American South.* New York: Oxford University Press, 1984.

Ball, Richard A., and G. David Curry. "The Logic of Definition in Criminology: Purposes and Methods for Defining 'Gangs.'" *Criminology* 33, no. 2 (May 1995): 225–45.

Barker, Tom. *North American Criminal Gangs.* Durham, NC: Carolina Academic Press, 2012.

Baskin, Jane A., Ralph G. Lewis, Joyce Hartweg Mannis, and Lester W. McCullough Jr. *The Long, Hot Summer? An Analysis of Summer Disorders, 1967–1971.* Waltham, MA: Lemberg Center for the Study of Violence at Brandeis University, 1972.

Behnken, Brian D. *Fighting Their Own Battles: Mexican Americans, African Americans, and the Struggle for Civil Rights in Texas.* Chapel Hill: University of North Carolina Press, 2011.

Benekos, Peter J., and Alida V. Merlo, eds. *Corrections: Dilemmas and Directions.* Cincinnati: ACJS Anderson, 1992.

Bernstein, Patricia. *The First Waco Horror: The Lynching of Jesse Washington and the Rise of the NAACP.* College Station: Texas A&M University Press, 2005.

Berryhill, Michael. *The Trials of Eroy Brown: The Murder Case That Shook the Texas Prison System.* Austin: University of Texas Press, 2012.

Bjerregaard, Beth, and Alan J. Lizotte. "Gun Ownership and Gang Membership." *Journal of Criminal Law and Criminology* 86, no. 1 (Fall 1995): 37–58.

Blight, David W. *Race and Reunion: The Civil War in American Memory.* Cambridge, MA.: Harvard University Press, 2001.

Bolden, Christian. "Friendly Foes: Hybrid Gangs or Social Networking." *Group Processes & Intergroup Relations* (May 2014): 1–20.

Bowden, Charles. *Down by the River: Drugs, Money, Murder, and Family.* New York: Simon & Schuster, 2002.

Bradshaw, Benjamin, David R. Johnson, Derral Cheatwood, and Stephen Blanchard. "A Historical Geographic Study of Lethal Violence in San Antonio." *Social Science Quarterly* 79, no. 4 (December 1998): 863–78.

Branch, Taylor. *At Canaan's Edge: America in the King Years, 1965–1968.* New York: Simon & Schuster, 2006.

———. *Parting the Waters: America in the King Years, 1954–63* (New York: Simon & Schuster, 1988.

Brown, Richard Maxwell. *No Duty to Retreat: Violence and Values in American History and Society.* Norman: University of Oklahoma Press, 1991.

———. *Strain of Violence: Historical Studies of American Violence and Vigilantism.* New York: Oxford University Press, 1975.

Brundage, W. Fitzhugh. *Lynching in the New South: Georgia and Virginia, 1880–1930.* Urbana: University of Illinois Press, 1993.

Buenger, Walter L. *The Path to a Modern South: Northeast Texas between Reconstruction and the Great Depression.* Austin: University of Texas Press, 2001.

Burran, James A. "Violence in an 'Arsenal of Democracy': The Beaumont Race Riot, 1943." *East Texas Historical Journal* 14, no 1 (1976): 39–52;

Caldwell, Clifford R., and Ron DeLord. *Eternity at the End of a Rope: Executions, Lynchings and Vigilante Justice in Texas, 1819–1923.* Santa Fe, NM: Sunstone Press, 2015.

Campbell, Howard. *Drug War Zone: Frontline Dispatches from the Streets of El Paso & Juarez.* Austin: University of Texas Press, 2009.

Campbell, Randolph B. *An Empire for Slavery: The Peculiar Institution in Texas, 1821–1861.* Baton Rouge: Louisiana State University Press, 1991.

———. *Gone to Texas: A History of the Lone Star State.* New York: Oxford University Press, 2003.

Cantrell, Gregg, and Elizabeth Hayes Turner, eds. *Lone Star Pasts: Memory and History in Texas.* College Station: Texas A&M University Press, 2007.

Carpenter, Dale. *Flagrant Conduct: The Story of Lawrence v. Texas.* New York: W. W. Norton and Company, 2013.

Carrigan, William. *The Making of a Lynching Culture: Violence and Vigilantism in Central Texas, 1836–1916.* Urbana: University of Illinois Press, 2004.

Carrigan, William, and Clive Webb. *Forgotten Dead: Mob Violence against Mexicans in the United States, 1848–1928*. New York: Oxford University Press, 2013.

Carter, Cecile Elkins. *Caddo Indians: Where We Come From*. Norman: University of Oklahoma Press, 1995.

Carter, David. *Stonewall: The Riots That Sparked the Gay Revolution*. New York: St. Martin's Press, 2004.

Cash, W. J. *The Mind of the South*. New York: Random House, 1941; Vintage, reprint, 1960.

Cepeda, Alice, Avelardo Valdez, Charles Kaplan, and Larry Hill. "Patterns of Substance Abuse Among Hurricane Katrina Evacuees in Houston, Texas." *Disasters* 34, no. 2 (December 2010): 426–46.

Chalmers, David M. *Hooded Americanism: The History of the Ku Klux Klan*. New York: New Viewpoints, 1981.

Chapman, David L. "Lynching in Texas." Master's thesis, Texas Tech University, 1973.

Chipman, Donald, and Harriet Denise Joseph. *Spanish Texas: 1519–1821*, 2nd ed. Austin: University of Texas Press, 2010.

Christianson, Scott. *With Liberty for Some*. Boston: Northeastern University Press, 1998.

Conover, Ted. *Newjack: Guarding Sing Sing*. New York: Random House, 2000.

Cooper, Hannah L. F. "War on Drugs Policing and Police Brutality." *Substance Use and Misuse* 508, no. 8/9 (2015): 1–7.

Correa-Cabrera, Guadalupe. "Security, Migration and the Economy in the Texas-Tamaulipas Border Region." *Politics & Policy* 41, no. 1 (February 2013): 65–82

Courtwright, David T. *Violent Land: Single Men and Social Disorder from the Frontier to the Inner City*. Cambridge, MA: Harvard University Press, 1996.

Crouch, Barry. *The Freedman's Bureau and Black Texans*. Austin: University of Texas Press, 1992.

Crouch, Ben, and James W. Marquart. *An Appeal to Justice: Litigated Reform of Texas Prisons*. Austin: University of Texas Press, 1989.

Cunningham, Sean P. *Cowboy Conservatism: Texas and the Rise of the Modern Right*. Lexington: University Press of Kentucky, 2010.

Curry, G. David, and Scott Decker. "What's in a Name? A Gang by Any Other Name Isn't Quite the Same." *Valparaiso University Law Review* 31, no. 2 (Spring 1997): 501–14.

Davidson, Theodore. *Chicano Prisoners: The Key to San Quentin*. New York: Holt, Rinehart and Winstaon, 1974.

Davis, Robert C. Davis, Barbara E. Smith, and Heather J. Davies. "Effects of No-Drop Prosecution of Domestic Violence on Conviction Rates." *Justice Research Policy* 3, no. 2 (Fall 2001): 1–13.

Dawson, Carol, and Carol Johnston. *House of Plenty: The Rise, Fall, and Revival of Luby's Cafeterias*. Austin: University of Texas Press, 2006.

Decker, Scott, ed. *Policing Gangs and Youth Violence*. Belmont, CA: Wadsworth, 2003.

Desmond, Scott, and Charis Kubrin. "The Power of Place: Immigrant Communities and Adolescent Violence." *Sociological Quarterly* 50, no. 4 (October 2009): 581–607.

DiIulio, John. *Governing Prisons: A Comparative Study of Correctional Management*. New York: Free Press, 1987.

Dulaney, W. Marvin, and Kathleen Underwood, eds. *Essays on the American Civil Rights Movement*. College Station: Published for the University of Texas at Arlington by Texas A&M University Press, 1993.

Durán, Robert. *Gang Life in Two Cities: An Insider's Journey*. New York: Columbia University Press, 2013.

———. *Gang Paradox: Inequality and Miracles on the U. S–Mexico Border*. New York: Colombia University Press, 2018.

Durham, Kenneth R. "The Longview Race Riot of 1919." *East Texas Historical Journal* 18, no. 2 (1980): 13–24.

Eisenbach, David. *Gay Power: An American Revolution*. New York: Carroll and Graf Publishers, 2006.

Elias, Norbert. *The Civilizing Process: The History of Manners*. New York: Urizen, 1978. First published 1939 by Urizen.

Equal Justice Initiative. *Lynching in America: Confronting the Legacy of Racial Terror*. Montgomery, AL: Equal Justice Initiative, 2015.

Esbensen, Finn-Aage, Thomas Winfree Jr., Ni He, and Terrance Taylor. "Youth Gangs and Definitional Issues: When Is a Gang a Gang and Why Does It Matter?" *Crime and Delinquency* 47, no. 1 (January 2001): 105–30.

Flitcraft, Anne. "Physicians and Domestic Violence: Challenges for Prevention." *Health Affairs*, 12, no. 4 (Winter 1993): 154–61.

Foley, Neil. *The White Scourge: Mexicans, Blacks, and Poor Whites in Texas Cotton Culture*. Berkeley: University of California Press, 1997.

Fong, Robert. "The Organizational Structure of Prison Gangs: A Texas Case Study." *Federal Probation* 54, no. 1 (1990): 36–44.

Fridel, Emma E., and James Alan Fox. "Gender Differences in Patterns and Trends in U.S. Homicides, 1976–2017." *Violence and Gender* 6, no. 1 (March 2019): 27–36.

Friedman, Lawrence M. *Crime and Punishment in American History*. New York: Basic Books, 1993.

Gabbidon, Shaun L., and Helen Taylor Greene. *Race and Crime*. Thousand Oaks, CA: Sage, 2009.

Galtung, Johan. "Cultural Violence." *Journal of Peace Research* 27, no. 3 (1990): 291–305.

Gaquin, D. A. "Spouse Abuse: Data from the National Crime Survey." *Victimology* 2, no. 3–4 (1977–78): 632–43.

Gastil, Raymond D. "Homicide and a Regional Culture of Violence." *American Sociological Review* 36, no. 3 (June 1971): 412–27.

Gee, P. W. "Ensuring Police Protection for Battered Women—The *Scott v. Hart* Suit." *Signs* 8, no. 3 (Spring 1983): 554–61.

Gelles, M. A., and R. J. Gelles. "Societal Change and Change in Family Violence from 1975 to 1985 as Revealed by Two National Surveys." *Journal of Marriage and the Family* 48, no. 3 (August 1986): 465–79.

Germany, Kent B. "Historians and the Many Lyndon Johnsons: A Review Essay." *Journal of Southern History* 75, No. 4 (November 2009): 1001–28.

Gerstenfeld, Phyllis B. *Hate Crimes: Causes, Controls, and Controversies.* Thousand Oaks, CA: Sage, 2004.

Gillon, Steven M. *Separate and Unequal: The Kerner Commission and the Unraveling of American Liberalism.* New York: Basic Books, 2018.

Glasrud, Bruce, ed. *Anti-Black Violence in Twentieth Century Texas.* College Station: Texas A&M University Press, 2015.

Gondolf, Edward W. *Gender-Based Perspectives on Battering Programs.* Lanham, MD: Lexington Books, 2015.

Goodman, Leigh. *Decriminalizing Domestic Violence: A Balanced Policy Approach to Intimate Partner Violence.* Oakland: University of California Press, 2018.

Gundur, Rajeev. "The Changing Social Organization of Prison Protection Markets." *Trends in Organized Crime* (February 2018): 1–20.

Hackney, Sheldon. "Southern Violence." *American Historical Review* 74, no. 3 (February 1969), 906–25.

Hagedorn, John. *People and Folks: Gangs, Crime, and the Underclass in a Rustbelt City.* Chicago: Lakeview Press, 1988.

Hall, Jacquelyn Dowd. *Revolt against Chivalry: Jessie Daniel Ames and the Women's Campaign against Lynching.* New York: Columbia University Press, 1993.

Hallinan, Joseph T. *Going up the River: Travels in a Prison Nation.* New York: Random House, 2001.

Hamalainen, Pekka. *The Comanche Empire.* New Haven: Yale University Press, 2008.

Hanhardt, Christina B. *Safe Space: Gay Neighborhood History and the Politics of Violence.* Durham, NC: Duke University Press, 2013.

Hansen, Mark. "Battered Child's Defense." *ABA Journal* 78 (May 1992): 28.

Harper, William T. *Eleven Days in Hell: The 1974 Carrasco Prison Siege at Huntsville, Texas.* Denton: University of North Texas Press, 2004.

Hewitt, Nancy, ed. *No Permanent Waves: Recasting Histories of U.S. Feminism.* Piscataway, NJ: Rutgers University Press, 2010.

Hindus, Michael S. *Prison and Plantation: Crime, Justice, and Authority in Massachusetts and South Carolina, 1767–1878.* Chapel Hill: University of North Carolina Press, 1980.

Hollon, W. Eugene. *Frontier Violence: Another Look.* New York: Oxford University Press, 1974.

Horton, David M., and George R. Nielson. *Walking George: The Life of George John*

Beto and the Rise of the Modern Texas Prison System. Denton: University of North Texas Press, 2005.

House, Aline. *The Carrasco Tragedy: Eleven Days of Terror in the Huntsville Prison*. Waco: Texian Press, 1975.

Howell, James. "Youth Gang Homicide." *Crime and Delinquency* 45, no. 2 (April 1999): 208–41.

Howell, Kenneth W., Keith J. Volanto, James M. Smallwood, Charles D. Grear, Jennifer S. Lawrence, and F. Todd Smith. *Beyond Myths and Legends: A Narrative History of Texas*, 5th ed. Wheaton, IL: Abigail Press, 2017.

Howell, Kenneth W., ed. *Still the Arena of Civil War: Violence and Turmoil in Reconstruction Texas, 1865–1874*. Denton: University of North Texas Press, 2012.

Huff, C. Ronald. "Youth Gangs and Public Policy." *Crime and Delinquency* 35, no. 4 (October 1989): 524–37.

Hutson, H. Range, Deirdre Anglin, and Marc Eckstein. "Drive-by Shootings by Violent Street Gangs in Los Angeles: A Five-Year Review from 1989 to 1993." *Academic Emergency Medicine* 3, no. 4 (April 1996): 300–303.

Irwin, John. *Prisons in Turmoil*. Boston: Little, Brown and Company, 1980.

Jacobs, James B., and Kimberly Potter. *Hate Crimes: Criminal Law and Identity Politics*. Oxford: Oxford University Press, 1998.

Jenness, Valerie, and Ryken Grattet. *Making Hate a Crime: From Social Movement to Law Enforcement*. New York: Russell Sage Foundation, 2001.

Jennings, Matthew. *New Worlds of Violence: Cultures and Conquests in the Early American Southeast*. Knoxville: University of Tennessee Press, 2011.

Jett, Brandon T. "'Detrimental to the Interests of the City:' Lynching and the Local Response in Bowie County, 1886–1922." *Journal of South Texas* 28, no. 1 (Spring 2015): 30–45.

———. "'Let Us Be Law Abiding Citizens': Mob Violence and the Local Response in Harrison County, Texas, 1890–1925." *East Texas Historical Journal* 54, no. 2 (Fall 2016): 22–52.

———. "Paris Is Burning: Lynching and Racial Violence in Lamar County, Texas, 1890–1920." *East Texas Historical Journal* 51, no. 2 (Fall 2013): 40–63.

Jillson, Cal. *Lone Star Tarnished: A Critical Look at Texas Politics and Public Policy*. New York: Routledge, Taylor and Francis Group, 2018.

John, Elizabeth A. H. *Storms Brewed in Other Men's Worlds: The Confrontation of Indians, Spanish, and French in the Southwest, 1540–1795*. Lincoln: University of Nebraska Press, 1975.

Johnson, Benjamin Heber. *Revolution in Texas: How a Forgotten Rebellion and Its Bloody Suppression Turned Mexicans Into Americans*. New Haven, CT: Yale University Press, 2003.

Johnson, Otis S. "Two Worlds: A Historical Perspective on the Dichotomous Relations between Police and Black and White Communities." *Human Rights* 42, no. 1 (2016): 6–9.

Kennedy, Randall. *Race, Crime, and the Law*. New York: Vintage Books, 1991.

King, Joyce. *Hate Crime: The Story of a Dragging in Jasper, Texas*. New York: Pantheon Books, 2002.

Klein, Malcolm. *Gang Cop: The Words and Ways of Paco Domingo*. Walnut Creek, CA: Alta Mira Press, 2004.

———. *The American Street Gang*. New York: Oxford University Press, 1995.

Koeninger, Rupert. "Capital Punishment in Texas, 1924–1968." *Crime and Delinquency* 15, no. 1 (January 1969): 132–41.

Kraska, Peter B., and Victor E. Kappeler. "Militarizing American Police: The Rise and Normalization of Paramilitary Units." *Social Problems* 44, no. 1 (February 1997): 1–18.

Krochmal, Max. *Blue Texas: The Making of a Multiracial Democratic Coalition in the Civil Rights Era*. Chapel Hill: University of North Carolina Press, 2016.

Kurz, Demie. "Emergency Department Responses to Battered Women: Resistance to Medicalization." *Social Problems* 34, no. 1 (February 1987): 69–81.

Lane, Roger. *Murder in America: A History*. Columbus: Ohio State University Press, 1997.

———. *Violent Death in the City: Suicide, Accident, and Murder in Nineteenth-Century Philadelphia*. Cambridge, MA: Harvard University Press, 1979.

Latzer, Barry. *The Rise and Fall of Violent Crime in America*. New York: Encounter Books, 2016.

Lavergne, Gary M. *A Sniper in the Tower: The Charles Whitman Murders*. Denton: University of North Texas Press, 1997.

———. *Worse Than Death: The Dallas Nightclub Murders and the Texas Multiple Murder Law*. Denton: University of Texas Press, 2003.

Levitt, Steven D., and Stephen J. Dubner. *Freakonomics: A Rogue Economist Explores the Hidden Side of Everything*. New York: William Morrow, 2009.

Levy, Peter B. *The Great Uprising: Race Riots in Urban American during the 1960s*. New York: Cambridge University Press, 2018.

Littlejohn, Jeffrey I., Charles H. Ford, Jami Horne, and Briana Weaver. "The Cabiness Family Lynching: Race, War, and Memory in Walker County, Texas." *Southwestern Historical Quarterly* vol. 122, no. 1 (July 2018): 1–30.

Glenn, Lon Bennett. *Texas Prison Tales: The Largest Hotel Chain in Texas*. Scotts Valley, CA: CreateSpace Independent Publishing, 2016.

Lundsgaarde, Henry P. *Murder in Space City: A Cultural Analysis of Houston Homicide Patterns*. New York: Oxford University Press, 1977.

Marquart, James W., Sheldon Ekland-Olson, and Jonathan R. Sorensen. *The Rope, the Chair, and the Needle: Capital Punishment in Texas, 1923–1990*. Austin: University of Texas Press, 1994.

Marquart, James W., Madhava Bodapati, Stephen J. Cuvelier, and Leo Carroll. "Ceremonial Justice, Loose Coupling, and the War on Drugs in Texas, 1980–1989." *Crime and Delinquency* 39, no. 4, (October 1993): 528–42.

Martin, Steve J., and Sheldon Ekland-Olson. *Texas Prisons: The Walls Came Tumbling Down*. Austin: Texas Monthly, 1987.

Martinez, Monica Muñoz. *The Injustice Never Leaves You: Anti-Mexican Violence in Texas*. Cambridge, MA: Harvard University Press, 2018.

Martinez, Jr., Ramiro. *Latino Homicide: Immigration, Violence, and Community*. New York: Routledge, 2002.

Martinez, Ramiro. *Latino Homicide*, 2nd ed. New York, Routledge, 2014.

Matsumoto, David. *Culture and Psychology*. Pacific Grove, CA: Brooks/Cole, 1996.

Maxson, Cheryl L. "Investigating Gang Migration: Contextual Issues for Intervention." *Gang Journal* 1, no. 2 (1993): 1–8.

Maxson, Cheryl L., Kristi J. Woods, and Malcolm W. Klein. "Street Gang Migration: How Big a Threat?" *National Institute of Justice Journal* 230 (1996): 26–31.

McComb, David G. *Houston: A History*. Austin: University of Texas Press, 1981.

McDonald, William F. *The Criminal Victimization of Immigrants*. Cham, Switzerland: Palgrave Macmillan, 2018.

McKinney, Wilson. *Fred Carrasco: The Heroin Merchant*. Austin, Texas: Heidelberg Publishing, 1975.

McNulty, Timothy and Brendan McNulty. *The Meanest Man in Congress: Jack Brooks and the Making of an American Century*. Montgomery, AL: NewSouth Books, 2019.

Miller, Jody, Cheryl L. Maxson, and Malcolm W. Klein, eds. *The Modern Gang Reader,* 2nd ed. Los Angeles: Roxbury, 2001.

Miller, J. Mitchell, and Jeff Rush, eds. *Gangs: A Criminal Justice Approach*. Cincinnati: ACJS/Anderson Monograph Series, 1996.

Modi, Monica N., et al. "The Role of Violence Against Women Act in Addressing Intimate Partner Violence: A Public Health Issue." *Journal of Women's Health* 23, no. 3 (March 2014): 253–59.

Monkkonen, Eric H. *Murder in New York City*. Berkeley: University of California Press, 2001.

Montejano, David. *Quixote's Soldiers: A Local History of the Chicano Movement, 1966–1981*. Austin: University of Texas Press, 2010.

Moore, Joan, and Raquel Pinderhughes, eds. *In the Barrios: Latinos and the Underclass Debate*. New York: Russell Sage Foundation, 1993.

Moreno, Mark E. "Mexican American Street Gangs, Migration, and Violence in the Yakima Valley." *Pacific Northwest Quarterly* 97, no. 3 (Summer 2006): 131–38.

Morrill, Robert. *The Mexican Mafia, La Eme: The Story*. San Antonio, TX: Mungia Printers, 2008.

Morris, Norval, and David J. Rothman, eds. *The Oxford History of the Prison: The Practice of Punishment in Western Society*. New York: Oxford University Press, 1998.

Myers, Toby. "Jewish Perspectives in Domestic Violence." In *Domestic Violence and Cross Cultural Perspective,* edited by M. Basheer Ahmed, 45–55. North Texas: MCC Human Services, 2009.

National Commission on the Causes and Prevention of Violence. *To Establish Justice, to Insure Domestic Tranquility: The Final Report.* New York: Bantam Books, 1970.

Nisbett, Richard E., and Dov Cohen. *Culture of Honor: The Psychology of Violence in the South.* Boulder: Westview Press, 1998.

Oshinsky, David M. *Worse than Slavery: Parchman Farm and the Ordeal of Jim Crow Justice.* New York: Simon & Schuster, 1996.

Payne, Darwin. *Big D: Triumphs and Troubles of an American Supercity in the 20th Century.* Dallas: Three Forks Press, 1994.

Pelz, Beth, James Marquart, and Terry Pelz. "Right-Wing Extremism in Texas Prisons: The Rise and Fall of the Aryan Brotherhood." *The Prison Journal* 71, no. 2 (September 1991): 23–37.

Perkinson, Robert. *Texas Tough: The Rise of America's Prison Empire.* New York: Metropolitan Books, 2010.

Petersen, Jennifer. *Murder, the Media, and the Politics of Public Feelings: Remembering Matthew Shepard and James Byrd Jr.* Bloomington: Indiana University Press, 2011.

Pfeifer, Michael J. *Rough Justice: Lynching and American Society, 1874–1947.* Urbana: University of Illinois Press, 2004.

Phelps, Wesley G. *A People's War on Poverty: Urban Politics and Grassroots Activists in Houston.* Athens: University of Georgia Press, 2014.

Phillips, Michael. *White Metropolis: Race, Ethnicity, and Religion in Dallas, 1841–2001.* Austin: University of Texas Press, 2006.

Pinker, Steven. *The Better Angels of Our Nature: Why Violence Has Declined.* New York: Penguin Books, 2011.

Pitney, Jr., John J. *After Reagan: Bush, Dukakis, and the 1988 Election.* Lawrence: University of Kansas Press, 2019.

Pyrooz, David C., and Scott H. Decker. *Competing for Control: Gangs and the Social Order of Prisons.* New York: Cambridge University Press, 2019.

Ramsdell, Charles. *Reconstruction in Texas.* New York: Columbia University Press, 1910.

Reavis, Dick J. *The Ashes of Waco: An Investigation.* Syracuse: Syracuse University Press, 1998.

Remington, Bruce. "Twelve Fighting Years: Homosexuals in Houston, 1969–1981." Master's thesis, University of Houston, 1983.

Renaud, Jorge Antonio. *Behind the Walls: A Guide for Family and Friends of Texas Inmates.* Denton: University of North Texas Press, 2002.

Resendez, Andres. *A Land So Strange: The Extraordinary Tale of a Shipwrecked Spaniard Who Walked across America in the Sixteenth Century.* New York: Basic Books, 2007.

Richardson, Chad. *The Informal and Underground Economy of the South Texas Border.* Austin: University of Texas Press, 2012.

Robertson, Christopher Everett. "Race, Class, and Attitudes toward Uses of Force by Police." Master's thesis, University of Texas at Arlington, 2018.

Roth, Randolph. *American Homicide*. Cambridge, MA: Harvard University Press, 2009.

Russell, Steve. "The Futility of Eloquence: Selected Texas Family Violence Legislation 1979–1991." *South Texas Law Review* 33 (1992): 353–76.

Sampson, Robert J., Jeffrey D. Morenoff, and Stephen Raudenbush. "Social Anatomy of Racial and Ethnic Disparities in Violence." *American Journal of Public Health* 95, no. 2 (February 2005): 225–32.

Santana, Juan, and Gabriel Morales. *Don't Mess with Texas: Gangs in the Lonestar State*. Columbia, SC: Create Space Publishing, 2014.

Santry, Shelley M. "Penny Wise But Pound Foolish in the Heartland: A Case Study of Decriminalizing Domestic Violence in Topeka, Kansas." *Journal of Law & Family Studies*, 14 (2012): 223–44.

Schechter, Susan. *Women and Male Violence*. Boston: South End Press, 1982.

Schildkraut, Jaclyn, and H. Jaymi Elsass. *Mass Shootings: Media, Myths, and Realities*. Santa Barbara, CA: Praeger, 2016.

Schildkraut, Jaclyn, ed. *Mass Shootings in America: Understanding the Debate, Causes, and Responses*. Santa Barbara, CA: ABC-CLIO, 2018.

Schutze, Jim. *The Accommodation: The Politics of Race in an American City*. Secaucus, NJ: Citadel Press, 1986.

Sikes, Gini. *8-Ball Chicks*. New York: Doubleday, 1997.

Sirin, Cigdim V. "From Nixon's War on Drugs to Obama's Drug Policies Today: Presidential Progress in Addressing Racial Injustices and Disparities." *Race, Class, and Gender* 18, no. 3–4 (2011): 82–99.

Smallwood, James, Barry A Crouch, and Larry Peacock. *Murder and Mayhem: The War of Reconstruction in Texas*. College Station: Texas A&M University Press, 2003.

Sokolow, Jayme A., and Mary Ann Lamanna. "Women and Utopia: The Woman's Commonwealth of Belton, Texas." *The Southwestern Historical Quarterly* 87, no. 4 (April 1984): 371–92.

Sorensen, Jon, and Rocky Leann Pilgrim. *Lethal Injection: Capital Punishment in Texas during the Modern Era*. Austin: University of Texas Press, 2006.

Spierenburg, Pieter. *A History of Murder: Personal Violence in Europe from the Middle Ages to the Present*. Cambridge: Polity Press, 2008.

Spruill, Marjorie J. *Divided We Stand: The Battle over Women's Rights and Family Values That Polarized American Politics*. New York: Bloomsbury Publishing, 2018.

Stets, Jan E., and Maureen A. Pirog-Good. "Violence in Dating Relationships." *Social Psychology Quarterly* 50, no. 3 (September 1987): 237–46.

Stoever, Jane K. *The Politicization of Safety Critical Perspectives on Domestic Violence Responses*. New York: New York University Press, 2019.

Sumner, Steven, James A. Mercy, Linda L. Dahlberg, Susan Hillis, Joanne Klevens, and Debra Houry. "Violence in the U.S.: Status, Challenges, and Opportunities." *Journal of the American Medical Association* 314, no. 5 (August 2015): 478–88.

Swanson, Doug J. *Cult of Glory: The Bold and Brutal History of the Texas Rangers.* New York: Viking, 2020.

Tapia, Mike, Corey Sparks, and J. Mitchell Miller. "Texas Latino Prison Gangs: An Exploration of Generational Shift and Rebellion." *Prison Journal* 94, no. 2 (March 2014): 159–79.

Tapia, Mike. *Gangs of the El Paso–Juarez Borderland.* Albuquerque: University of New Mexico Press, 2020.

———. "Latino Street Gang Emergence in the Midwest: Strategic Franchising or Natural Migration?" *Crime and Delinquency* 60, no. 4 (June 2014): 592–618.

———. "Texas Latino Gangs and Large Urban Jails: Intergenerational Conflict and Issues in Management." *Journal of Crime and Justice* 37, no. 2 (February 2013): 256–74.

———. *The Barrio Gangs of San Antonio, Texas, 1915–2015.* Ft. Worth: Texas Christian University Press, 2017.

Temple-Raston, Dina. *A Death in Texas: A Story of Race, Murder, and a Small Town's Struggle for Redemption.* New York: Henry Holt and Company, 2002.

Teske, Jr., Raymond H. C., ed. *Crime and Justice in Texas.* Huntsville, TX: Sam Houston Press, 1995.

Thompson, Heather Ann. *Blood in the Water: The Attica Prison Uprising in 1971 and Its Legacy.* New York: Pantheon Books, 2016.

———. "Why Mass Incarceration Matters: Rethinking Crisis, Decline, and Transformation in Postwar American History." *Journal of American History* 97, no. 3 (December 2010): 703–34.

Tienda, Marta and Michael Rutter, eds. *Ethnicity and Causal Mechanisms.* New York: Cambridge University Press, 2005.

Tierney, Kathleen J. "The Battered Women Movement and the Creation of the Wife Beating Problem." *Social Problems* 29, no. 3 (February 1982): 207–20.

Wood, Amy Louise, ed. *Violence.* Chapel Hill: University of North Carolina Press, 2011.

Tuttle, Jr., William M. "Violence in a 'Heathen' Land: The Longview Race Riot of 1919," *Phylon* 33, no. 4 (4th Qtr. 1972): 324–33

Valdez, Avelardo, Alice Cepeda, and Charles Kaplan. "Homicidal Events among Mexican American Street Gangs: A Situational Analysis." *Homicide Studies* 13, no. 3 (July 2009): 288–306.

Valdez, Avelardo. "Mexican American Youth and Adult Prison Gangs in a Changing Heroin Market." *Journal of Drug Issues* 35, no. 4 (October 2005): 843–68.

Valdez, Avelrado, and Rene Enriquez. *Urban Street Terrorism: The Mexican Mafia and the Sureño Trece.* Santa Ana, CA: Police and Fire Publishing, 2011.

Villanueva, Jr. Nicholas. *The Lynching of Mexicans in the Texas Borderlands.* Albuquerque: University of New Mexico Press, 2017.

Waldorf, Dan. "When the Crips Invaded San Francisco: Gang Migration." *Gang Journal* 1, no. 4. (1993): 11–16.

Walker, Leonore A. *The Battered Woman*. New York: Harper and Row, 1979.

Ward, T. W. *Gangsters without Borders: Ethnography of a Salvadoran Street Gang*. New York: Oxford University Press, 2013.

Watson, Dwight W. "'In the Name of Progress and Decency': The Response of Houston's Civic Leaders to the Lynching of Robert Powell in 1928." *Houston Review* 1, no. 2 (1995), 26–30.

———. *Race and the Houston Police Department, 1930–1990: A Change Did Come*. College Station: Texas A&M University Press, 2005.

Weiner, Merle H. "From Dollars to Sense: A Critique of Government Funding for the Battered Women's Movement." *Law & Equality* 9, no. 2 (1991): 185–277.

White, Walter. *Rope and Faggot: A Biography of Judge Lynch*. New York: Alfred A. Knopf, Inc., 1929.

Wilson, K. J. *When Violence Begins at Home*. Alameda, CA: Hunter House, 2006.

Wong, Felicia J., Susan R. Holmberg, Andrea Flynn, and Dorian T. Warren. *The Hidden Rules of Race: Barriers to an Inclusive Economy*. Cambridge: Cambridge University Press, 2017.

Wyatt-Brown, Bertram. *Southern Honor: Ethics & Behavior in the Old South*. New York: Oxford University Press, 1983.

Xie, Min, and Eric Baumer. "Reassessing the Breadth of the Protective Benefit of Immigrant Neighborhoods." *Criminology* 56, no. 2 (February 2018): 302–32.

Yearwood, Douglass, and Alison Rhyne. "Hispanic/Latino Gangs: A Comparative Analysis of Nationally Affiliated and Local Gangs." *Journal of Gang Research* 14: (Winter 2007): 1–18.

CONTRIBUTORS

Brandon T. Jett is an assistant professor of history at Florida SouthWestern State College. He is the author of *Race, Crime, and Policing in the Jim Crow South: African Americans and Law Enforcement in Birmingham, Memphis, and New Orleans, 1920–1945*, as well as several articles on lynching in Northeast Texas, homicides in Memphis, Tennessee, and police brutality and activism in Birmingham, Alabama. His work has been featured in several venues, including the *East Texas Historical Journal*, the *Journal of South Texas*, the *Tennessee Historical Quarterly*, the *Alabama Review*, *Washington Post*, and *Ft. Myers News-Press*, and on WGCU's Gulf Coast Life.

Kenneth W. Howell is a professor of history and head of the history department at Blinn College and the executive director of the Central Texas Historical Association. He is the author of *Texas Confederate, Reconstruction Governor: James Webb Throckmorton* and coauthor of *The Devil's Triangle: Ben Bickerstaff, Northeast Texans, and the War of Reconstruction in Texas* and *Beyond Myths and Legends: A Narrative History of Texas*. He is also the editor of *The Seventh Star of the Confederacy: Texas during the Civil War*, winner of the prestigious A. M. Pate Jr. Award in Civil War History, *Still the Arena of Civil War: Violence and Turmoil in Reconstruction Texas, 1865–1874*, and the coeditor of *Single Star of the West: The Republic of Texas, 1836–1845*, named the Alamo Society's Best Book of 2017.

Jeffrey L. Littlejohn serves as professor of history at Sam Houston State University. He is the coauthor or coeditor of *Elusive Equality: Desegregation and Resegregation in Norfolk's Public Schools; The Enemy Within Never Did Without: German and Japanese Prisoners of War at Camp Huntsville, Texas, 1942–1945;* and *The Seedtime, the Work and the Harvest: New Perspectives on the Black Freedom Struggle in America*. He has published numerous articles with his coauthor Charles H. Ford, including "The Cabiness Family Lynching: Race, War, and Memory in Walker County, Texas." He is also the creator of the digital history projects Lynching in Texas and East Texas History.

Ashley Baggett is the director of the Women and Gender Studies program and an associate professor of history at North Dakota State University. Baggett's research focuses on gender-based violence and sociolegal reform. She is the author of *Intimate Partner Violence in New Orleans: Gender, Race, and Reform, 1840 to 1900*. Other publications include "'Alleged Crusades' and 'Self-Fooled Reformers': The Rise and Fall of White Slavery Hysteria in the 1910s" in *Historical Sex Work: New Contributions from History and Archaeology* as well as an article in the *Journal of Mississippi History*. She has also served as an expert consultant on the television show *Who Do You Think You Are?* and for *USA Today*.

Christopher P. Haight is a professor of history at Houston Community College. He earned his Ph.D. in history from the University of Houston in 2016. His work, which focuses on LGBTQ activism and the history of violence, has previously been published in the *Southwestern Historical Quarterly*. His first book, *The Silence Is Killing Us: The Anti-Hate Crime Movement in Texas*, is under contract with the University of Texas Press.

Betsy Friauf was a journalist and assistant metropolitan editor at the *Fort Worth Star-Telegram* from 1980 to 2007. She served from 2007 to 2009 as a communications officer for the City of Fort Worth, Texas from 2007 to 2009 and with the University of North Texas Health Science Center from 2011 to 2020. In 2021, she became a senior communications specialist for Children's Health (hospital)–Dallas. With Michael Phillips, she conducted oral histories of alumni and former faculty of historically black colleges and universities in Texas. A 2013 Baylor University Charlton Oral History grant funded the project God Carved in Night: Black Intellectuals in Texas. Also with Phillips, she won the 2018 C. K. Chamberlain Award for Best Article of the Year in the *East Texas Historical Journal* and the 2019–2020 Texas Oral History Association Kenneth E. Hendrickson, Jr. *Sound Historian* Best Article Award.

Michael Phillips is a scholar of American race relations, Texas history, right-wing politics, and apocalyptic religions. A former reporter for the *Fort Worth Star-Telegram*, his book, *White Metropolis: Race, Ethnicity and Religion in Dallas, 1841–2001*, won the 2007 Texas Historical Commission's prize for best book on Texas history. In 2019, he was named one of the first group of community college professors to receive a Mellon/American Council of Learned Societies Community College research fellowship for his project on the history of eugenics in the state of Texas. Phillips and his wife and research partner, Betsy Friauf, are under contract with the University of Oklahoma Press to write an upcoming book, *The Strange Career of Eugenics in Texas, 1854–1940*. Since 2007, he has taught American history at Collin College in Plano, Texas.

Mike Tapia is a faculty member in the Department of Sociology & Criminal Justice at Texas A&M University–Commerce. His research interests include delinquency and juvenile justice, street and prison gangs, tests of crime theory, and race-ethnicity. Much of his research describes the role of migration, age-structure, social class, and organizational context on various individual and group-level outcomes for the gang population. Tapia's latest works examine Chicano street and prison gang organization in historical perspective. He has recently published *The Barrio Gangs of San Antonio 1915–2015* and *Gangs of the El Paso-Juarez Borderland Region*.

Mitchel P. Roth is a professor of criminal justice and criminology at Sam Houston State University. He has published widely and his work includes *Power on the Inside: A Global History of Prison Gangs, Fire in the Big House: The Worst Prison Disaster in American History, A History of Crime and the American Criminal Justice System, An Eye for An Eye: A Global History of Crime and Punishment*, and *Convict Cowboys: The Untold History of the Texas Prison Rodeo*. He is editor in chief of the *International Journal of Criminology and Sociology*. In 2020, Dr. Roth received the Frederic Milton Thrasher award for excellence in gang research.

INDEX

Index